Praise for *Hands-On Differential Privacy*

This book fills a pressing need for practicing data scientists who wish to perform and publish statistical analyses or machine learning on sensitive data. It offers a comprehensive treatment of the fundamental concepts and issues needed for one to learn about, experiment with, and properly deploy differential privacy. It grounds the abstract mathematics with down-to-earth explanations and concrete code examples. It is unique in the way it integrates open source differential privacy software libraries, so that readers can immediately benefit from state-of-the-art implementations. I highly recommend it!

—Salil Vadhan, Vicky Joseph Professor of Computer Science and Applied Mathematics, Harvard University, and co-director of OpenDP

In the past 18 years, differential privacy (DP) has firmly established itself as the de facto standard for privacy protection. The core promise of DP is straightforward: regardless of what an adversary knows about the data, an individual's privacy remains safeguarded when it comes to the output of data analysis or machine learning models.

Hands-On Differential Privacy is a groundbreaking textbook designed specifically for data scientists and engineers who may lack a background in privacy but find themselves needing to perform computations involving sensitive data while avoiding privacy breaches. Covering all essential differentially private algorithms, this book provides numerous examples and exercises based on the OpenDP library. It serves as an invaluable resource for anyone seeking to apply differential privacy in practical scenarios.

—Sergey Yekhanin, partner research manager, Microsoft Research

Hands-On Differential Privacy

Introduction to the Theory and Practice
Using OpenDP

Ethan Cowan, Michael Shoemate, and Mayana Pereira

Hands-On Differential Privacy

by Ethan Cowan, Michael Shoemate, and Mayana Pereira

Published by O'Reilly Media, Inc., 1005 Gravenstein Highway North, Sebastopol, CA 95472.

O'Reilly books may be purchased for educational, business, or sales promotional use. Online editions are also available for most titles (*http://oreilly.com*). For more information, contact our corporate/institutional sales department: 800-998-9938 or *corporate@oreilly.com*.

Acquisitions Editor: Aaron Black
Development Editor: Corbin Collins
Production Editor: Kristen Brown
Copyeditor: Brandon Hashemi
Proofreader: Piper Editorial Consulting, LLC

Indexer: Judith McConville
Interior Designer: David Futato
Cover Designer: Karen Montgomery
Illustrator: Kate Dullea

May 2024:   First Edition

Revision History for the First Edition
2024-05-16:   First Release
2024-11-15:   Second Release

See *http://oreilly.com/catalog/errata.csp?isbn=9781492097747* for release details.

978-1-492-09774-7

[LSI]

Table of Contents

Part II.   Differential Privacy in Practice

Part III.   Deploying Differential Privacy

Preface

In this book, you will learn the mathematically rigorous definition of privacy known as *differential privacy* (DP). Differential privacy can be used to accurately release statistical information about a data set that does not reveal information about specific individuals in the data set. Such an analysis leads to the publication of information about the data set, known as a *DP data release*. This book shows you how to design data analysis workflows for sensitive data sets in a way that guarantees privacy.

DP is the preferred and trustworthy solution for data privatization needs:

- DP guarantees are robust against adversaries with unbounded resources, like auxiliary data and unlimited computational power.
- DP guarantees are interpretable in terms of the risk of individuals in the data.
- DP guarantees degrade gracefully as more data releases are made.

Data privacy is a vast topic. If you've previously studied data privacy, you might have learned about securing databases from hacking or creating cryptographic hashes. You may have also studied virtual private networks (VPNs) and other tools to prevent tracking online. These concepts are focused on guaranteeing privacy by not revealing anything about the data. However, the notion of privacy addressed in this book relates to privacy-preserving data releases. The goal of a privacy-preserving data release is to release information about a data set without revealing information about specific individuals in the data. Differential privacy is a mathematically rigorous definition for privacy-preserving data releases, applied specifically to controlled releases of information about a data set.

What is privacy?

Privacy is a term used in daily life—think of signs like "Private property" hanging in a yard or "Privacy please" on a hotel door. There is a general agreement about what these signs mean—in the first case, walking through the yard is considered trespassing (and makes you an inconsiderate neighbor), and in the second, you can expect that hotel staff will not knock or enter your room. This guarantees privacy of the guest from the establishment. Keep in mind, you have just seen two examples where a person can establish a private domain from other people but not from the government. A "private property" sign or "privacy please" on a hotel door certainly will not invalidate a warrant. This leads to another layer in the term *privacy*—you should ask, "Privacy from *whom* and under what circumstances?"

Another aspect of privacy is related to identification. For example, HIPAA[1] guarantees that patients have a reasonable right to the privacy of their medical records. Clearly, hacking into a database of hospital records is a privacy violation. But can you release aggregate statistics of hospital patients while protecting their privacy? In this book, you will learn various relevant techniques for such scenarios with sensitive data.

Why *differential*?

You may see the word *differential* and immediately think of differential equations and derivatives. While this is a sensible guess, the concept of DP is not connected to calculus in this sense. Rather, DP is connected to the notion of *differences*.

The term *differential* here is really about obscuring the *difference* between data releases on data sets that only differ by a single individual.

After learning the theoretical fundamentals of differential privacy, you will come to understand a variety of differentially private techniques as well as how to apply them in real-world situations. With this knowledge, you will be able to translate data workflows into differentially private data workflows capable of analyzing sensitive data. An example of this includes training machine learning models on sensitive data sets by modifying well-known algorithms to satisfy DP. Developing an understanding of

---

1 The Health Insurance Portability and Accountability Act is a US law passed in 1996 that covers the access and distribution of patient medical records. The law states the patient health information (PHI) is only accessed by authorized parties and not released or disclosed without the permission of the patient.

how and why differential privacy constrains algorithms will also help you recognize vulnerabilities to privacy attacks.

The underlying theories of DP are materialized in a wide variety of algorithms, and those algorithms are then demonstrated with accessible examples. The many examples given in this book survey effective DP data analysis techniques across many contexts. This involves more than just understanding the algorithms involved; you will also gain a deep intuitive understanding of the theories that underlie—and the guarantees provided by—differential privacy.

On the implementation side, you will also learn how to construct common differentially private data analysis pipelines. Both non-DP and DP data analysis pipelines tend to break down into simpler, modular pieces that are often largely interchangeable. DP pipelines, in particular, are modeled as a sequence of stable transformations, a private mechanism, and then postprocessing.

To construct this pipeline, you will need to know the query you want to make, the perturbation necessary to protect privacy, and the postprocessing steps needed for the final result (perturbation and postprocessing are covered in Chapter 2).

When applying differential privacy, you will face a trade-off between privacy and utility. While it is possible to make the trade-off more forgiving through careful algorithm design, there's no escaping the fact that your final algorithm will need to balance privacy and utility in a way that makes sense for your specific use cases. This trade-off between privacy and utility is controlled by how you preprocess (possibly introducing bias) and perturb (introducing variance) the data you release to satisfy DP. Intuitively, the more noise you add to a statistic, the less likely you are to learn its true value.

The Structure of This Book

This book is self-contained and divided into three parts. Part I defines and introduces the theory behind differential privacy, explaining each concept that you will need to prepare your data and execute a differentially private data release. Part II addresses applications, from querying different data formats such as search logs to adding differential privacy to machine learning algorithms. Part III talks about important topics for practitioners, such as understanding privacy attacks, setting privacy parameters, and deploying your first differentially private data release.

Part 1: Differential Privacy Concepts

- Chapter 1, "Welcome to Differential Privacy", contextualizes how and why differential privacy was created and gives an intuitive sense of how it works.

- Chapter 2, "Differential Privacy Fundamentals", defines differential privacy and introduces key concepts. This chapter offers an understanding of the mathematics behind differential privacy and why it provides strong privacy guarantees.

- Chapter 3, "Stable Transformations", defines the concept of stable transformations. Stable transformations are the workhorse of differentially private data analyses, as they model nearly the entire data pipeline. Stable transformations also give a foundation to develop a deeper understanding of differentially private mechanisms.

- Chapter 4, "Private Mechanisms", introduces a variety of differentially private mechanisms. Private mechanisms provide the substantive privacy guarantees that motivate the use of differential privacy.

  This chapter covers mechanisms for local DP, output perturbation, private selection, and data streams.

- Chapter 5, "Definitions of Privacy", covers relaxations of pure differential privacy, as well as a number of private mechanisms that these relaxations make possible.

  This chapter will also deepen your understanding of privacy loss, making it possible to achieve tighter privacy guarantees when answering many queries.

- Chapter 6, "Fearless Combinators", shows how more complex private mechanisms can be constructed out of simpler private mechanisms. The tools that combine these mechanisms, called *combinators*, exploit the modular nature inherent to DP algorithms.

Part 2: Differential Privacy in Practice

- Chapter 7, "Eyes on the Privacy Unit", applies the concepts introduced in Part I to an end-to-end data release. In particular, it is essential that the unit of privacy is meaningful and that the unit of privacy remains protected even in the setting of unbounded contributions.

- Chapter 8, "Differentially Private Statistical Modeling", applies differential privacy to linear regression and classification models. There are many diverse approaches for fitting models, each with their own trade-offs.

- Chapter 9, "Differentially Private Machine Learning", explores techniques for private training of machine learning models and private inference on machine learning models.

- Chapter 10, "Differentially Private Synthetic Data", introduces differentially private algorithms for generating synthetic data. This chapter explains the main aspects of differentially private synthetic data generation algorithms, as well as their usages and limitations.

Part 3: Deploying Differential Privacy

- Chapter 11, "Protecting Your Data Against Privacy Attacks", demonstrates privacy attacks that can be used to violate the privacy of individuals in a data set.
- Chapter 12, "Defining Privacy Loss Parameters of a Data Release", highlights important aspects of differential privacy in real-world applications, including how to think about setting privacy loss parameters.
- Chapter 13, "Planning Your First DP Project" wraps up everything you've learned in the book by highlighting important steps in the deployment of a DP data release.

If you are completely new to differential privacy, we recommend focusing on Chapters 1 and 2 first, then proceeding when you are comfortable with the concepts found in them. In these chapters, you will learn the basic language of differential privacy and prepare for the more advanced concepts found later in the book.

Further dependencies on read order are shown in Figure P-1.

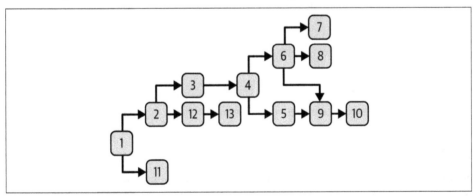

Figure P-1. Chapter dependencies

Conventions Used in This Book

The following typographical conventions are used in this book:

Italic
    Indicates new terms, URLs, email addresses, filenames, and file extensions.

Constant width

> Used for program listings, as well as within paragraphs to refer to program elements such as variable or function names, databases, data types, environment variables, statements, and keywords.

Constant width bold

> Shows commands or other text that should be typed literally by the user.

Constant width italic

> Shows text that should be replaced with user-supplied values or by values determined by context.

 This element signifies a tip or suggestion.

 This element signifies a general note.

 This element indicates a warning or caution.

Definition

> This contains the definition of a key term.

Using Code Examples

Solutions to exercises and other supplemental materials (code examples, etc.) are available for download at *https://oreil.ly/HODP_GitHub*.

If you have a technical question or a problem using the code examples, please send an email to *bookquestions@oreilly.com*.

You can contact the authors at *ethan@lakeside.tech*.

This book is here to help you get your job done. In general, if example code is offered with this book, you may use it in your programs and documentation. You do not need to contact us for permission unless you're reproducing a significant portion of the code. For example, writing a program that uses several chunks of code from this book does not require permission. Selling or distributing examples from O'Reilly books does require permission. Answering a question by citing this book and quoting example code does not require permission. Incorporating a significant amount of example code from this book into your product's documentation does require permission.

We appreciate, but generally do not require, attribution. An attribution usually includes the title, author, publisher, and ISBN. For example: "*Hands-On Differential Privacy* by Ethan Cowan, Michael Shoemate, and Mayana Pereira (O'Reilly). Copyright 2024 Ethan Cowan, Michael Joseph Shoemate and Mayana Pereira, 978-1-492-09774-7."

If you feel your use of code examples falls outside fair use or the permission given above, feel free to contact us at *permissions@oreilly.com*.

O'Reilly Online Learning

 For more than 40 years, *O'Reilly Media* has provided technology and business training, knowledge, and insight to help companies succeed.

Our unique network of experts and innovators share their knowledge and expertise through books, articles, and our online learning platform. O'Reilly's online learning platform gives you on-demand access to live training courses, in-depth learning paths, interactive coding environments, and a vast collection of text and video from O'Reilly and 200+ other publishers. For more information, visit *http://oreilly.com*.

How to Contact Us

Please address comments and questions concerning this book to the publisher:

O'Reilly Media, Inc.
1005 Gravenstein Highway North
Sebastopol, CA 95472
800-889-8969 (in the United States or Canada)
707-827-7019 (international or local)
707-829-0104 (fax)
support@oreilly.com
https://www.oreilly.com/about/contact.html

We have a web page for this book, where we list errata, examples, and any additional information. You can access this page at *https://oreil.ly/hands-on-diff-privacy*.

For news and information about our books and courses, visit *https://oreilly.com*.

Find us on LinkedIn: *https://linkedin.com/company/oreilly-media*

Watch us on YouTube: *https://youtube.com/oreillymedia*

Acknowledgments

This book wouldn't have been possible without the thoughtful feedback and comments from the following readers: Salil Vadhan, Christian Covington, and Anderson Nascimento.

Thank you to our O'Reilly reviewers: Curtis Mitchell and Aileen Nielsen.

Special thanks to Jayshree Sarathy for contributing her deep DP knowledge and working with us on Chapter 12.

Thank you to Joshua Allen, Juan Lavista, Rahul Dodhia, and Kevin White from Microsoft for their support during this writing process.

Thank you to Mengyuan Cai, for her endless support.

Thank you to Raman Prasad, who championed this book from the beginning.

Thank you to Corbin Collins, Kristen Brown, and the rest of the O'Reilly staff!

## PART I

Differential Privacy Concepts

## CHAPTER 1

Welcome to Differential Privacy

If you are new to the concept of differential privacy, you've found the right place. This chapter will present the historical background and conceptual intuition of differential privacy. This chapter is designed to achieve two main objectives:

1. Offer a brief history of data privatization, culminating in contemporary examples of differential privacy deployments

2. Provide a simple practical example of data privatization risks in a classroom setting that demonstrates basic key terms

This chapter is meant to be a soft introduction to differential privacy. You will learn about core DP concepts with less of a focus on math and code. The book will gradually mix in more formal mathematical language and implementations of algorithms as you progress through the chapters.

History

The idea that computing statistics on a data set can leak information about individual data points is not new. In fact, many of the fundamental differential privacy papers[1,2] from the 21st century cite research from the 1970s and '80s.

---

1 Cynthia Dwork et al., "Calibrating Noise to Sensitivity in Private Data Analysis," in *Theory of Cryptography*, ed. S. Halevi and T. Rabin. Lecture Notes in Computer Science. (Berlin: Springer, 2006): 265–84, *https://doi.org/10.1007/11681878_14*.

2 Cynthia Dwork, "Differential Privacy," in *Automata, Languages and Programming*, ed. M. Bugliesi et al. Lecture Notes in Computer Science. (Berlin: Springer, 2006): 1–12, *https://doi.org/10.1007/11787006_1*.

In 1977, Tore Dalenius sought to formalize the notion of statistical disclosure control.[3] As part of this work, Dalenius contended that the goal should be disclosure control rather than elimination, adding that "elimination of disclosure is possible only by elimination of statistics." This idea of controlling disclosure will be important throughout the book; the goal is to quantify and calibrate the risk of disclosure, rather than eliminate it altogether. In 1980, Dorothy E. Denning further raised the *inference problem* as the "deduction of confidential data by correlating the declassified statistical summaries and prior information."[4]

These previous studies acknowledge challenges that are of widespread concern today. The problem of preserving privacy has gained increased attention, as data storage and computation are significantly more pervasive now than in 1980. In addition, "prior information" is more readily available for purchase and analysis, increasing the risk of privacy violations via inference. Denning's paper also identifies a key concept in privacy: if you compute a statistic on a data set and then compute the same statistic on the data set minus one of the data points, you have learned something about that missing data point. In her words, "Comparing the mean salary of two groups differing only by a single record may reveal the salary of the individual whose record is in one group but not the other."[5]

A variety of approaches were proposed to counter these vulnerabilities. Some early statistical disclosure control systems would add a fixed value to all queries or swap values within the data. Many approaches suffered from a significant reduction in utility, vulnerability to *averaging attacks*,[6] and a lack of formal guarantees.

One promising approach, *output perturbation*, involves modifying (perturbing) the result of a query so that statistical inference is less likely to cause a privacy violation. Irit Dinur and Kobbi Nissim validated this approach by showing that output perturbation can be mathematically proven to provide immunity to *data-set reconstruction attacks*.[7]

---

3 Tore Dalenius, "Towards a Methodology for Statistical Disclosure Control," accessed June 21, 2023, *https://ecommons.cornell.edu/handle/1813/111303*.

4 Dorothy E. Denning, "Secure Statistical Databases with Random Sample Queries," *ACM Transactions on Database Systems* 5, no. 3 (September 1980): 291–315, *https://doi.org/10.1145/320613.320616*.

5 Denning, "Secure Statistical Databases."

6 An averaging attack is a process where an attacker executes a large number of queries and averages the results to de-noise the outputs. You will learn more about privacy attacks in Chapter 11.

7 Irit Dinur and Kobbi Nissim, "Revealing Information While Preserving Privacy," in *Proceedings of the Twenty-Second ACM SIGMOD-SIGACT-SIGART Symposium on Principles of Database Systems*. PODS '03. (New York, NY, USA: Association for Computing Machinery, (2003): 202–10, *https://doi.org/10.1145/773153.773173*.

The attack exploits what was later termed the *Fundamental Law of Information Recovery*:[8] privacy can be destroyed by giving overly accurate answers to a sufficient number of questions.

In 2006, the paper "Calibrating Noise to Sensitivity in Private Data Analysis" (*https://oreil.ly/IXV6K*) was published by Cynthia Dwork, Frank McSherry, Kobbi Nissim, and Adam Smith to address the problem of scaling noise to satisfy a privacy guarantee. In this paper, the authors address "privacy-preserving statistical databases"[9] and demonstrate privacy guarantees when adding noise to any statistical query. Let's carefully look at the words in the previous sentence—you may have encountered these words before, but they have subtly different meanings in this context:

Statistical database
> A *statistical database* is a "system that enables its users to retrieve only aggregate statistics for a subset of the entities represented in the database."[10] You may already be familiar with databases like PostgreSQL or SQLite; with these databases, you can execute queries to search for individual rows based on certain conditions. By contrast, a statistical database only allows you to ask questions like, "What is the average age of the people in this database?" and prevents you from executing queries like:

```
SELECT * FROM users WHERE age = 32;
```

If this syntax looks unfamiliar to you, or you want a refresher on the type of database queries you will see throughout the book, check out Appendix D.

Noise
> In the context of privacy, *noise* refers to values sampled from a statistical distribution. You will encounter terms like *Laplace noise* and *Gaussian noise* that specify the kind of distribution that the values were sampled from.

Privacy
> Depending on context, the term *privacy* can mean the absence of surveillance, or the inability to be identified. In contrast to the previous two terms, which are technical in nature, the word *privacy* is used in philosophical and legal literature under various definitions. In fact, even the Stanford Encyclopedia of Philosophy

---

8 Cynthia Dwork and Aaron Roth, "The Algorithmic Foundations of Differential Privacy," *FNT in Theoretical Computer Science* 9, nos. 3–4, (2013): 211–407, *https://doi.org/10.1561/0400000042*.

9 Cynthia Dwork et al., "Calibrating Noise to Sensitivity in Private Data Analysis," in *Theory of Cryptography*, ed. S. Halevi and T. Rabin. Lecture Notes in Computer Science. (Berlin: Springer, 2006): 265–84, *https://doi.org/10.1007/11681878_14*.

10 Nabil Adam et al., "Statistical Databases," in *Encyclopedia of Cryptography and Security*, ed. H. C. A. van Tilborg and S. Jajodia. (Berlin: Springer, 2011): 1256–60, *https://link.springer.com/reference work/10.1007/978-1-4419-5906-5*.

(*https://oreil.ly/V6u01*) admits that "there is no single definition or analysis or meaning of the term."[11]

DP has enjoyed significant research and a gradual implementation in data releases since its establishment. Spurred by the work of Dinur and Nissim, the US Census Bureau conducted a data-set reconstruction attack (*https://oreil.ly/pqB3P*) against its own statistical releases to gauge the risk of violating its statutory obligations to protect confidentiality.

This attack validated confidentiality concerns, motivated the development of a differentially private statistical publication system, and led to a 2018 announcement that the US Census would privatize the results of the *End-to-End (E2E) Census Test*.[12] This process was a practice run for future censuses and systems that passed validation in 2018 and were expected to be put into production for the 2020 census. The stakes were serious; the data in question is used to construct legislative districts and ensure that the 1965 Voting Rights Act is being followed.

The use of differential privacy in the census has not been without challenges. In 2021, the State of Alabama sued the US Census for its use of differential privacy, alleging that the census was providing "manipulated redistricting data to the States."[13] There is prior precedent of the US Census introducing techniques to protect individual privacy. For example, in 1930, census releases stopped including data from small areas (*https://oreil.ly/ZQUQa*) to protect residents in sparsely populated regions from being re-identified. A panel of three judges ultimately rejected Alabama's complaint (*https://oreil.ly/z_-95*), responding that the state had no claim of harm stemming from skewed results since they had yet to be released.[14]

Privatization Before Differential Privacy

Differential privacy is certainly not the first technique that has been developed to analyze data while protecting individuals in the data. Consider a situation where a researcher releases aggregate statistics about hospital patients over the past year. The

---

11 For further demonstrations of many concepts that will be centrally important in this book, see Chapters 1–3, 7, and 13 in Cynthia Dwork and Aaron Roth, "The Algorithmic Foundations of Differential Privacy," *FNT in Theoretical Computer Science* 9, nos. 3–4, (2013): 211–407, *https://doi.org/10.1561/0400000042*.

12 John M. Abowd, "The U.S. Census Bureau Adopts Differential Privacy," in *Proceedings of the 24th ACM SIGKDD International Conference on Knowledge Discovery & Data Mining.* (New York: ACM, 2018): 2867, *https://doi.org/10.1145/3219819.3226070*.

13 The State of Alabama v. United States Department of Commerce & United States Census Bureau, United States District Court for the Middle District of Alabama.

14 The full case is called "Memorandum Opinion and Order, The State of Alabama v. United States Department of Commerce & United States Census Bureau, United States District Court for the Middle District of Alabama." A brief of *amicus curae* (*https://oreil.ly/OWrza*) was filed by the Electronic Privacy Information Center (EPIC) in support of the US Census.

---

researcher publishes a paper stating that there have been three cases of a particular type of cancer in that hospital this year. On the surface, you may assume this is safe; there were no names, addresses, Social Security numbers, or other sensitive, personally identifiable aspects released about these patients.

Previously, standard privatization techniques relied on anonymization to protect privacy—for example, removing or modifying the names of individuals. This is insufficient and can lead to privacy leakages. Consider the case of Dr. Latanya Sweeney who, while still a graduate student, purchased Massachusetts voter registration information and was able to identify the governor of Massachusetts within anonymized medical data.[15] She was able to do this by isolating those individuals in the data with the same attributes as the governor, finding that "six people had [the governor's] particular birthdate, only three of them were men, and, he was the only one in his 5-digit zip code."[16]

This work led Sweeney to the discovery that many people are uniquely identifiable using only these three pieces of information: birthdate, government-recorded gender, and zip code.[17] A 2006 study estimated that about 63% of the US population can be uniquely identified from these three attributes,[18] while 44% of the population in the 2010 census is identifiable via census block, age, and sex.[19]

To protect against vulnerabilities like this, Sweeney introduced *k-anonymity* in 2002. K-anonymity is a generalized protection against this specific type of identification. The *k* in k-anonymity refers to its central principle—that an individual cannot be distinguished from at least *k-1* other individuals in the data set. Using the Massachusetts scenario, this would mean a hypothetical scenario where Sweeney could not distinguish between the governor and *k-1* other individuals in the voter roll, preventing her from re-identifying his medical records. Thus, k-anonymity has vulnerabilities to *linking*; if an attribute is considered non-identifying, but can be linked to another data set, it can become an identifying attribute and lead to privacy violations.

The two major attacks on k-anonymity are:

---

15 Latanya Sweeney, "Simple Demographics Often Identify People Uniquely." (Carnegie Mellon University, 2000).

16 Latanya Sweeney, "Recommendations to Identify and Combat Privacy Problems in the Commonwealth," October 2005. Testimony before the Pennsylvania House Select Committee on Information Security (House Resolution 351), Pittsburgh, PA.

17 Latanya Sweeney, "Simple Demographics Often Identify People Uniquely." (Carnegie Mellon University, 2000)

18 Philippe Golle, "Revisiting the Uniqueness of Simple Demographics in the US Population," in *Proceedings of the 5th ACM Workshop on Privacy in Electronic Society* (New York: 2006): 77–80.

19 John M. Abowd. Supplemental Declaration, 2021. State of Alabama v. US Department of Commerce.

Homogeneity attack

> This attack takes advantage of a situation where the data has many identical values. Consider a situation where a hostile actor knows that someone has been admitted to the hospital on a certain date and looks at the admission logs. If everyone admitted to the hospital on that day had cancer, then the attacker has learned that this individual has cancer. Clearly, this attack relied on the *homogeneity* of the data—if everyone admitted on that date had a different disease, then the attacker would have learned nothing.

Background knowledge attack

> This attack relies on the attacker knowing things about the individual that are not present in the relevant data set. For example, if the attacker wants to know what type of cancer the individual has, and knows that the hospital admissions were all for prostate or cervical cancer, then the attacker simply needs to know whether the individual has a prostate or a cervix in order to learn their cancer diagnosis with certainty.[20]

As you can see, k-anonymity does not always prevent a bad actor from identifying individuals in a data set. Even if the data is sufficiently heterogeneous to not fall victim to a homogeneity attack, with the availability of third-party data for sale, the risk of a linkage attack is significant. Methods that suppress individual features in a data set are not sufficient to guarantee privacy.

Differential privacy gives a more general definition of privacy than techniques like k-anonymity. Instead of focusing on removing or anonymizing certain attributes from a data set, DP gives an analyst a quantitative guarantee about how distinguishable an individual's information can be to a potential attacker.

Case Study: Applying DP in a Classroom

This section covers a simple case study that demonstrates the risks of nonprivate statistical releases. Though the stakes are relatively low (an exam score), the principles are the same for more sensitive types of data. This example highlights an important pattern when working with sensitive data: seemingly innocuous releases can lead to privacy violations.

By the end of this section, you should understand what makes two data sets *adjacent* and what the *sensitivity* of a function is.

---

20 Abou-el-ela Abdou Hussien, Nermin Hamza, and Hesham A. Hefny, "Attacks on Anonymization-Based Privacy-Preserving: A Survey for Data Mining and Data Publishing," *Journal of Information Security* 4, no. 2 (2013): 101–12, *https://doi.org/10.4236/jis.2013.42012*.

Privacy and the Mean

Imagine you are in a class with 10 students total. You've just taken an exam and are eagerly awaiting the results. One day, the professor walks into the room and writes a number on the board: 85%. They announce that this was the average grade on the exam and that they will be passing back papers shortly. Suddenly, you get a text from your good friend Ari: "Big news! Just got a job with the circus and had to drop the class. See you this summer!" You mention to the professor that your friend is no longer enrolled in the class. With this information, they open their computer, type for a moment, then walk over to the board, erase the old average, and write 87%.

This scenario is innocent enough, right? After all, they didn't write your friend's score on the board.

"Well, in a way, they just did," says a voice behind you.

Who said that? You turn around to find a demon sitting in the back row (yes, this connects to privacy—bear with us for a second). You are curious about his claim that the professor just essentially wrote your friend's score on the board.

"What do you mean?" you ask.

He begins to explain that you know how to calculate an average in general. Suppose each student's score is denoted by x_i, the set of all such scores is X, and the size of this set is n. Then:

$$\bar{x} = \frac{1}{n} \sum_{i=1}^{n} x_i$$

You know there were 10 people in the class before your friend dropped it:

$$\bar{x}_{\text{before}} = \frac{1}{10} \sum_{i=1}^{10} x_i = 85$$

where each x_i is an exam score. Further, you know there were 9 people after he left and that the average score was 87:

$$\bar{x}_{\text{after}} = \frac{1}{9} \sum_{i=1}^{9} x_i = 87$$

Subtract the two equations from each other:

$$\bar{x}_{\text{before}} - \bar{x}_{\text{after}} = \frac{1}{10}\sum_{i=1}^{10} x_i - \frac{1}{9}\sum_{i=1}^{9} x_i = -2$$

Let's call your friend x_{10}, then:

$$\left(\frac{1}{10} - \frac{1}{9}\right)\sum_{i=1}^{9} x_i + \frac{1}{10}x_{10} = -2$$

Simplify the subtraction term and use the definition of $\bar{x}_{\text{after}}$:

$$-\frac{1}{90} \cdot 9 \cdot \bar{x}_{\text{after}} + \frac{1}{10}x_{10} = -2$$

and simplify the fraction to its lowest common denominator:

$$-\frac{1}{10} \cdot \bar{x}_{\text{after}} + \frac{1}{10}x_{10} = -2$$

Now you just need to isolate x_{10}, your friend's exam score:

$$x_{10} = 10 \cdot \left(-2 + \frac{1}{10}\bar{x}_{\text{after}}\right) = -20 + \bar{x}_{\text{after}}$$

You already know $\bar{x}_{\text{after}}$, it is simply the average written on the board:

$$x_{10} = -20 + 87 = 67$$

Hold on—that's your friend's exam grade. What just happened? This demon just determined your friend's grade using several pieces of information: the mean before he left, the mean after he left, and the number of students in the class. As you've just learned, releasing statistics about a data set can also release sensitive information about individuals in the data.

How Could This Be Prevented?

What could the professor have done? He could have instead written a possible range for the mean, like "80–90", on the board. Unfortunately, this would be a poor trade-off for everyone, because it wouldn't necessarily help privacy, and it would damage utility, because less information is being communicated to the students. The privacy of your friend could still be violated if dropping his score caused the range to shift, and the broad ranges don't give the students very much specificity. All in all, this is suboptimal for the students and their privacy.

Randomized response

Another potential approach is *randomized response*, where the value is changed with a certain probability.[21] In this case, the professor could have categorized every student as either "passed" (P) or "failed" (F). For each student, the professor flips a coin. If heads, they share the truth (either P or F) for that student. If tails, they flip again. They share P for heads or F for tails, regardless of the student's true performance (see Figure 1-1). By building a histogram with the result of randomized response, the professor could present the students with a distribution that estimates the class's overall performance on the exam.

Randomized response

> Randomized response is a method that modifies the value of each item in a data set according to certain probabilistic rules. For each item, if a coin flip returns tails (false), then the value recorded may not be the true value. This algorithm originated in the social sciences, where the goal was to prevent embarrassment to survey participants who were answering sensitive questions about their health or behavior.

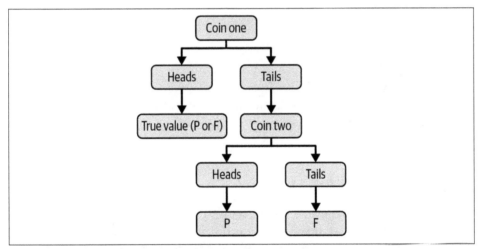

Figure 1-1. Randomized response via a coin flip

Randomized response certainly adds plausible deniability to the data set, since it is expected that 25% of the students will appear to be failing, even if none are (note that

---

21 Stanley L. Warner, "Randomized Response: A Survey Technique for Eliminating Evasive Answer Bias," *Journal of the American Statistical Association* 60, no. 309, (1965): 63–69, *https://doi.org/10.2307/2283137*.

this just requires two flips of "tails" in a row). For this situation, randomized response may not be ideal; it places every student into one of two subsets and does not provide as accurate information about the overall class performance. This approach is preferable if the professor wants to share whether each student passed or failed in a way that gives each student plausible deniability. As written, it will also bias the pass/fail rate toward 0.5.

If the professor modifies their first coin to only return heads with lower probability (say, in 1 out of 100 flips), then they give greater privacy/more plausible deniability to each student but less accurate information.

Adding noise

Alternatively, what if the professor samples a value from a distribution and adds it to the mean? For example, if the professor tells you that the mean has noise added to it, then reconstructing your friend's score becomes impossible, since the equation has two unknowns: the exam score and the amount of noise added. In this case, the means from the previous section become:

$$\bar{x}_{\text{before}} = \left(\frac{1}{10} \sum_{i=1}^{10} x_i \right) + N_1 = 85$$

$$\bar{x}_{\text{after}} = \left(\frac{1}{9} \sum_{i=1}^{9} x_i \right) + N_2 = 87$$

where N_1 and N_2 are values drawn from some distribution and are not disclosed to the students. With this noise added, attempting to calculate your friend's grade yields the following equation:

$$\left| \bar{x}_{\text{before}} - \bar{x}_{\text{after}} \right| = \left| \frac{1}{10} \sum_{i=1}^{10} x_i + N_1 - \frac{1}{9} \sum_{i=1}^{9} x_i + N_2 \right| = \left| 1 + N_1 - N_2 \right|$$

You now have three unknowns: x_{10}, N_1, and N_2, so the equation can no longer be solved analytically. At best, if you know the distribution that N_1 and N_2 were drawn from, then you can estimate the probabilities of different scores, without knowing with perfect information the true score. The question becomes: how do you add noise in such a way that you strike a balance between protecting privacy and keeping the statistic as useful as possible? If you know that your friend is the only person who is leaving, you can choose the noise from a known distribution in such a way that you sufficiently protect his score.

Yet this raises an important point—you aren't just protecting privacy for one scenario (your friend leaving) but for *all* such scenarios where one person joins or leaves the class. You can't know who will leave the class or when, which means it is insufficient to look at only one outcome; you must instead prepare for all possible changes to the class roster.

Adjacent Data Sets: What If Someone Else Had Dropped the Class?

Back to this demon. He comes to you and says, "You will live this day over and over, but each time, a different person will drop the class. When this happens, I will use the definition of the mean to uncover their score." Now, if you have put sufficient privacy protections in place, you would shrug this demon off, knowing he will be frustrated or simply think he has the true scores computed. However, if you have only protected against the scenario where your friend leaves the class, then that leaves everyone else vulnerable.

Now suddenly you are sitting in a room, exactly like the classroom in the previous example but with one major difference—your friend is sitting next to you. His application to the circus was tragically rejected, but he is still happy to be with you in class. Right before class starts, you get a text from another classmate, Bobby, who is going on tour with his band and has to drop the class. At least he promises you VIP passes next time they come through town. You are relieved that Ari's score is private, but in the back row, you see the demon ready to calculate Bobby's score, and understand that it will be leaked.

The professor comes in and writes the mean exam score on the board, and you point out that Bobby has dropped the class. Just like last time, they update the score based on this new information. But this time, they remove a different score, so the mean changes: 84. In this parallel universe, the exam average drops one point instead of increasing by two. Regardless of the change in the average, the demon still sits in the back row calculating the score of whoever dropped the class. There is nothing special about this particular parallel universe; in fact, you need to prepare for all of them. Obviously, we are more concerned with human actors, but the demon serves as a useful foil for what information someone *might* have about a data set and what they could do with it.

In a classroom of 10 students, there are 10 possible adjacent classrooms where exactly one person drops the class. These are the types of events that can cause privacy leakage, as was shown earlier in the chapter. This concept of adjacency is crucial to providing rigorous privacy guarantees.

Since the class enrollment is public information, it is not necessary to configure the differential privacy guarantee to conceal a student's inclusion in the data set. It is only necessary to conceal the value of the individual's data.

Data set adjacency

Two data sets x and x' are adjacent if they differ by changing a single individual. (This definition will be made more general in Chapter 3.)

In the DP literature, and in common usage, *neighboring* is used interchangeably with *adjacent*.

There are many senses in which two data sets may differ by a single individual. In the classroom example, we consider two data sets to be adjacent if they differ by the *change* of a single individual. In Chapter 3, you will learn a generalization of the concept of adjacent data sets.

For example, rosters A and B are adjacent in this sense because they differ by exactly one student (Carol). Let's examine these student rosters as *tabular data*, that is, data organized in rows and columns, as seen in Tables 1-1 and 1-2.

Table 1-1. Student roster A

ID	Name
1	Alice
2	Bob
3	Carol

Table 1-2. Student roster B

ID	Name
1	Alice
2	Bob
3	Eustace

Let's recap what you know so far:

- Releasing a statistic can "leak" private information about individuals in a data set.

  In particular, if you know that one data point has been removed and you know how much a given statistic has changed, you can reconstruct the value of the missing data point. This means that you have to protect against all possible scenarios like this.

- Adding noise to a statistic can prevent this type of reconstruction from learning anything with perfect certainty. However, you don't yet know how much noise to add.

Sensitivity: How Much Can the Statistic Change?

How do you define the possible changes in the exam score mean over these possible classes? To determine this, you need to understand *sensitivity*. You know that the mean can change when a person's score changes: in one case, it increased by two points, and in the other, it decreased by one point. First, think about the largest change possible that can occur when any one person leaves the class.

This is the *local sensitivity*.

Local sensitivity of the mean
> The local sensitivity of the mean for a data set x is the greatest possible value of $|\bar{x} - \overline{x'}|$ over every adjacent data set x'.

Notice that the local sensitivity varies depending on your own data. If the class mean is around 50, then the mean computed on adjacent data sets could differ by less than a situation where the class mean was 100. Unfortunately, this means that the local sensitivity itself can reveal information about the structure of data in the data set. Because of this, the local sensitivity is not actually strong enough to defend against the demon.

You instead need the *global sensitivity*.

Global sensitivity of the mean
> The global sensitivity of the mean is the greatest possible value of $|\bar{x} - \overline{x'}|$ over every pair of adjacent data sets x, x'.

You can think of the global sensitivity as the greatest possible local sensitivity, for any initial data set. The sensitivities can be understood by thinking about pairs of neighboring data sets that maximize the difference between outputs of a function. Based on this intuition, in the most extreme case, let's say your friend got a 0 and everyone else in the class got a 100—how embarrassing! In this situation, how much can *changing* his answer change the mean?

$$\bar{x}_{before} = \frac{1}{10} \sum_{i=1}^{10} x_i = \frac{900}{10} = 90$$

and after changing the exam score to 100:

$$\bar{x}_{after} = \frac{1}{10} \sum_{i=1}^{10} x_i = 100$$

which means the change in the mean is:

$$|\bar{x}_{\text{before}} - \bar{x}_{\text{after}}| = 10$$

Alternatively, examine another extreme case: what if everyone else in the class got a 0 and your friend got a 100?

$$\bar{x}_{\text{before}} = \frac{1}{10}\sum_{i=1}^{10} x_i = \frac{0 + 0 + ... + 100}{10} = 10$$

and after:

$$\bar{x}_{\text{after}} = \frac{1}{10}\sum_{i=1}^{10} x_i = \frac{0}{10} = 0$$

and again the change is:

$$|\bar{x}_{\text{before}} - \bar{x}_{\text{after}}| = 10$$

Plugging in any values for the class, you will find that the maximum change in the mean is 10. For the mean of this data set, this number is special: it is the global sensitivity.

The global sensitivity tells us how much the statistic can change for any possible pair of initial data sets. Often, people refer only to the sensitivity without qualifying it as *local* or *global*.

In this book, and in popular use, assume *global* when the kind of sensitivity is not specified.

For the classroom mean, our sensitivity is 10, since in the most distinguishable case, the exam score average changes by 10 points. Note that the justification given earlier is somewhat ad hoc: it relies on correctly identifying the choice of x and x' for which the difference is the greatest. This kind of justification is prone to human error, which is why this kind of analysis is better handled by a mathematical proof. Throughout this book, you will encounter examples of proofs of important DP concepts.

Now that you've seen this scenario from the perspective of the students, let's look at the professor's role as the only person with access to the full data set. Since the students don't have access to the full data set, the change in a statistic value is the only signal they can use to learn anything about the underlying data. On the other hand, those with access to the complete data set don't need to infer anything because they can look directly at each individual row.

Adding Noise

As you've now seen, adding random noise can help obscure your friend's exam grade—but from which distribution should you sample noise? The *Laplace distribution* is a particularly useful distribution, as it tends to minimize the amount of noise added while maximizing the privacy afforded (see Figure 1-2) The Laplace distribution has two tunable parameters: its center (μ) and its width (b). The probability density function shows how the tails decrease exponentially, meaning the likelihood of sampling a value further from the center decreases exponentially:

$$\Pr\left[\mathrm{Lap}(\mu, b) = y\right] = \frac{1}{2b} \cdot \exp\left(-\frac{|y - \mu|}{b}\right)$$

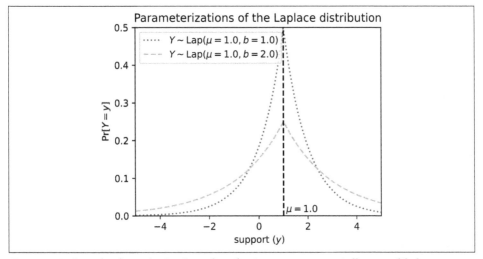

Figure 1-2. Samples from the Laplace distribution are exponentially more likely nearer the center

Let's apply this method to the classroom example, where $\bar{x}$ represents the mean. Notice that $\bar{x}$ perturbed by a sample from a zero-centered Laplace distribution is identically distributed to sampling from a Laplace distribution centered at $\bar{x}$. Therefore, Laplacian output perturbation is the same as sampling from a Laplace distribution centered at $\bar{x}$ (where $\mu = \bar{x}$).

Imagine the professor wants to choose a noise scale of either $b_1 = 1$ or $b_2 = 2$. As shown in the figure, since b_1 is smaller, the distribution is more tightly concentrated around $\overline{X}$, likely resulting in an estimate with greater utility (less error) than b_2. On the other hand, adding noise scaled based on b_2 will result in better privacy protection because more noise is likely to be added. Choosing a parameter that balances the trade-off between privacy and utility is a common motif in differential privacy. Chapter 2 will provide you with tools to numerically quantify both the privacy and utility, which will help eliminate the guesswork when addressing this tension.

What Is a Trusted Curator?

Let's examine this example from the professor's point of view. In this scenario, the professor has total access to all the student data, while the students are only given access to aggregate statistics. This means that the professor is a *trusted curator*.

Trusted curator
   An individual or organization with complete access to a sensitive data set.

The students are the individuals in the data set, and the school staff and students represent the public that will receive the data analysis.

Suppose the professor has the student scores in a data set:

```
exam_scores
-----------
85
84
85
89
92
95
100
83
70
67
```

The professor then queries the student database using a mean function to get the mean test score for the class:

```
exam_scores.mean()
>>> 85.0
```

As before, student *0* joins the circus and drops the class. The professor computes a new mean and updates the score on the board:

```
exam_scores[:-1].mean()
>>> 87.0
```

You now know that anyone who knows how many students the school has could easily calculate the student's grade, which is 67.

To protect the student's privacy, the professor needs a function; let's call it *dp_mean*. Under the hood, this function is calculating the mean and adding noise sampled from a Laplace distribution. With this function, the scenario looks like the following:

```
dp_mean(exam_scores)
>>> 83.84393665240519

dp_mean(exam_scores[:-1])
>>> 84.49003889353587
```

Now when the professor releases these statistics, the students cannot calculate their friend's grade, even if they know the type of noise and scale parameters used!

As you've just seen, *disclosing statistics about a data set leaks information about individuals in the data set.* The professor certainly wasn't trying to disclose sensitive information to their students, but the combination of a statistic and information about how the data set had changed was enough to isolate an individual. This will be a common theme throughout the book: how can you responsibly release statistics about sensitive data without disclosing data about individuals in the data set?

Available Tools

In data privacy, implementation is key to guaranteeing protection—a flawed implementation can leak information and cause privacy violations. Luckily, there are already high-quality open source tools available for working with data in a differentially private manner.

The majority of the code examples you will see in this book are written under the OpenDP Framework. Code examples that use libraries will typically use the OpenDP Library or SmartNoise, which contains higher-level abstractions over the OpenDP Library:

The OpenDP Library
The OpenDP Library is a "modular collection of statistical algorithms" (*https://opendp.org*) written under the OpenDP Framework. It can be used to build differentially private data analysis pipelines using a number of different models of privacy. The architecture of the OpenDP Library is based on a conceptual framework for expressing privacy-aware computations.[22]

The following OpenDP Library sample (*https://oreil.ly/UycF4*), taken from the documentation, creates a chain of three operations and applies them to a data set:

---

22 Michael Hay, Marco Gaboardi, and Salil Vadhan, "A Programming Framework for OpenDP," 6th Workshop on the Theory and Practice of Differential Privacy (2020). *https://salil.seas.harvard.edu/publications/programming-framework-opendp*.

```
import opendp.prelude as dp

context = dp.Context.compositor(
    data=exam_scores,
    privacy_unit=dp.unit_of(contributions=2),
    privacy_loss=dp.loss_of(epsilon=1.),
    split_evenly_over=1,
    domain=dp.vector_domain(dp.atom_domain(T=float), size=10)
)

query = context.query().clamp((50., 100.)).sum().laplace()
print(query.release())
```

The OpenDP Library is part of the larger OpenDP Project (*https://opendp.org*), a community effort to build trustworthy, open source software tools for analysis of private data. The full documentation for OpenDP can be found at the OpenDP website (*https://docs.opendp.org*).

SmartNoise

SmartNoise is a collaboration between Microsoft, Harvard's Institute for Quantitative Social Science (IQSS), and the OpenDP Project. The project aims to connect solutions from the research community with the lessons learned from real-world deployments to make differential privacy broadly accessible. Building upon the foundation of the OpenDP Library, the SmartNoise SDK includes two Python packages:

`smartnoise-sql`

Allows data owners to run differentially private SQL queries. This package is useful when generating reports or data cubes over tabular data stored in SQL databases or Spark, or when the data set is very large.

`smartnoise-synth`

Provides utilities for generating differentially private synthetic data sets. This is useful when you can't predict the workload in advance and want to be able to share data that is structurally similar to the real data with collaborators.

Tumult Labs

Tumult Core is a set of components for building differentially private computations. Tumult Analytics is a Python library, built on top of Tumult Core, that allows the user to perform differentially private queries on tabular data. Tumult also has an online platform for both batch and interactive data analysis. In May 2023, Tumult and Google announced a strategic partnership (*https://oreil.ly/dGqwA*) integrating Tumult's differential privacy techniques into Google's BigQuery platform. This allows BigQuery users to make differentially private queries on the platform by adding a *differential privacy clause* to their query. That is, you only have to add WITH DIFFERENTIAL PRIVACY to your SELECT statement along with several options in order to make the query differentially private:

```
SELECT
  WITH DIFFERENTIAL_PRIVACY
    OPTIONS(epsilon=1.0, delta=.01, privacy_unit_column=id)
    item,
    AVG(quantity) average_sales
FROM inventory
GROUP BY item;
```

Opacus

Opacus (*https://oreil.ly/RVPRi*) is a library for training differentially private PyTorch models. Training a DP model with Opacus requires minimal code changes, and in many cases does not have a significant impact on training performance. The library also supports online tracking of the privacy budget.

Tensorflow Privacy

Tensorflow Privacy (*https://oreil.ly/fXxKH*) (also known as TF Privacy) was created by Google Research. The library includes DP implementations of Tensor-Flow optimizers for training ML. TF Privacy was designed so that users can train DP models with TensorFlow by changing a minimal amount of code. Differentially private implementations of some Keras models are available as well.

Diffprivlib

Diffprivlib (*https://oreil.ly/10hl5*), from IBM, is a "general-purpose library for experimenting with" differential privacy. The library has Python bindings that can be used to compare DP and non-DP ML models and to build DP-preserving applications. It includes a variety of mechanisms, including differentially private implementations of common scikit-learn machine learning models.

If you have a background with scikit-learn, this code sample from the diffprivlib documentation (*https://oreil.ly/IYbma*) will likely seem familiar:

```
from diffprivlib.models import GaussianNB

clf = GaussianNB()
clf.fit(X_train, y_train)
```

Summary

Differential privacy, though a relatively recent development, has led to the creation of powerful tools for analyzing sensitive data. It is not enough to simply remove sensitive attributes from data, nor is it sufficient to anonymize data in order to protect privacy. Relatively simple methods can be used to re-identify individuals in a data set, for example, cross-referencing demographic information with voter rolls in order to identify patients in a medical data set. With the weaknesses of previous privatization techniques in mind, you can begin to weigh your options so that you will be able to safely work with sensitive data in the future. The goal of this book is that, upon completing it, you will have a firm grasp of the concepts behind differential privacy and also feel confident and prepared to work with sensitive data without falling into common traps.

Each chapter has a set of exercises at the end. These exercises are divided between conceptual, theoretical, and programming:

- A conceptual question will ask you to answer a "why" question in sentences. These questions will probe whether you understand the fundamentals that have been covered in the chapter.
- Theoretical questions will rely on mathematical reasoning; sometimes answering them will involve solving a problem, other times proving a theorem.
- Programming questions will challenge you to implement concepts in Python with the OpenDP Library.

All exercises are answered in the book's repository (*https://oreil.ly/HODP_GitHub*), with explanations and further comments.

Now that you have become familiar with some introductory material in differential privacy, you may have started to think more about how data is shared (or not shared) around you. While differential privacy can give fantastic privacy guarantees about data releases you make, you haven't yet seen *why* differential privacy can make these guarantees.

The next chapter will provide a slightly more technical look into the same concepts, more formally define what the differential privacy guarantee means, and expand on the implications of the definition.

Exercises

1. Assuming an individual can contribute at most one record, which of the following database pairs are adjacent?
   a. X = [1,2,3] Y=[1,2,3]
   b. X = [A,B,C] Y=[C,A,D]
   c. X = [A,B] Y=[B,A,C]
   d. X = [D,E,F] Y=[E,F,D,G]
   e. X = [A,B] Y=[A,A,A,B]
   f. X = [A,B] Y=[A,B]

2. Consider a COUNT(x) function that takes as input a database and returns the number of rows in the database. Instead of saying two data sets are neighboring by counting the number of edits needed to turn one data set into another, instead

consider two data sets to be neighboring if adding or removing an individual can add or remove one row.

   a. Given $x = [1, 2, 3, 4, 5, 6, 7, 8, 9, 10]$, calculate COUNT(x).

   b. Calculate COUNT(x') for each possible adjacent data-set x' where one record is removed. Can the distance between counts ever be more than 1?

   c. What is the global sensitivity of COUNT(x)?

3. Imagine the exam from the previous example had an extra-credit question, and the maximum score is actually 110.

   a. What is the sensitivity of the mean exam score?

   b. Now do the same for several max scores {120, 130, 140,...}

   c. What is the relationship between sensitivity and the max exam score?

   d. If there is no limit to the exam score, is the sensitivity still well-defined?

4. Consider the mean for data bounded on $[0, U]$. What is the global sensitivity when the data set size is known?

5. Now consider the more general case where the data is bounded on $[L, U]$. What is the global sensitivity when the data set size is known?

## CHAPTER 2

Differential Privacy Fundamentals

This chapter introduces the fundamentals of differential privacy. Take your time getting familiar with the definitions and ideas in this and the next two chapters, as the framework covered in these chapters forms the structure of nearly all differentially private algorithms.

This chapter builds on the scenario from Chapter 1, where a professor releases mean queries about the test results of a class of students.

By the end of this chapter, you will:

- Understand the basic terminology of differential privacy
- Understand distance bounds, such as adjacency, sensitivity, and privacy loss parameters
- Understand how postprocessing affects a DP release
- Understand how DP mechanisms compose, both sequentially and in parallel
- Understand the *local* and *central* models of privacy
- Be able to execute DP queries with the SmartNoise Library

There is a saying in software development: "If it's not tested, it's broken." A similar mantra holds for differential privacy: "If it's not proven, it's not private." In practice, you should not trust an algorithm to be differentially private unless it is accompanied by a proof. For this reason, algorithms in this book are accompanied by proofs—or at minimum, where to find one.

You will gain a deeper understanding of differential privacy if you follow along with the proofs. On the other hand, if you don't consider yourself a mathematician, don't fret. Focus on understanding the setup and purpose (what are we proving?), directions of inequalities (does it get bigger?), and final statement (what are we concluding?). By the end of Chapter 6, showing that an algorithm satisfies DP should start to feel routine.

Intuitive Privacy

Let's start with a notion of privacy you may find intuitive:

> A data release is considered private if it can't be used to infer anything useful about any one individual.

A private data release should qualify as a statistical inference in the sense that it exclusively infers a property about a population. If, however, a data release can be used to infer a property about an individual in the population, then it doesn't qualify as a statistical inference. This is why *statistical inference is not a privacy violation.*

You can use this to restate the original idea:

> A data release is considered private if it doesn't distinguishably change due to the influence from any one individual.

That is, if the input to the function changes by at most a small amount (*influence from any one individual*), then the output of the function also changes by at most a small amount (*[release] doesn't distinguishably change*). Privacy is not a property inherent to a data release: it is impossible to determine if a data release is private through any careful inspection of it. Instead, only the function used to compute the release is able to guarantee that its release is private.

While this makes the statement more actionable, there are still two open questions:

1. *Privacy unit*: how do you quantify the influence of an individual?
2. *Privacy loss*: how do you quantify how distinguishable releases are?

The next two sections explain how differential privacy addresses these questions.

Privacy Unit

Let's start with the first question: *how do you quantify the influence of an individual?*

The *privacy unit* or *unit of privacy* quantifies how much influence an individual may have on the data set. Since the purpose of differential privacy is to obscure the influence of an individual on a data release, the unit of privacy characterizes what you are trying to protect.

An individual is a natural choice for the unit of privacy. In the classroom example, you want to protect students but don't need to conceal whether a student is in the data set or not. Therefore, the unit of privacy is the change in any one student, which corresponds to the change in any one record in your data set.

Broadly speaking, differential privacy can be applied to any medium of data for which you can define a unit of privacy. In other contexts, the unit of privacy may correspond to the addition or removal of a certain number of rows, a user ID, or nodes or edges in a graph.

The unit of privacy may also be more general or more precise than a single individual:

- More general: the unit of privacy is an entire household or a company
- More precise: the unit of privacy is a device or a person operating in a particular time period

To obtain meaningful privacy guarantees, it is highly recommended to choose a unit of privacy that is at least as general as an individual. The unit of privacy in examples in this book corresponds to an individual, and any departures from this assumption are clearly noted.

For a more in-depth discussion on the unit of privacy, see Chapter 7.

The greater the influence any one unit may have on the data set, the more noise will be necessary to obscure your privacy units. That is, the amount of uncertainty you will need to add to your data release scales in accordance with the greatest influence any one privacy unit may have on your data set.

Privacy Loss

Now, let's address the next key question: *how do you quantify how distinguishable releases are?*

As demonstrated in the classroom example ("Privacy and the Mean" on page 9), when the function is *deterministic*,[1] it is trivial to violate privacy via a differencing attack. This is a distinguishable change in outputs that does not provide privacy.

This is why randomized functions are used instead. *Randomized* functions output a sample y from a probability distribution conditioned on a given input x. Randomized functions make attacks like differencing more difficult for adversaries, because each time you invoke one, it returns a different sample.[2] The randomness allows you to smoothly control the amount of information an adversary gains about any one individual in a data release.

Assume that $M(\cdot)$ is a randomized function, and x and x' are data sets differing by one targeted individual, Alice. An adversary is given access to a data release y, and wants to violate Alice's privacy by determining whether y was released from $M(x)$ or $M(x')$.

The adversary compares the probability of observing y if the underlying data is x against the probability of observing y if the underlying data is x', and then chooses the one with higher probability.

Depending on how different the probabilities are, the adversary may be more or less confident in their choice of underlying data set. The privacy loss quantifies how confident a potential adversary can be based on the odds-ratio of the two possibilities.

Privacy loss

Let $M(\cdot)$ be a randomized function and x and x' be adjacent data sets. The privacy loss for a given output y is:[3]

$$L(M(x), M(x'), y) = \ln\left(\frac{\Pr\left[M(x) = y\right]}{\Pr\left[M(x') = y\right]}\right).$$

---

1 *Deterministic* functions always produce the same output y for a given input x.

2 See "Differencing Attack" on page 261 for more about this.

3 More discussion can be found in "The Privacy Loss Random Variable" on page 112.

This allows you to measure the distance between output distributions for any one specific release y:

- When the loss is zero, the probabilities match each other, and the adversary gains no advantage.
- When the privacy loss is positive, the adversary picks the data set Alice is in, x.
- When the privacy loss is negative, the adversary is misled into picking x'.

When y is drawn from $M(x)$, the privacy loss variable tends to be positive. Otherwise, there would be no utility. A privacy violation occurs if the privacy loss is very large in magnitude.

You now have the tools to talk about changes on both the input (privacy unit) and output (privacy loss) of a randomized function. The next section uses these tools to define differential privacy.

Formalizing the Concept of Differential Privacy

Differential privacy is defined in terms of the privacy unit and privacy loss. Throughout this book, we will use the term *(private) mechanism* to describe a randomized function that satisfies differential privacy. Any function can be a mechanism, so long as you can mathematically prove that the function satisfies the following definition of differential privacy. When you invoke this mechanism on a sensitive data set, the output is a private data release. The output carries the privacy guarantees derived for the function.

Pure differential privacy
A mechanism $M(\cdot)$ satisfies ϵ-differential privacy if, for all possible neighboring data sets x and x', and every outcome y:[4]

$$\Pr\left[M(x) = y\right] \leq \Pr\left[M(x') = y\right] \cdot e^{\epsilon}$$

Pure differential privacy is a requirement that, regardless of the data set you are trying to privatize, the privacy loss will never exceed ϵ *(epsilon)*, a non-negative number. The definition of ϵ-differential privacy ensures that the probability of observing any given output of the mechanism $M(\cdot)$ is almost the same for any pair of neighboring data sets. More specifically, they can differ at most by a multiplicative factor of e^{ϵ}.

---

4 This definition is technically point-wise DP. This definition will be generalized in Chapter 4.

Using the instructions in "Privacy Loss" on page 28, the previous inequality can be reworded as:

$$L(M(x), M(x'), y) \leq \epsilon$$

Following the intuition from the previous section, no matter which pair of data sets x, x' an adversary is trying to pick between, and no matter which outcome/release y an adversary is provided, the adversary will only gain a limited advantage when trying to violate privacy by distinguishing between x and x'.

At some point when conducting a differentially private analysis, you will need to determine what level of privacy protection to provide to your units of privacy. This choice may be governed by a variety of factors, such as the amount of harm that individuals could experience if their data were revealed, and your ethical and legal obligations as a data custodian.

A common rule of thumb is to limit ϵ to one, but this limit will vary depending on the considerations previously mentioned. See Chapter 12 for a more detailed investigation into setting your privacy loss parameters. For a discussion of choosing ϵ values as the probability of being re-identified, see "How Much Is Enough? Choosing ε for Differential Privacy" (*https://oreil.ly/9VhuH*).

Notice that both the limit on how far apart input data sets can be (via the privacy unit) and the limit on how far apart the output distributions can be (via ϵ) can be viewed as upper bounds on distances. Together, the privacy unit and privacy loss parameter characterize the privacy properties of a differentially private query: when an individual has limited influence on the data set, then they also have limited influence on the data release.

Randomized Response

You first encountered randomized response (RR) in Chapter 1, in the context of flipping coins to change an input value. Now, you will learn about RR as a differentially private mechanism. In this case, the data set has only one individual. RR is one of the simplest mechanisms that satisfies differential privacy and can be calibrated based on a truthfulness parameter p, where $0.5 \leq p \leq 1.0$, that controls how private the mechanism is.

RR samples from the *Bernoulli distribution* with parameter p to provide privacy.

Bernoulli distribution
For $y \in \{0, 1\}$, the Bernoulli distribution represents the probability of a binary, discrete random variable B taking the value $y = \top$ (true) with probability p and the value $y = \bot$ (false) with probability $1 - p$:

$$\Pr[B = y] = \begin{cases} p & \text{if } y = \top \\ 1 - p & \text{if } y = \bot \end{cases}$$

The following code demonstrates a single-line implementation of randomized response:

```
from scipy.stats import bernoulli
```

```
def randomized_response(x, p):
    # .rvs is short for random variates and draws a value
    # from the Bernoulli distribution with parameter p
    return x == bernoulli.rvs(p)
```

Think about how this function behaves when $p = 1$. In this case, you are sampling from $\Pr[B = \top] = p = 1$, so every value of bernoulli.rvs(1) = 1. This means that the function will return whether x equals 1, which completely negates the obfuscating power of RR, meaning no privacy is offered. On the other hand, when $p = 0.5$, no utility is offered. The function returns True and False in equal proportion, telling us nothing about x.

Randomized response is ϵ-DP

To show that RR is private, first isolate ϵ in the definition from "Formalizing the Concept of Differential Privacy" on page 29:

$$\ln\left(\frac{\Pr[M(x) = y]}{\Pr[M(x') = y]}\right) \leq \epsilon$$

By continuity arguments, the log-ratio can be considered zero when both probabilities are zero. For the mechanism to satisfy differential privacy, the log-ratio on the lefthand side must always be finite.

To demonstrate that the mechanism satisfies ϵ-DP, you need to find the maximum value that the lefthand side can take, over every choice of adjacent data sets x and x', and every possible outcome y. Let's show these requirements in the formula.

There is a convenient shorthand to denote when x and x' are adjacent: $x \sim x'$. You also know that y must be a value that the mechanism $M(\cdot)$ outputs. The *support* (denoted *supp*) denotes the set of all possible values that a random variable can take, so $\text{supp}(M(x))$ is the set of all possible outcomes of the mechanism. Using these new notations, you can incorporate these requirements into the lefthand side of the equation as follows:

$$\max_{x \sim x'} \max_{y \in \text{supp}(M(x))} \ln\left(\frac{\Pr[M(x) = y]}{\Pr[M(x') = y]}\right) \leq \epsilon$$

In other words, the mechanism is only as private as the maximally distinguishable pair of potential output distributions:

$$\max_{x \sim x'} \max_{y \in \{\top, \bot\}} \ln \left(\frac{\Pr\left[M(x) = y\right]}{\Pr\left[M(x') = y\right]} \right)$$

$$= \max_{x \sim x'} \max \left(\ln \left(\frac{\Pr\left[M(x) = \top\right]}{\Pr\left[M(x') = \top\right]} \right), \ln \left(\frac{\Pr\left[M(x) = \bot\right]}{\Pr\left[M(x') = \bot\right]} \right) \right)$$

$$= \max \left(\ln \left(\frac{p}{1 - p} \right), \ln \left(\frac{1 - p}{p} \right) \right)$$

Of the two terms, $\ln(p/(1 - p))$ dominates for the acceptable range of p (when $p > 0.5$). Therefore, the output distributions on neighboring data sets are never more distinguishable than $\ln(p/(1 - p)) = \epsilon$.

Now that you have proven that a mechanism satisfies differential privacy, you should have an intuitive understanding of how ϵ relates to privacy. Next, you'll learn how privacy can be violated, especially when ϵ is set improperly.

Privacy Violation

A *privacy violation* occurs when information specific to an individual is made available to someone who should not have access to it.

Consider the following scenario: Anna, a data analyst, is doing research that requires querying a data set. Barb is a member of the data set (see Figure 2-1). Assume that the unit of privacy is a single person, who contributes at most one row to the sensitive data set.

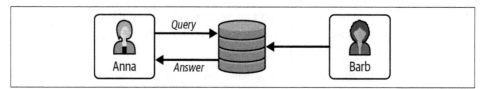

Figure 2-1. One of the individuals in the data set is Barb; Anna gaining information specific to Barb constitutes a privacy violation

Now suppose Anna does the same research on a neighboring data set without Barb's data. Anna's research violates Barb's privacy whether or not her research conclusion changes by querying the neighboring data set. This is important to note—querying the data without Barb can leak information about her, even if the outcome is the same without her.

Privacy is not preserved if it is possible for Anna to learn something different from the adjacent data without Barb (Figure 2-2).

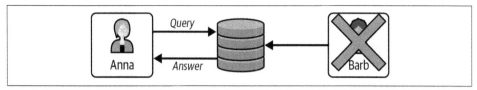

Figure 2-2. If it is algorithmically impossible for Anna to learn something different from the same data set less Barb, then there is no privacy violation

Differential privacy comes from the notion that the presence or absence of any individual in a data set should not provide extra information about such individual when inspecting the data analysis results.

Moreover, if the output of a query is differentially private, the presence or absence of Barb in the data set should not significantly change the data analysis result. However, as mentioned previously, the definition of differential privacy is tightly connected to the privacy loss parameter ϵ. A violation can occur when using a differentially private mechanism with a value of ϵ that is set too large.

Recall from "Privacy Loss" on page 28 that the privacy loss is the log-odds-ratio of the release y being from x or from x'. When ϵ is set too large, this log-odds-ratio quickly becomes large, as shown in Figure 2-3.

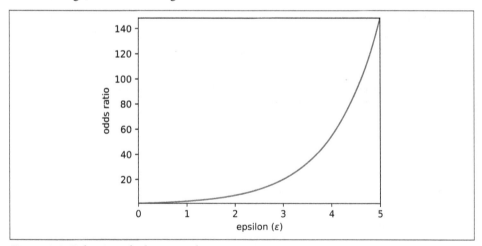

Figure 2-3. Behavior of a large ϵ value

Notice that for a choice of $\epsilon = 5$, an adversary benefits from over a 140-times ratio, meaning the adversary can feel extremely confident when attempting to distinguish the change in an individual's data between x and x'. This is why, as a rule of thumb, it is recommended to keep epsilon small: in the region where the curve is still somewhat flat ($\epsilon \leq 1$).

Recommended parameters do change depending on your mechanism. Randomized response sharply characterizes the privacy/utility curve: auxiliary data is not needed to attack the randomized response, so it is much more efficient for adversaries to analyze. In contrast, many other algorithms make releases that involve data mixed together from many individuals. While the benefit you get from being a part of a data release with many individuals doesn't help the formal guarantee, it does make attacks less practical.

The next section will give more details about models of privacy.

Models of Differential Privacy

The two most common models of differential privacy are the *local model* and the *central model*.[5] The models differ based on how much trust individuals in the data have in a central authority data system.

In the *central model*, the data of all individuals is collected on a trusted central authority and then privatized. In the *local model*, individuals in the data do not rely on a trusted central authority, given that the individuals privatize their own data before sharing it with anyone else.

Deployments of DP that use the local model apply differentially private mechanisms to individuals' data *before* sharing it. The responses are then aggregated into statistical estimates. On the other hand, the local model requires significantly more data to satisfy the same privacy guarantee as in the central model.

A rule of thumb in differential privacy is to privatize as late as possible to get better utility and to collect as little data as possible.

Central DP privatizes later than local DP, resulting in greater utility, but the central authority collects more data. The local model tends to be used by companies who have a very large amount of data, which can offset the loss in utility. In addition, keeping sensitive customer data off company servers can have its own benefits. Randomized response is an example of an algorithm that is used in the local model.

Next, you'll learn about a mechanism that is used in the central model. To understand this mechanism, you'll first need to learn about sensitivity.

---

5 The *shuffle model* is briefly discussed in "Privacy Amplification by Shuffling" on page 163.

Sensitivity

In the classroom example (Chapter 1), the (global) sensitivity of a function was defined as the maximum possible variation in a function's output when the function is applied to neighboring data sets. The output of the function can change no more than the sensitivity on any two adjacent data sets. In other words, the sensitivity is the greatest amount that a function output can change when computed on any two adjacent data sets.

The sensitivity is an important input parameter for differentially private mechanisms, as it influences how much noise must be added to satisfy a privacy guarantee. One way to express the sensitivity of a function is via the *absolute distance* metric:

Absolute distance metric
> The absolute distance is the absolute value of the difference between two scalars a and b:

$$d_{Abs}(a, b) = |a - b|$$

The absolute distance arises in contexts where the output of a function is scalar-valued, like sums, means, and counts.

Global sensitivity
> The sensitivity Δf of a function $f(\cdot)$ is the *maximum absolute distance* between scalar outputs $f(x)$ and $f(x')$, over all possible adjacent data sets x and x':[6]

$$\Delta f = \max_{x \sim x'} d_{Abs}(f(x), f(x')) = \max_{x \sim x'} |f(x) - f(x')|$$

To illustrate the definition of global sensitivity, let's derive Δf for COUNT. While you saw this in the exercises for Chapter 1, this version has a modification.

Given a function COUNT that returns the number of elements in a data set, what is its global sensitivity, where adjacent data sets may differ by up to k removals and additions?

The global sensitivity of a function is defined as:

$$\Delta\text{COUNT} = \max_{x \sim x'} d_{Abs}(f(x), f(x')) = \max_{x \sim x'} |\text{COUNT}(x) - \text{COUNT}(x')|$$

---

6 $x \sim x'$ means x is a neighbor of x'.

where x and x' are neighboring data sets. Assuming data sets differ by at most k additions or removals, then the sensitivity of COUNT query is k:

$$\Delta COUNT = k$$

Now that you have a more generalized understanding of the sensitivity, you are ready to learn about mechanisms.

Differentially Private Mechanisms

Let's return to the classroom example for a moment. Suppose there exist two data sets x and x' that differ by exactly one student, via either addition or subtraction of a single student. Using the student data set, we will define x as the data set with all students and x' as the data set x minus student #0. This time, when the teacher releases the average exam score to the students, they release a DP statistic on x. This release is generated by a mechanism that returns similar outputs for adjacent data sets. From the students' perspective, they cannot distinguish whether the mechanism was applied to x or x', as shown in Figure 2-4. Moreover, this distinction should hold true for the removal or addition of any student.

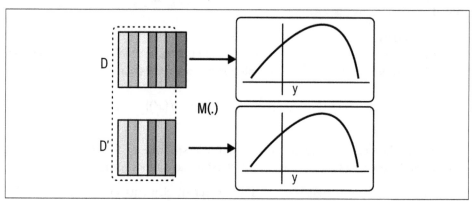

Figure 2-4. Differentially private mechanisms applied to neighboring data sets should produce indistinguishable results

 Recap: why do we use the concept of two adjacent data sets? The concept of neighboring data sets helps rationalize how much an individual can contribute to the output of a query. This concept will help you understand how to construct mechanisms that mask changes in data sets based on the unit of privacy.

Laplace Mechanism

Now you are ready to learn how to construct the *Laplace mechanism,* which is a very popular algorithm in the practice of DP. The mechanism achieves privacy via output perturbation: perturbing (modifying) the output with Laplacian noise. For now, we'll focus on the case where the Laplace mechanism privatizes a single scalar:

$$M(x) = x + \text{Lap}(\mu = 0, b)$$
$$= \text{Lap}(\mu = x, b) \qquad \text{equivalent representations}$$

An equivalent perspective is that the mechanism outputs a sample from the Laplace distribution, centered at the input.

The Laplace distribution is a particularly useful distribution, as it tends to minimize the amount of noise added while maximizing the privacy afforded. The Laplace distribution has two tunable parameters: its center (μ) and its width (b). The b parameter can be tuned freely along a privacy/utility trade-off: a higher noise scale results in lower utility (see Figure 2-5).

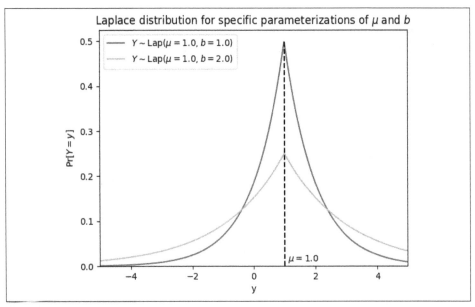

Figure 2-5. Samples from the Laplace distribution are exponentially more likely nearer the center

The Laplace distribution is also known as the *double exponential distribution* because it is exponentially more likely to return samples closer to the quantity of interest (x) than further away. This behavior of the tails gives the mechanism its utility.

The sensitivity (Δ), privacy loss parameter (ϵ), and Laplace mechanism's scale (b) are related through the inequality (to be proven in "The Laplace Mechanism Is ϵ-DP" on page 38):

$$\frac{\Delta}{b} \leq \epsilon$$

You can think of the sensitivity as a fixed value since it is derived via public properties of the data set, data preprocessing, and the specific statistical query. Once you fix the sensitivity, the privacy loss parameter and the scale of the Laplace mechanism are inversely proportional: the larger the noise parameter, the smaller the privacy loss parameter (meaning more privacy).

Next, we will answer a key question about the Laplace mechanism: how can you be sure that the Laplace mechanism guarantees differential privacy? Don't take our word for it; read through the proof and follow along. For each step, try to understand the mathematical reasoning that is happening and work step-by-step until you arrive at the conclusion.

The Laplace Mechanism Is ϵ-DP

As seen in Chapter 1, the probability density at y, when sampling from the Laplace distribution, is given by:

$$\Pr\left[\text{Lap}(\mu, b) = y\right] = \frac{1}{2b} \exp\left(\frac{-|y - \mu|}{b}\right)$$

The density is parameterized by a shift of μ and scale of b.

To show that the Laplace mechanism is private, let's take the same approach as we did for the proof in "Randomized Response" on page 30. First, isolate ϵ in the definition of pure differential privacy:

$$\max_{x \sim x'} \max_{y \in supp(M(x))} \ln\left(\frac{\Pr\left[M(x) = y\right]}{\Pr\left[M(x') = y\right]}\right) \leq \epsilon$$

Just like in randomized response, the goal is to simplify the lefthand side into an expression that is as small as possible: the smaller you can get it, the better the privacy-utility trade-off will be. This expression gives the smallest acceptable ϵ that satisfies differential privacy:

$$= \max_{x \sim x'} \max_{y \in \mathbb{R}} \ln \left(\frac{\frac{1}{2b} \exp\left(\frac{-|y-x|}{b}\right)}{\frac{1}{2b} \exp\left(\frac{-|y-x'|}{b}\right)} \right) \qquad \text{substitute densities}$$

$$= \max_{x \sim x'} \max_{y \in \mathbb{R}} \ln \left(\exp\left(\frac{-|y-x|}{b} - \frac{-|y-x'|}{b}\right) \right) \qquad \text{by exponentiation rules}$$

$$= \max_{x \sim x'} \max_{y \in \mathbb{R}} \frac{|y-x'| - |y-x|}{b} \qquad \text{algebraic simplification}$$

$$\leq \max_{x \sim x'} \frac{|x-x'|}{b} \qquad \text{by triangle inequality}$$

$$= \frac{\Delta}{b} \qquad \text{by sensitivity definition}$$

Therefore, ϵ must always be greater than or equal to $\frac{\Delta}{b}$. In practice, we always choose the smallest ϵ, even though larger choices of ϵ are also valid.

You must now choose the scale (b), which presents a privacy versus utility trade-off. If the scale is smaller, the spike will be thinner, which will preserve the utility of the statistic but degrade privacy. Conversely, if the scale is larger, the spike will be wider. A wider distribution provides more privacy protection but less utility because samples have greater variance. Choosing an ideal scale parameter depends on your use case: what choice of scale strikes an acceptable balance between privacy and utility?

To make a suitable trade-off between privacy and utility, you should consider how much noise is acceptable for the release to be useful and what ϵ expenditure is acceptable for the individuals in the data. Since the choice of scale can be shared freely, you may want to construct a confidence interval to help inform your utility assessment.

Mechanism Accuracy

It is common for differentially private mechanisms to be characterized as (α, β)-accurate.

(α, β)-*accurate*
A function $f(\cdot)$ is (α, β)-accurate with respect to any input x and true output y if:

$$\Pr\left[\,|f(x) - y| \geq \alpha\right] \leq \beta$$

That is, the release will only differ from the true value by more than α with probability at most β.

In the case of the Laplace mechanism, this works out to:

$$\alpha = b \cdot \ln\left(1/\beta\right)$$

where b is the mechanism's scale. Consider this geometrical interpretation: if you were to cut the tails of the probability distribution at α, the probability mass in the tails is at most β, as shown in Figure 2-6.

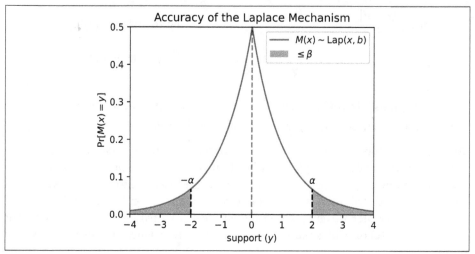

Figure 2-6. Accuracy of the Laplace mechanism

A confidence interval spans a region for which you expect the exact value to live in, at a given confidence level. For symmetric distributions like the Laplace, an interval can be constructed by first deriving an accuracy estimate (the radius of the interval). Using the definition of (α, β)-accurate, you can work out a $100(1 - \beta)\,\%$ confidence interval of $[y - \alpha, y + \alpha]$, where y is the output of the Laplace mechanism.

Most Common Family Type Among Students

Let's see an application of the Laplace mechanism. This example and other examples in this chapter utilize the student data set (*https://oreil.ly/02an9*).

Suppose a school is interested in understanding the distribution of the family size of each family (denoted by *famsize*). In the student data set, students are classified as either having a family with at most three individuals (LE3) or having a family with more than three individuals (GT3).

Use the Laplace mechanism to privately count how many students fall into each classification. You can filter the data without affecting the privacy guarantee. Let x_{LE3} denote the data set of records where famsize is equal to LE3, and likewise for x_{GT3}.

In this setting, assume that neighboring data sets differ by the addition or removal of one student, resulting in the addition or removal of at most one row to the data set. Therefore, the sensitivity of the count on each of x_{LE3} and x_{GT3} are both still just one. The computation of the two differentially private count queries proceeds as follows:

$$M(x_{LE3}) = \text{COUNT}(x_{LE3}) + \text{Lap}\left(\mu = 0, \frac{1}{\epsilon}\right)$$

$$M(x_{GT3}) = \text{COUNT}(x_{GT3}) + \text{Lap}\left(\mu = 0, \frac{1}{\epsilon}\right)$$

"Composition" on page 43 will help you work out the privacy loss of these two releases (try using parallel composition).

When $\epsilon = 1$, you compute the following values:

$$M(x_{LE3}) = 192 + \text{Lap}\left(\mu = 0, \frac{1}{\epsilon}\right)$$

$$M(x_{GT3}) = 457 + \text{Lap}\left(\mu = 0, \frac{1}{\epsilon}\right)$$

Let's say that the output of the mechanisms $M(x_{LE3})$ and $M(x_{GT3})$ are 190.34 and 459.67, respectively. With the noisy counts in hand, you conclude that the most common family type among students is when the family size is greater than three.

Exponential Mechanism

The *exponential mechanism* is used to privately select the best-scoring response from a set of candidates. This is done by randomly choosing from the candidate set in a way that is exponentially more likely to select candidates associated with higher scores.

The mechanism associates a score s with each candidate c via a scoring function $q(x, c)$. The signature of the scoring function is $q: X \times C \to \mathbb{R}$, where X is the set of possible sensitive data sets and C is a publicly known set of candidates/potential outcomes/support of the mechanism.

A tricky drawback of the mechanism is that, often, there are an infinite number of candidates to choose from. Because of this, it is helpful to view the exponential mechanism not as an algorithm that is directly implemented and run, but as a tool that can be used to design differentially private mechanisms that suit your needs.

The Laplace mechanism is an example of the exponential mechanism, where the candidate set is all real numbers (an infinite set) and the scoring function is $q(x, c) = -|f(x) - c|$. This scoring function assigns more negative scores to candidates further away from your data. Your choice of scoring function encodes implicit assumptions about the utility of each candidate: in this case, that small perturbations to the answer won't significantly impact utility.

 Notice that there are an infinite number of candidates to evaluate (C is the set of all real numbers), and yet the Laplace mechanism runs nearly instantaneously. It is common to design and prove that a mechanism is differentially private via the exponential mechanism, and then implement it with a more efficient and specialized algorithm that has an identical output distribution.

The primary benefit of the exponential mechanism is that it is flexible. Imagine, for example, another scoring function that counts how many times a candidate c appears in a data set x, where C is a finite set of categorical values. This choice of scoring function is maximized when c is the *mode*. Lower scores are assigned to candidates observed fewer times in the data set and are thus less likely to be selected.

A necessary constraint for privacy is that the scoring function Δq must have finite sensitivity:

$$\Delta q = \max_{x \sim x'} \max_{c \in C} |q(x, c) - q(x', c)|$$

The sensitivity of the Laplace scoring function works out to the sensitivity of $f(\cdot)$, and the sensitivity of the mode scoring function works out to be the number of rows an individual may contribute to the data set.

$\Pr[M(x) = c]$ is the probability that the outcome of the mechanism is c, and is defined by:

$$\Pr[M(x) = c] = \frac{\exp\left(\frac{\epsilon q(x, c)}{2\Delta q}\right)}{\sum_{c' \in C} \exp\left(\frac{\epsilon q(x, c')}{2\Delta q}\right)}$$

This is what makes high-scoring outputs (according to q) exponentially more likely to be selected. The rate at which likelihoods change depends on the sensitivity of the quality scoring function and the privacy loss parameter ϵ.

A more thorough treatment of the exponential mechanism will be given in "Exponential Mechanism" on page 94.

Let's revisit the problem introduced in "Most Common Family Type Among Students" on page 40. The query you are interested in is "What is the most common family type among students?" We can define the quality scoring function q as the count of students of each family type, as previously defined for the mode, where $C = \{GT3, LE3\}$, and the sensitivity of q, denoted Δq, is one.

The probability of selecting GT3 as the most common family type, when $\epsilon = 1$ is:

$$\Pr\left[M(x) = GT3\right] = \frac{\exp\left(\frac{1 \cdot 457}{2 \cdot 1}\right)}{\exp\left(\frac{1 \cdot 192}{2 \cdot 1}\right) + \exp\left(\frac{1 \cdot 457}{2 \cdot 1}\right)} \approx 1.0$$

Since the two candidates have such vastly differing scores, the probability that GT3 will be selected is nearly one. Notice that the use of the exponential mechanism does not tell you what the scores were. However, since you are releasing less information with a more specialized query, you are more likely to choose an answer that matches the underlying data set.

The exponential mechanism will be given a more thorough treatment in "Exponential Mechanism" on page 94, where a proof that the mechanism satisfies ϵ-DP will be provided.

Now that you have some familiarity with several mechanisms in differential privacy, let's take a closer look at how you might use more than one mechanism in the same differentially private analysis.

Composition

It is common to release multiple differentially private queries on the same data set. When releasing more than one query, you must calculate an overall privacy loss based on the privacy loss of each query. In the terminology of differential privacy, the *composition* of differentially private queries is itself a differentially private query.[7]

As you would expect, increasing the number of differentially private queries increases the privacy loss. There are many variations of composition: the most fundamental is *sequential composition*, where a set of queries are computed and released together in a single batch. The privacy loss of sequential composition is easy to calculate, as it tends to increase linearly in the number of queries.

---

7 Take care not to confuse the DP composition with functional composition, where the output of one function is used as the input to another function.

Sequential composition

Given a data set x and a batch of DP mechanisms $\{M_0, \ldots, M_k\}$, where each M_i is ϵ_i-DP, then apply the batch sequentially to data set x, $M_0(x), M_1(x)\cdots M_k(x)$ provides $\sum_i^k \epsilon_i$-DP.[8]

Going back to the classroom example, suppose the teacher decides to release the mean score of the midterm and the final exams. If the teacher uses an ϵ_1-differential privacy mechanism to release the mean scores of the midterm and an ϵ_2-differential privacy mechanism to release the mean scores of the final exam, the entire release (the mean scores of midterm and final exam) provides $(\epsilon_1 + \epsilon_2)$-differential privacy.

A special case of DP composition is when distinct queries are applied to disjoint subsets of the database. In this case, the privacy loss is not the sum of all the epsilons but rather is the maximum epsilon. This composition is known as *parallel composition*.

Parallel composition

Given a sequence of disjoint subsets x_i of a data set x and a sequence of ϵ_i-differentially private queries $\{M_0, \ldots, M_k\}$, the parallel composition of the mechanisms $M(x) = (M_1(x_1), \ldots, M_k(x_k))$ satisfies $\max_i \epsilon_i$-differential privacy.[9]

In the classroom example, suppose the teacher is interested in understanding the mean score of the final exams of two disjoint subsets of students: group 1 comprises the students with at least one parent who is a teacher, and group 2 comprises students with parents who are not teachers. If the teacher uses an ϵ_1-differential privacy mechanism to release the mean scores of group 1 and an ϵ_2-differential privacy mechanism to release the mean scores of group 2, the entire release (the mean score of the midterm and the final exam) provides $\max(\epsilon_1, \epsilon_2)$-differential privacy. See Appendix E for a generalization of parallel composition to an arbitrary number of partitions.

Postprocessing Immunity

We say that differentially private mechanisms are "immune" to postprocessing, which means that you can apply transformations (either random or deterministic) to a DP release and know that the result is still differentially private. For example, scaling a DP release with $f(y) = 2y$, where y is the output of a DP mechanism, will not affect its privacy guarantees.

---

8 See Appendix E for the proof of this claim.

9 This depends on the notion of adjacency and how the partitions are determined. For a more specific treatment, see "Partitioned Data" on page 156.

Immunity to postprocessing

Let M be an ϵ-differentially private mechanism and $g: R \to R'$ be an arbitrary mapping. Then the composition $g \circ M$ is ϵ-differentially private.[10]

A notable application of postprocessing is generating a histogram with randomized response, which you learned about in Chapter 1. In the example presented in Chapter 1, you learned how to apply randomized response to a binary data set of size n, resulting in a count of "yes" values and a count of "no" values. Since this data has been modified, you will want to estimate the proportion of the true values in the original, unmodified data. Given the observed count of yes values in the modified data set, what is the best estimate for the true number of yes values? If you know that the randomized response algorithm reported the true value with probability p, and y is the observed count of yes values, then you can construct an estimator. First, you can divide y by the size of the data set n; this is your first preprocessing function, and you can be sure that it doesn't affect the privacy guarantees of the mechanism. If t is the true number of yes values, then the expected proportion of yes values is:

$$\frac{y}{n} = pt + (1-p)(1-t)$$

This is the probability of "yes" times the true number of yes values, plus the probability of "no" times the true number of no values. We want to solve for t:

$$\frac{y}{n} = pt + 1 - p - t + pt$$

Combining the pt terms:

$$\frac{y}{n} = 2pt + 1 - p - t$$

Isolating t:

$$2pt - t = \frac{y}{n} + p - 1$$

$$t(2p - 1) = \frac{y}{n} + p - 1$$

---

10 See Appendix E for a proof of this theorem.

$$t = \frac{\frac{y}{n} + p - 1}{2p - 1}$$

From the initial modified count of values returned by randomized response, you've now been able to use the postprocessing immunity property of differential privacy to construct an estimator from the DP release without worrying that it no longer has the same privacy guarantees.

Implementing Differentially Private Queries with SmartNoise

SmartNoise (*https://www.smartnoise.org*) is a set of tools for creating differentially private reports, dashboards, synopses, and synthetic data sets.

SmartNoise includes an SQL processing library and a synthetic data library. The SQL processing library provides a method to query Spark and other popular database engines. You can also use the library to issue queries against a pandas dataframe.

For most common SQL queries, Table 2-1 lists the default mechanisms.

Table 2-1. Default mechanisms for SQL queries in SmartNoise SQL

Query	Default mechanism
Count	Geometric mechanism
Sum (int)	Geometric mechanism
Sum (float)	Laplace mechanism
Threshold	Laplace mechanism

The SmartNoise SQL library can be installed via the `pip` command:

```
pip install smartnoise-sql
```

Example 1: Differentially Private Counts

The SmartNoise library works as a wrapper for the OpenDP Library and simplifies common database queries, such as counts, sums, and averages.

SmartNoise requires the trusted curator to load the data set, specify data set metadata, and choose the privacy loss parameters. The library automatically calculates the sensitivity based on the data set metadata and query. Although the library offers default mechanisms for each query type, the user can easily change the desired mechanism.

As mentioned earlier, the student data set (*https://oreil.ly/02an9*) is used in examples in this chapter:

```
import pandas as pd

df = pd.read_csv('student.csv') ## load the data set
```

To use the SmartNoise SQL library, you need to specify data set metadata via a YAML file. The metadata describes the data types of columns and some additional metadata depending on the data type. For numeric columns, the metadata should include the lower and the upper values in the column. For categorical columns, the metadata should include the cardinality of the categorical variable:

```
Database:
    MySchema:
        MyTable:
            row_privacy: True
            age:
                type: int
                lower: 15
                upper: 25

            G3:
                type: int
                lower: 0
                upper: 20

            famsize:
                cardinality: 2
                type: string

            school:
                cardinality: 2
                type: string

            absences:
                type: int
                lower: 0
                upper: 50
```

To load the data, you need to define three things: the path to the YAML file, a per-query privacy loss parameter, and the pandas dataframe.

Recall that the Laplace mechanism satisfies ϵ-differential privacy. The following example sets the per-query privacy loss parameter ϵ to 1:

```
from importlib.metadata import metadata
from snsql.sql._mechanisms.base import Mechanism
from snsql import Privacy
from snsql import from_df
from snsql.sql.privacy import Stat
```

```
metadata = 'student.yaml' ## load metadata
privacy = Privacy(epsilon=1.0) ## set privacy loss parameter
reader = from_df(df, privacy=privacy, metadata=metadata)
```

The total privacy loss will increase by ϵ each time you execute a query on reader. You can adaptively set the privacy loss parameter of each query by creating new readers. Once the data is initialized by the SmartNoise Library, you can construct queries using SQL syntax to query the dataframe. You can use privacy.mechanisms.map to define which differential privacy mechanism to use in the data analysis.

The following executes a count query to get the number of students in the dataframe:

```
query = 'SELECT Count(*) AS students FROM MySchema.MyTable'

privacy.mechanisms.map[Stat.count] = Mechanism.laplace
print("Running query with Laplace mechanism for count:")
print(privacy.mechanisms.map[Stat.count])
print(reader.execute_df(query))

Running query with Laplace mechanism for count:
Mechanism.laplace
    students
0      650
```

The result of the private count query is 650 students. The same query without privacy-preserving mechanisms would return a result of 649 students.

Example 2: Differentially Private Sum

Using the same dataframe from the previous example, you can make other kinds of queries that illustrate how to use SmartNoise. To query the number of absences of all students, you can define an SQL query and run the private analysis as follows:

```
query = 'SELECT SUM(absences) AS sum_absences FROM MySchema.MyTable '

privacy.mechanisms.map[Stat.sum_int] = Mechanism.laplace
print("Running query with Laplace mechanism for count:")
print(privacy.mechanisms.map[Stat.sum_int])
print(reader.execute_df(query))

Running query with default mechanisms:
Mechanism.geometric
    sum_absences
0      2192
```

The result of the private sum is 2,192, while the data analysis without privacy-preserving mechanisms would return a result of 2,255. What happened in the preceding sum mechanism for the result to return 2,192? The sum mechanism is computing two terms: the non-private sum of the number of absences and the Laplace noise to privatize the sum. The Laplace mechanism (as defined in "Laplace Mechanism" on page 37) adds noise to the output of the non-private result of the function. In the preceding example, the mechanism computes the sum and then adds Laplace noise to it.

Consider a scenario where a new student enrolls in the school. If the results from the privatized data analysis are published, and the analyses are republished after the new student has enrolled, then the new student's number of absences is kept private via differential privacy.

Example 3: Multiple Queries from a Single Database

Using the same dataframe from the previous examples, let's query the average grade for exam 3 (column G3). Now, there are two different partitions of the data: students whose family size is greater than 3 and students whose family size is less than or equal to 3:

```
query =
"""
SELECT
  famsize as Family_Size,
  AVG(G3) AS average_score
FROM MySchema.MyTable
GROUP BY famsize
"""

print("Running query with default mechanisms:")
res = reader.execute_df(query)
print(res)

Running query with default mechanisms:
  Family_Size  average_score
0         GT3      11.825019
1         LE3      12.018476
```

Now let's try another partition of the data: students from school GP and students from school MS:

```
query =
"""
SELECT
    school,
    AVG(G3) AS average_score
FROM MySchema.MyTable
GROUP BY school
"""

print("Running query with default mechanisms:")
print(reader.execute_df(query))
```

```
Running query with default mechanisms:
  school  average_score
0    GP       12.755956
1    MS       10.721144
```

Now let's calculate the privacy loss after the two preceding queries.

The first query returns the average score for two groups of students. Both queries utilize the Laplace mechanism with privacy loss parameter $\epsilon = 1$. From the definition of parallel composition, a sequence of ϵ-differentially privacy queries applied to disjoint partitions of a data set provides ϵ-differential privacy. Note that in this case, ϵ is the same for each query, so $\max_i \epsilon_i = \epsilon$.

The second query also provides the average score for two disjoint groups of students. Just like the first query, it provides ϵ-differential privacy with $\epsilon = 1$.

The final privacy guarantee can be computed using sequential composition. We have a sequence of two queries that each provide ϵ-differential privacy, so the final privacy guarantee will be $\epsilon + \epsilon = 2\epsilon$-differential privacy.

Summary

With an understanding of these definitions and theorems, you are ready to dive into use cases and deeper theories in differential privacy. By now, you should be comfortable answering basic questions about the approach for a DP data analysis: does noise from a particular distribution satisfy DP? Is the sensitivity of a mechanism small enough to allow for meaningful noise addition? Is the sensitivity even defined? You should also understand what DP guarantees (and what it doesn't) and how your ϵ changes the output of your DP data release.

The next chapter will cover *stability*, a term that generalizes adjacency and sensitivity. With this concept, you will be able to answer a more general question: given a change in the input, what is maximum change in the output?

Exercises

1. What is the sensitivity (in terms of the absolute distance) of the following functions, where x is a binary array of size n?

   a. $f(x) = \sum_{i=1}^{n} 2 \cdot x_i + 1$

   b. $f(x) = \sum_{i=1}^{n} x_i^2$

2. Which privacy loss parameter provides stronger privacy guarantees: $\epsilon = 0.1$ or $\epsilon = 1$?

3. Using the SmartNoise Library and the student data set (*https://oreil.ly/7c8I6*), make the following queries:

   a. With a privacy loss parameter of $\epsilon = 0.1$, query the number of students that study in school GP.

   b. With a privacy loss parameter of $\epsilon = 1.0$, query the average score of students in school GP with Family = GT3 and with Family = LE3.

4. If an ϵ-DP data release returns a value x, show that $f(x)$ is still ϵ-DP:

   a. $f(x) = nx$ for some real number n

## CHAPTER 3

Stable Transformations

In this chapter, you will learn about data transformations and how they will help you convert a non-private data analysis into a differentially private data analysis. Understanding if a data transformation is stable will help you identify whether your data analysis can be transformed into a DP data analysis.

Data transformations encompass any function from a data set to a data set. In the context of transformations, consider a data set to be any form of data that has not been made private. Transformations are mathematical abstractions that represent any manipulations, modifications, and computations performed on a data set.

Non-private data analysis pipelines can typically be broken down into three distinct phases: data preprocessing, a statistical query, and postprocessing. In the pipeline shown in Figure 3-1, data passes sequentially through each phase.

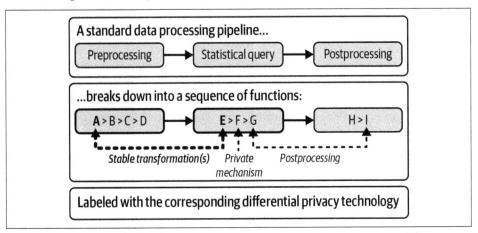

Figure 3-1. A data processing pipeline from both the non-DP perspective and the DP perspective

In a non-DP context, *preprocessing* consists of any modifications you may make to *microdata*. Microdata is a data set where each row corresponds to data from one individual.

An example is a function that modifies each record in a data set, one at a time, while preserving the dimensions of the data. Consider a preprocessing that doubles the value of each numeric element in a column. In differential privacy, these operations must qualify as stable transformations.

Statistical queries are functions that help you understand a property, or statistic, of your data. A statistic aggregates many records into a summary, like a sum, mean, standard deviation, or even regression parameter(s). In differential privacy, the value of a computed statistic (such as a sum or mean estimate) is also considered a data set. When in the central model, private mechanisms are applied after aggregation. When in the local model, private mechanisms are applied before aggregation.

In a non-DP context, *postprocessing* consists of any computation you may perform on the output of a statistical query. However, in differential privacy, postprocessing consists of any computation you may perform after applying a private mechanism. This means you only need to translate computations that happen before applying a private mechanism into stable transformations, which are typically only data preprocessing and statistical queries. Anything that qualifies as postprocessing can stay as is without impacting the privacy guarantees.

Understanding if the transformations that compose a (non-private) data analysis are stable will help you convert a non-private data analysis pipeline into a differentially private data analysis. Having a stability guarantee for the transformations you apply to your data will make it possible to establish a privacy guarantee later.

Informally, a transformation $T(\cdot)$ is stable under the following condition: if the distance between two data sets x and x' is bounded, then the distance between the respective outputs $T(x)$ and $T(x')$ is also bounded. The intuition is that when inputs to a stable transformation are close to each other, the outputs will also be close to each other. Therefore, in the context of differential privacy, the absence or presence of a record in a data set will not significantly affect the result of the transformation.

Since the sensitivity (see "Sensitivity" on page 35) is a special case of the stability, the contents of this chapter will also help you learn how to calibrate how much noise will be necessary when choosing the parameters of a differentially private mechanism.

This chapter discusses the general concept of stability and the stability of data set transformations that are typically used in differentially private releases. You will first study a series of simple examples to get the fundamentals down before picking up speed.

Terms like *similar, close,* or *distance* are useful to develop intuition, but to obtain well-defined stability guarantees, you'll need to be precise when describing how similar two data sets are. This can be done with *metrics.*

Distance Metrics

A metric is a function that computes the distance between any two members a and b of a domain $\mathbb{D}$. A more rigorous definition of a metric is given in Appendix A. The distance with respect to some metric M is computed via $d_M(a, b)$.

This section presents the definition of several distance metrics that will be used throughout this book, the first of which was already defined in the previous chapter:

Absolute distance
> The absolute distance between two real numbers a and b is the absolute value of their difference:

$$d_{Abs}(a, b) = |a - b|$$

> where, for some value c, $|c|$ denotes the absolute value.

The next two metrics are typically used to compute the distance between microdata data sets.

Symmetric distance
> The symmetric distance between data sets is the number of elements appearing in either x or x', but not both. The symmetric distance between data sets x and x' is the cardinality of the symmetric difference:[1]

$$d_{Sym}(x, x') = |x \triangle x'|_C,$$

> where $x \triangle x'$ stands for the set difference between data sets x and x', and $|\cdot|_C$ denotes the cardinality.

The symmetric distance counts mismatches: it is the number of elements that do not have matches in the other data set. You can think of it as taking the pairs out and then counting what's left. This metric considers microdata data sets to be *multisets.*[2]

Consider sets x and x' in Figure 3-2. Let's compute the symmetric distance between x and x'.

---

[1] The symmetric difference between multisets x and x' is the multiset of elements that are either in x or x', but not in their intersection. For more, see Appendix A.

[2] For the definition of *multisets,* see Appendix A.

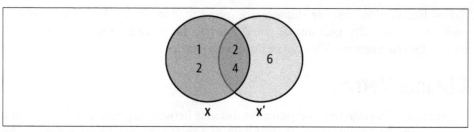

Figure 3-2. Three elements are not part of the intersection when $x = \{1, 2, 2, 4\}$ *and* $x' = \{2, 4, 6\}$

By utilizing the definition of symmetric distance, you have the following:

$$d_{Sym}(\{1, 2, 2, 4\}, \{2, 4, 6\}) = |\{1, 2, 2, 4\} \triangle \{2, 4, 6\}| = |\{1, 2, 6\}| = 3$$

The symmetric distance of x and x' is equal to 3:

```
from collections import Counter

def d_Sym(x, x_p):
    """symmetric distance between x and x'"""
    # NOT this, as sets are not multisets. Loses multiplicity:
    # return len(set(x).symmetric_difference(set(x_p)))
    u_counter, v_counter = Counter(x), Counter(x_p)
    # indirectly compute symmetric difference via union of asymmetric differences
    return sum(((u_counter - v_counter) + (v_counter - u_counter)).values())

# consider two toy data sets, x and x'
#       [Anne, Ava, John, Jack]
x   = [1,     2,    2,    4]

#       [John, Jack, Blake]
x_p = [2,     4,    6]

# compute the symmetric distance between these two example data sets:
assert d_Sym(x, x_p) == 3
```

This example illustrates how to compute the distance between data sets and should strengthen your understanding of the metric. However, in practice, these distances are not directly computed. Metrics are the tools you can use to describe the distance between adjacent data sets rigorously. In practice, this information should be known independently of the data: for example, if each individual may contribute at most k records, then the symmetric distance between adjacent data sets is at most k.

Under some conditions, you may want to compute the distance between data sets by the number of edits:

Hamming distance
> The Hamming distance d_{Ham} between two ordered data sets of the same size $x = \{x_1, x_2, ..., x_n\}$ and $x' = \{x'_1, x'_2, ..., x'_n\}$ counts the number of records that differ between x and x':

$$d_{Ham}(x, x') = \sum_{i=1}^{N} x_i \neq x'_i$$

As you continue through the book, other choices of metrics will arise naturally.

Data Set Adjacency

You have already seen a definition of adjacent/neighboring data sets when it was initially defined in "Adjacent Data Sets: What If Someone Else Had Dropped the Class?" on page 13:

> Two data sets x and x' are adjacent if they differ by changing a single individual.

Now that you have become familiar with a few metrics, you can use them to generalize this definition:

Data set adjacency
> Two data sets x and x' are p-neighboring (or p-adjacent) with respect to a metric M, if $d_M(x, x') \leq p$.

For instance, you could say two scalar data sets $x = 1$ and $x' = 2$ are 1-neighboring with respect to the absolute distance metric. The first time adjacency was defined, the choice of metric M was the Hamming distance, and $p = 1$.

In this generalized definition, the privacy unit (an individual) is more precisely described by the metric M and distance parameter p.

Bounded Versus Unbounded Differential Privacy

A distinction is often made between *bounded* and *unbounded* differential privacy. This distinction is based on the existence of one piece of public information: the data set size.

These correspond to two different ways to define data set adjacency:

1. Counting the number of row-edits needed to transform one data set into another. In this case, the Hamming distance metric is the natural choice.

2. Counting the number of row additions and row removals needed to transform one data set into another. In this case, the *symmetric distance* is the natural choice.

When the data set size is unknown, then you are operating under *unbounded* differential privacy. In unbounded differential privacy, the set of possible data sets includes data sets of any size. The symmetric distance works well under unbounded DP.

When the data set size is known, then you are operating under *bounded* differential privacy. In bounded differential privacy, all possible data sets under consideration are of exactly the known size. In this regime, the distance between any two data sets is computed by counting the number of rows that must be edited to convert any one data set into another data set. The *Hamming distance* metric works well under bounded DP.

Bounded differential privacy can be seen as a special case of unbounded differential privacy when the set of possible data sets is restricted to those with a known size. If this restriction is in place, then the number of edits is equivalent to two times the number of additions and removals, because each edit constitutes one addition and one removal. This relationship makes it possible to convert between different definitions of neighboring data sets.

 When you find yourself using differentially private libraries or reading differential privacy literature, be mindful of how the authors define adjacency. This can significantly change the interpretation of the privacy guarantee.

Now that you are acquainted with metrics for measuring distances and concepts such as microdata, let's define what a stable transformation is.

Definition of a c-Stable Transformation

A solid understanding of stability will set you up to understand the definition of privacy, which will be discussed in the next chapter and is defined in a very similar way. This makes stability an important building block in your conceptual understanding of differential privacy. A stability guarantee does not carry privacy guarantees (that's what a privacy guarantee is for), but it does allow us to break differentially private data pipelines and algorithms into manageable and composable pieces.

Let's start with two key facts:

- A stability guarantee is always associated with a transformation.
- A transformation is a function from one data set to another data set.

Then you can understand this key intuition for stability: if you know that any two data sets passed into a transformation are neighboring, then the transformation is stable if you can also say that the respective outputs are neighboring.

Before formally defining stability, let's bootstrap the concept by defining the slightly simpler notion of a c-stable transformation.

c-stable transformation

A transformation $T(\cdot): X \rightarrow Y$ is *c-stable* with respect to an input metric IM and output metric OM, if, for every choice of data sets x and x' in X, and $c \geq 0$:

$$d_{OM}(T(x), T(x')) \leq c \cdot d_{IM}(x, x')$$

This is a more formal way of stating the key intuition: if you know the inputs are b_{in}-neighboring, then you know the outputs are b_{out}-neighboring, where $b_{out} = c \cdot b_{in}$.

Each time you define a new transformation $T(\cdot)$, you'll need to derive its stability constant c. The derivation is always set up the same way. In the following expression, start with the lefthand side and simplify it into the form on the righthand side:

$$\max_{x \sim x'} d_{OM}(T(x), T(x')) \leq c \cdot \max_{x \sim x'} d_{IM}(x, x')$$

The following sections demonstrate this process to derive the stability of several functions.

Transformation: Double

Let's start by analyzing the stability of the *double* transformation. The double transformation takes as an input a value x and outputs $2 \cdot x$:

```
def double(x: int):
    return 2 * x
```

The double transformation maps integer values to integer values. In this case, both the input metric and output metric are the absolute distance.

Doing a similar analysis on the output of the transformation, the absolute distance of the transformation outputs is a real value defined by $|2 \cdot a - 2 \cdot b|$. Putting it all together:

$$\max_{a \sim b} d_{Abs}(T(a), T(b)) \quad\quad \text{you want the greatest change in outputs}$$

$$= \max_{a \sim b} |2 \cdot a - 2 \cdot b| \quad\quad \text{substitute the metric and transformation}$$

$$= 2 \cdot \max_{a \sim b} |a - b| \quad\quad\quad\quad \text{algebraic wizardry}$$

$$= 2 \cdot \max_{a \sim b} d_{Abs}(a, b) \quad\quad\quad \text{success! you've shown that } c = 2$$

You can now say that if input data sets differ by at most b_{in}, then output data sets differ by at most $b_{out} = 2 \cdot b_{in}$, matching what your intuition would lead you to for the function.

You can derive the same quantity, but wait to apply the $\max_{a,b}$ until later:

$$d_{Abs}(T(a), T(b)) = |2 \cdot a - 2 \cdot b| = 2 \cdot |a - b| \le 2 \cdot \max_{a \sim b} d_{Abs}(a, b)$$

Future proofs will be presented in this way to make them more concise.

Transformation: Row-by-Row

Consider a transformation $T(\cdot)$ that applies a function $f(\cdot)$ to each element in a data set x of size n:

$$T(x) = [f(x_1), f(x_2), \ldots, f(x_n)]$$

where x_i $(1 \le i \le n)$ are rows of a data set x.

For now, assume $f(\cdot)$ is a deterministic function without side effects. You might choose to let f be the log function, to log-transform your data, for example.

Such a transformation $T(x)$ is called a *row-by-row* transformation. The transformation operates on each row independently and returns a transformed data set with the same number of rows.

You can intuit that, for any single record change on the input, at most a single record will change on the output, so the output distance is the same as the input distance.

To prove that the row-by-row transformation is actually 1-stable, set up the usual expression and then simplify.

This proof operates under the assumption that M is either the symmetric distance or Hamming distance. Try to think through the implications of each choice of metric on this proof.

.

$$d_M(T(x), T(x'))$$ interested in the change in outputs

$$= d_M([f(x_1), f(x_2), \ldots], [f(x_1'), f(x_2'), \ldots])$$ substitute $T(\cdot)$

$$\le d_M([x_1, x_2, \ldots], [x_1', x_2', \ldots])$$ inputs are even farther apart

$$= d_M(x, x') \le 1 \cdot b_{in}$$ inputs are no further apart than b_{in}

In the worst case, the resulting data sets are just as far apart as they were before, and no more. The first inequality is because, in the best case, the data sets may be transformed to be closer together. This can happen if f maps into a smaller domain. It is easiest to observe this if you let f be a constant function.

This proof requires that the input metric and output metric match (are both M). In addition, since the proof assumes the structure of the data (a microdata vector), the proof only works with metrics on microdata, like the symmetric distance and Hamming distance.

Altogether, it has been shown that row-by-row is 1-stable, under some conditions on the function $f(\cdot)$ and the input/output metric M.

The fact that row-by-row transformations are 1-stable is incredibly useful. Many kinds of data transformations and data preprocessing functions easily qualify as row-by-row, making them 1-stable transformations. Think of data frames or arrays, where each individual may influence a limited number of rows. Row-by-row transformations can be used to project or remove columns. Selecting one column is a row-by-row transformation from a data frame to a vector. This opens the door to many kinds of data preprocessing in your differentially private analysis.

While you can do many things with row-by-row transformations, they are still quite limited. Many transformations are still stable but are not row-by-row: as you will see in the next section, stable transformations may more generally have different input and output metrics, change the order or number of records, or change an individual's influence on the data set.

Stability Is a Necessary and Sufficient Condition for Sensitivity

Chapter 2 defined the sensitivity of a function $f(\cdot)$ to be the maximum distance between $f(x)$ and $f(x')$, over all possible adjacent data sets x and x'.

The sensitivity and stability are tightly connected. $f(\cdot)$ qualifies as a stable transformation, meaning the definition of sensitivity is a special case of the definition of stability.

The sensitivity of a transformation $T(\cdot)$ is the maximum distance between $T(x)$ and $T(x')$, over all possible adjacent data sets x and x' with respect to a metric OM. This results in a very familiar expression:

$$\Delta T = \max_{x \sim x'} d_{OM}(T(x), T(x'))$$

The prior terminology, ΔT, is the smallest possible b_{out}.

If $T(\cdot)$ is c-stable, and you know that all data sets x and x' are b_{in}-neighboring, then you can further simplify the expression:

$$\Delta T \le c \cdot \max_{x \sim x'} d_{IM}(x, x') \le c \cdot b_{in}.$$

Figure 3-3 illustrates the relation between the distance b_{in} of adjacent data sets and the sensitivity ΔT of a stable transformation.

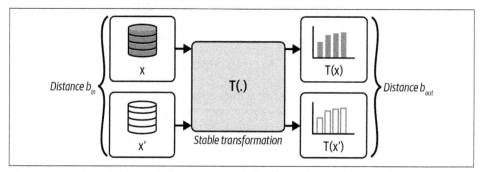

Figure 3-3. When the distance between data sets x and x' is bounded by b_{in}, the distance between the respective outputs of a stable transformation $T(x)$ and $T(x')$ is bounded by b_{out}; the greatest distance between the outputs is the sensitivity of the transformation $T(\cdot)$

In the next chapters, you will notice that converting non-private data releases into DP data releases is a simpler task than you might think. If you start a data analysis knowing the maximum contribution an individual can make to a data set (denoted b_{in}), and all transformations in the pipeline are stable, then you will know that the distance between outputs is also bounded. That is, the entire pipeline behaves as a single stable transformation.

Notice that this is the key property you need to derive the sensitivity, which will, in turn, determine the amount of noise you will need to apply to the output to satisfy ϵ-differential privacy.

The following sections discuss the stability (sensitivity, in this case) of common data aggregations.

Transformation: Count

The *count* transformation simply computes a count of the number of records in the data set. For this transformation, the symmetric distance is a natural input metric, and the absolute distance is a natural output metric.

To show that the count transformation is stable, you need to demonstrate that for any two b_{in}-neighboring data sets x and x', the following inequality holds:

$$d_{Abs}(\text{count}(x), \text{count}(x')) \leq c \cdot d_{Sym}(x, x'),$$

for some constant c.

Reframing the data set as a histogram is a useful technique for analyzing the stability of transformations. Suppose you have a vector data set x. The corresponding histogram representation contains one bin for each possible unique value the vector elements may take on. Each histogram element contains a count of the number of instances of said value.

Imagine you can access the histogram for a data set x through a function $h_x(u)$. The function takes u, a unique value, and returns the number of instances of that value.

For example, consider a data set x, where the elements in x can assume three possible values: {"No_high_school", "High_school", "Bachelors_degree"}.

The histograms for each value in column w are:

- $h_x(\text{"No\_high\_school"}) = 10$
- $h_x(\text{"High\_school"}) = 14$
- $h_x(\text{"Bachelors\_degree"}) = 13$

In the example, $h_x(\text{"Bachelors\_degree"}) = 13$ means that there are 13 occurrences of *Bachelors_degree* in the data set x.

A count of the number of elements in the data set can be framed as a sum of histograms. Suppose you want to count all individuals in the data set x. Then the count is the sum of the occurrences of each value:

$$count(x) = \Sigma_u h_x(u).$$

Using this representation of count(x), you want to show that count(x) is a stable function by demonstrating $d_{Abs}(\text{count}(x), \text{count}(x'))$ is bounded by $d_{Sym}(x, x')$. Let's evaluate when x and x' differ by a single row, $d_{Sym}(x, x') = 1$:

$$d_{Abs}(\text{count}(x), \text{count}(x')) \qquad\qquad (1)$$

$$= \left| \text{count}(x) - \text{count}(x') \right| \qquad (2) \text{ substitute the definition of } d_{Abs}$$

$$= \left| \sum_u h_x(u) - \sum_u h_x(u) \right| \qquad\qquad (3) \text{ histogram trick!}$$

The difference between the sum of histograms can be rewritten as the sum of the differences. Since x and x' differ by a single individual, all terms of the sum will be canceled except for one:

$$= \left| h_x(v) - h'_x(v) \right| \qquad (4) \text{ only the vth cell is affected}$$

$$\leq 1 \qquad\qquad (5) \text{ by the single-row assumption}$$

The preceding demonstration can then be generalized to data sets that differ in up to p additions or removals. If two data sets are p-neighboring under the symmetric distance, then there exists a path of up to p data sets that each differ by one record from the next data set in the path. The first and last data sets in the path are x and x'. You can use this to extend the previous analysis to the case where x and x' differ by up to b_{in} rows by repeatedly applying the analysis that only considers a single row. This gives you the result that $d_{Abs}(\text{count}(x), \text{count}(x'))$ is no greater than $1 \cdot d_{Sym}(x, x')$ and that the count is therefore 1-stable.

Putting this in the terminology of sensitivity, you can use this to say:

$$\Delta\text{count} = \max_{x \sim x'} d_{Abs}(\text{count}(x), \text{count}(x')) = b_{in}$$

Changing the distance metric you use to compute the distance between adjacent data sets can significantly impact the sensitivity. Earlier in the chapter, when discussing bounded DP and the Hamming metric, it was mentioned that data set size is fixed and must be public information. Verify this by working out the sensitivity of the count when data sets may differ under the Hamming distance. You will find that, under bounded-DP, the count transformation is 0-stable, when counting all elements in the data set.

Transformation: Unknown-Size Sum

Now, let's compute the stability of the sum transformation. The sum function is defined as $\text{sum}(x) = \sum_i x_i$, where each $x_i \in \mathbb{R}$ is an element of data set x. For this transformation, assume that the input metric is the symmetric distance and the output metric is the absolute distance.

From the definition of stability, a function sum(x) is c-stable if:

$$d_{Abs}(\text{sum}(x), \text{sum}(x')) \le c \cdot d_{Sym}(x, x')$$

To solve for c, focus on simplifying the left side of the preceding inequality:

$$d_{Abs}(\text{sum}(x), \text{sum}(x')) = \left| \sum_i x_i - \sum_i x_i' \right|$$

You can again narrow the problem to the case where x and x' differ by a single record. Moreover, let's assume that x' has the same records as x plus an extra record. Therefore $\sum_i^N x_i' = \sum_i^N x_i + x_{N+1}'$, where N is the size of data set x. With these simplifications, the preceding expression becomes:

$$= \left| \sum_i^N x_i - \left(\sum_i^N x_i + x_{N+1}' \right) \right| = |x_{N+1}'|$$

Unfortunately x_{N+1}' can be arbitrarily large, meaning the function is *not* stable—at least, not in its current state.

All you need is an assumption that all elements of the data set x are bounded between some constants L and U. This would imply that $|x_{N+1}'| \le \max(|L|, |U|)$.[3] This results in:

$$d_{Abs}(\text{sum}(x), \text{sum}(x')) \le \max(|L|, |U|)$$

Just like in the count proof, you can generalize this to work with data sets that differ by up to b_{in} records via the path property of the symmetric distance. Putting the pieces together, for a data set where the value of each element is within $[L, U]$, the sum(x) is a $\max(|L|, |U|)$-stable transformation.

Now that you have a stability guarantee, then you also have the sensitivity, since the sensitivity is a special case of stability.

We'll demonstrate this with the OpenDP Library. Suppose you have a data set that is bounded by $[0, 10]$. Additionally, suppose the symmetric distance between adjacent data sets is 2:

---

3 $max(a, b)$ denotes the function that takes as inputs $a, b \in \mathbb{R}$ and returns the maximum value between a and b.

```
import opendp.prelude as dp
# starting with an assumption that data is bounded
#   (the domain of vectors of bounded ints)
domain = dp.vector_domain(dp.atom_domain(bounds=(0, 10)))
metric = dp.symmetric_distance()

# construct a stable transformation
t_sum = dp.t.make_sum(domain, metric)

# compute the sensitivity by invoking the stability map
assert t_sum.map(2) == 20
```

When an individual may contribute up to two records, then the sum may change by up to 20.

Domain Descriptors

When proving the stability of a transformation, you may need to make assumptions about the properties of the data. In the previous section, to show that the sum transformation was stable, you needed to assume that the value of each row in the input data is bounded. *Domain descriptors* fulfill these assumptions.

A domain descriptor restricts the set of possible data sets that are members of a domain. An example of this is restricting numeric data to within some given lower bound L and upper bound U. The data set size N is another example of a domain descriptor.

Most data you will want to privately analyze will lack these domain descriptors. Consider data where each row is a numeric value that represents the monthly salary of the residents of the city of Seattle. In this case, although there is a clear lower bound of zero, there is no clear upper bound for the maximum salary.

Data domain descriptors come from two sources:

- Descriptors may be public information about the data set.
- Descriptors may be established via data preprocessing.

In the first case, descriptors may only be safely considered public information about a data set if, for all potential data sets under consideration, that descriptor holds invariant regardless of the actions of any one individual. In many real-world applications, descriptors can be derived from common-sense relationships. For example, in a data set of families, the age of the parents may not be less than the age of their children.

It is, however, good practice to acquire domain descriptors via data preprocessing. The reason is that, in practice, data is messy and may not be consistent with your prior expectations or public information. In addition, you generally only want to use public information in settings where not using public data would damage utility. For instance, you may expect ages to fall within a given range but someone in the data has a higher age than you expected. If you don't acquire the domain descriptor via clamping, their privacy loss would exceed the privacy guarantee. Acquiring domain descriptors via data preprocessing avoids the risk of these kinds of mistakes degrading your privacy guarantees.

Now that you understand the importance of bounds on the input data, and why there is a preference for acquiring these bounds via data preprocessing, let's take a closer look at the clipping transformation.

Transformation: Data Clipping

Use a clipping transformation to establish a domain descriptor for the lower and upper bound of values in your data.

Clipping
Clipping replaces each value outside pre-defined bound(s) with the nearest neighbor within the bound(s).

Implementations of the clipping transformation are straightforward. Python's NumPy library has a function for clipping scalar values:

```
import numpy as np

v = [0, 1, 2, 3, 4, 5, 6, 7, 8, 9]  # values to be clipped
v_min = 3  # minimum value
v_max = 6  # maximum value

np.clip(v , v_min , v_max)

>>>> [3, 3, 3, 3, 4, 5, 6, 6, 6, 6]
```

Similarly, the OpenDP Library has a constructor for clipping data (named clamp):

```
import opendp.prelude as dp

# when working with microdata in the domain of vectors
input_space = dp.vector_domain(dp.atom_domain(T=int)), dp.symmetric_distance()

# create a 1-stable clamp transformation
t_clamp = dp.t.make_clamp(*input_space, bounds=(0, 10))

# check the transformation behaves as expected
assert t_clamp([-10, 0, 10, 20]) == [0, 0, 10, 10]
assert t_clamp.map(1) == 1
```

Since the clamp function $f(\cdot)$ satisfies the requirements of the row-by-row transformation, clipping is 1-stable. Clipping establishes a domain descriptor on the output domain of the clamp transformation.

This is a common pattern in differential privacy: preprocessing transformations are used to establish domain descriptors that will facilitate proving the stability of later transformations.

The general advice for choosing clipping bounds is to choose them conservatively wide based on either domain expertise or similar public data sets, if they exist. It is possible to estimate them with some of your privacy budget, but unless you have no idea, these methods tend to give lower utility than rough, conservative guesses.

Notice that there is a trade-off when choosing bounds: choosing bounds too small will bias your results toward the clipping bounds, and choosing them too large will result in larger sensitivity. As you learned in Chapter 2, sensitivity is one of the parameters that influence the amount of noise needed to be added to satisfy ϵ-differential privacy.

If you do choose to privately estimate bounds for your data, keep in mind that the max and min are highly sensitive to a single individual. Most techniques opt to estimate less extreme values, such as the .05 and .95 quantiles ("Piecewise-Constant Support Exponential Mechanism" on page 100), or by postprocessing a histogram ("Example: Bounds Estimation" on page 143).

Chaining

You now have two separate transformations (a clamp and a sum) and would almost certainly rather have one transformation that does both. Luckily, the definition of stability is designed to enable the functional composition of transformations.

If the output domain of the clamp matches the input domain of the sum (and similarly for the metrics), then the two transformations can be chained.

The resulting transformation guarantees that if the input data set is in the input domain of the clamp transformation, then the output data set is in the output domain of the sum transformation. Just like for domains and data, the same holds for metrics and distances: if the input distance b_{in} is with respect to the input metric of the clamp transformation, then the output distance b_{out} is with respect to the output metric of the sum transformation.

More generally, if you chain any c_1-stable transformation $T_1(\cdot)$ with any c_2-stable transformation $T_2(\cdot)$, then you'll get a new c_3-stable transformation $T_3(\cdot) = T_2(T_1(\cdot))$ where $c_3 = c_2 \cdot c_1$.

You can construct entire data processing pipelines that have stability guarantees by repeatedly chaining transformations together.

Now that you've become more familiar with how domains and metrics work together, it is time to explain their relationship.

Metric Spaces

Together, a domain and a metric form what is called a *metric space*. Your sensitive data set is a member of a domain, or set, of possible data sets.

Metric space
> A metric space is a set (domain) equipped with a metric to compute the distance between any two members of the set.

A stable transformation maps data from one metric space to another. When you build up a differentially private algorithm from a series of chained transformations, you are mapping your data from one space to another space, to another space, and so on (see Figure 3-4). It is the responsibility of every transformation to ensure that, once a series of transformations have been applied to neighboring data sets that are quantifiably "close," the resulting outcomes are also quantifiably "close."

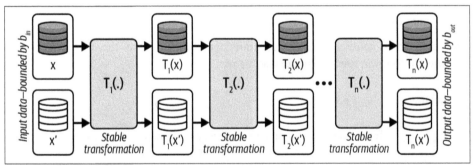

Figure 3-4. Path of stable transformations; when the inputs of a chain of stable transformations are bounded, the outputs will also be bounded

The overarching goal is to transform the data into a metric space that can be used as the input to a private mechanism, in a way that always remains as close as possible to its neighbors. Private mechanisms were discussed briefly in Chapter 2, and will be discussed in more depth in the next two chapters. With this bigger picture in mind, let's continue to enrich the set of building blocks and gain more practice reasoning about the stability of transformations.

Definition of Stability

The definition of c-stability unnecessarily requires the relationship between b_{in} and b_{out} to be linear. While transformations discussed thus far exhibit a linear relationship between b_{in} and b_{out}, the stability of many transformations is nonlinear.

Stable transformation

A transformation $T(\cdot)$ is (b_{in}, b_{out})-*stable* with respect to input metric IM and output metric OM if, for any choice of data sets x and x' such that $d_{IM}(x, x') \le b_{in}$, then $d_{OM}(T(x), T(x')) \le b_{out}$.

This final definition of stability allows the relationship between b_{in} and b_{out} to be captured by a function, called a *stability map*. A stability map translates an upper bound on the distance between neighboring inputs (b_{in}) to an upper bound on the distance between neighboring outputs (b_{out}).

Just like with c-stability, you always derive the stability map in the same way. In the following expression, start with the lefthand side and simplify it into the form on the righthand side:

$$\max_{x \sim x'} d_{OM}(T(x), T(x')) \le \text{stability\_map}\left(\max_{x \sim x'} d_{IM}(x, x') \right)$$

A stability map derived in this way upholds the guarantee that, if you know the inputs are b_{in}-neighboring, then you know the outputs are b_{out}-neighboring, where $b_{out} = \text{stability\_map}(b_{in})$.

This definition generalizes c-stable transformations, where the stability map is assumed to follow a specific functional form:

$$\text{stability\_map}(b_{in}) = c \cdot b_{in}$$

 Transformations have a second requirement, which is useful for chaining. Since transformations explicitly describe the output domain, you must be able to prove that, assuming input data is in the input domain, the output of the function is a member of the output domain.

The definition of stability mirrors the definition of privacy. For this reason, gaining an understanding of the definition of stability now will aid in understanding the definition of privacy, which will be discussed in the next chapter. This chapter discusses several examples of nonlinear stability maps, starting with the known-size sum.

Transformation: Known-Size Sum

Let's revisit the sum, but this time assume you know that neighboring data sets differ in terms of the Hamming distance. Since you're working with the Hamming distance under bounded DP, the size of the data sets N is a known integer.

For an ordered data set $x = [x_1, x_2, ..., x_N]$, assume x' is the same as x except for the first b_{in} records. Which records are changed doesn't matter, but in this case, changing the first records will make the analysis easier.

Since all but the first b_{in} records are the same, you can break apart the sum:

$$\sum_i x_i' = \sum_{i=1}^{b_{in}} x_i' + \sum_{i=r+1}^{N} x_i,$$

This property will be useful in the following analysis: as always, you want to work out how much the output can change, for any choice of adjacent data sets:

$$d_{Abs}(\text{sum}(x), \text{sum}(x'))$$ outputs of the transformation

$$= \left| \sum_{i=1}^{N} x_i - \sum_{i=1}^{N} x_i' \right|$$ substitute the function

$$= \left| \sum_{i=1}^{b_{in}} (x_i' - x_i) \right|$$ trailing sums cancel (they weren't changed)

$$\leq \sum_{i=1}^{b_{in}} |x_i' - x_i|$$ by triangle inequality

assuming that the data is bounded by a lower bound L and an upper bound U,

$$\leq \sum_{i=1}^{b_{in}} |U - L|$$ each datum is bounded

$$= b_{in} \cdot |U - L|$$ since summands are constants

 This proof departs from previous proof approaches in that it doesn't start with an assumption that only one record is changed and then generalizes via the path property. While it would still be valid to use the path property, this proof directly derives the stability in one pass.

Intuitively, the change in the sum is greatest when you remove values at the lower bound and replace them with values at the upper bound. Therefore, the stability map is $b_{out} = b_{in} \cdot |U - L|$ when the input metric is the Hamming distance.

This transformation is also in the OpenDP Library but with a twist: since unbounded DP is a superset of bounded DP, all transformations use unbounded DP metrics (e.g., symmetric distance). The library distinguishes between the two cases (bounded and unbounded) based on the existence of a data set size descriptor in the domain.

Luckily, it is easy to translate to unbounded DP, as the change of one record equates to one additional record and one removed record. Therefore, when the input metric is the symmetric distance, the stability map is $\lfloor b_{in}/2 \rfloor \cdot |U - L|$ (nonlinear in b_{in}):

```
domain = dp.vector_domain(dp.atom_domain(bounds=(90, 100)), size=100)
metric = dp.symmetric_distance()

sum_trans = dp.t.make_sum(domain, metric)
# two changed records (four additions/removals) can change the sum by up to 20
assert sum_trans.map(4) == 20
```

When $b_{in} = 4$ and $L, U = [90, 100]$, the sensitivity is 400 under unbounded DP, but the sensitivity is only 20 under bounded DP. By making use of domain descriptors, the utility of bounded DP dominates that of unbounded DP, especially as the bounds become larger in magnitude.

Transformation: Known-Size Mean

The bounded-DP mean is a natural follow-up case to the bounded-DP sum:

$$\max_{x \sim x'} d_{Abs}\left(\frac{\text{sum}(x)}{N}, \frac{\text{sum}(x')}{N}\right)$$

Since you are in the bounded-DP regime and the data set size N is available to you, you can think of the mean as a stable bounded-DP sum transformation, chained with a stable division transformation, resulting in a stability of $\frac{|U - L|}{N}$ when the input metric is the Hamming distance.

While this result is indeed correct from a theoretical point of view, it introduces unnecessary complexity to practical implementations. There are many ways an implementation like this can go wrong: if you are working with integers, did you account for rounding when dividing by N? If the quantity were to round to an integer of greater magnitude (means can be negative), how might that increase the bound $\frac{|U - L|}{N}$? What would happen if someone made a mistake and the input data had fewer records than was expected? Would the transformation still fail gracefully, or would the sensitivity be underestimated?

This kind of adversarial perspective on DP proofs and implementations is important to nurture because it is surprisingly difficult, in practice, to write or use DP software that is immune to vulnerabilities.

It is generally considered a best practice to move all computations you can to postprocessing, since postprocessing cannot degrade the privacy guarantee. In the case of our example, that means moving the division by N to a postprocessing phase. This reduces the risk of mistakes and often simplifies the implementation of algorithms.

Transformation: Unknown-Size Mean

Now consider the stability/sensitivity of the mean under unbounded-DP (unknown data set size N):

$$\max_{x \sim x'} d_{Abs}(\text{mean}(x), \text{mean}(x'))$$

Unfortunately, even when the data is clipped, this quantity goes to infinity, meaning the transformation is not stable under unbounded DP.

To prove this, it suffices to show one example pair of neighboring data sets x and x' with extremely unstable outputs. Take a pair of neighboring data sets where x has b_{in} records, and x' has zero records. The difference between their respective means is undefined, as the mean of an empty data set is undefined. Since the differences in outputs on neighboring data sets tend toward infinity as the size of the data set approaches zero, and no prior information is known about the data set size, it is shown (by counterexample) that the transformation is not stable under unbounded-DP.

Often, people privately estimate the unknown-size sum and count separately and then postprocess the output into a mean. A benefit of this approach is that, if you have multiple queries to run that need a count, you can reuse the same count query across them.

By this point, you may have begun to notice a pattern—domain descriptors can help prove stability. In this case, for example, if you had a domain descriptor for having no fewer than l records in the data, you could use l to prove the stability of the mean. It is left as an exercise to prove this statement.

Transformation: Resize

Resizing is a preprocessing transformation that establishes a data set size domain descriptor. The resizing transformation is useful as it can allow you to employ algorithms that only satisfy bounded DP to data sets with an unknown data set size.

To use this transformation, you first set a target data set size. If there are fewer records in the data than the target size, the transformation will increase the data size by imputing missing records. If there are more records in the data than the target size, the transformation will return a simple sample. The resize transformation is defined as follows:

```
import opendp.prelude as dp
import random

def make_resize(target_size, constant):
    def f_resize(x):
        if len(x) > target_size:
            random.shuffle(x) # data should be considered unordered
            return x[:target_size]
        if len(x) < target_size:
            return x + [constant] * (target_size - len(x))
        return x

    atom_domain = dp.atom_domain(T=type(constant))

    return dp.t.make_user_transformation(
        input_domain=dp.vector_domain(atom_domain),
        input_metric=dp.symmetric_distance(),
        output_domain=dp.vector_domain(atom_domain, size=target_size),
        output_metric=dp.symmetric_distance(),
        function=f_resize,
        stability_map=lambda b_in: 2 * b_in
    )
```

Notice that the transformation is 2-stable, where both the input metric and output metric are the symmetric distance.

Instead of giving a proof, this section will walk you through how you might think about the stability of this transformation. Consider the stability when the sizes of neighboring data sets x and x' induce an imputed record and when it induces a discarded record. In this table, t denotes the *target* data set size:

len(x)	len(x')	$d_{Sym}(x,x')$	$d_{Sym}(resize(x),resize(x'))$
t - 1	t	1	2
t + 1	t	1	2

In the first row of the table, the resize transformation adds a row to x, but does nothing to x'. The symmetric distance between the transformed data sets is at most two, because the transformed data sets now differ by one changed record.

The second line of the table considers what happens when you sample down. In the second row of the table, the resize transformation samples down, discarding one row uniformly at random from x, and doing nothing to x'. The symmetric distance between the transformed data sets is also at most two, because the transform could have discarded any record, not necessarily the one missing from x'.

Take the union bound over these two cases to get the overall stability: the resize transformation is 2-stable.

This kind of exploration demonstrates why labels like bounded DP and unbounded DP are not exhaustive. In general, there are many gradations of descriptors and preprocessors for your data that you may leverage to restrict the stability of your transformations.

Recap of Scalar Aggregators

In this table, assume that x and x' differ by the addition or removal of at most b_{in} rows. The expression in each cell is the sensitivity $(max_{x \sim x'} d_{OM}(T(x), T(x')))$ of various statistics ($T(\cdot)$) when certain domain descriptors are known:

Statistic	Any numeric vector	With L, U	With L, U, N
Count	b_{in}	b_{in}	0
Sum	∞	$b_{in} \cdot max(|L|, U)$	$b_{in}/2 \cdot (U - L)$
Mean	∞	∞	$b_{in}/2 \cdot (U - L)/N$
Variance	∞	∞	$b_{in}/2 \cdot (U - L)^2/(N - 1)$
STD	∞	∞	$b_{in}/2 \cdot (U - L)/\sqrt{N - 1}$

Here is an explanation of the table data:

1. The first column contains several choices of $T(\cdot)$: count, sum, mean, variance, and standard deviation.
2. The second column shows the sensitivity when the input domain is not bounded and the input vector can be any length.
3. The third column shows the sensitivity when elements in the input vector are bounded within $[L, U]$ and the input vector can be any length.
4. The fourth column shows the sensitivity when elements in the input vector are bounded within $[L, U]$ and the input vector has a fixed length N.

Observe how more data descriptors result in lower sensitivities, leading to lower variance, whereas, using more data preprocessing to get tighter data descriptors and reduce variance results in higher bias.

Vector-Valued Aggregators

Transformations that compute vector-valued aggregates can also be stable.

For example, consider a tabular data set of individuals' criminal convictions. Each row corresponds to a different individual, each column corresponds to a type of offense, and each cell contains the number of convictions. You may want to prepare differentially private releases of how many people committed each type of offense or how many offenses of each type were committed. Answering these questions with vector-valued queries will give you better utility than answering independent queries for each offense type under composition.

To understand these transformations, you'll need to become familiar with their input and output metric spaces:

1. The *input space* typically consists of the domain of tabular microdata data sets, differing in terms of the symmetric distance or Hamming distance. You can still compute the distance between tabular data sets via the symmetric and Hamming distances by counting added/removed or changed rows, respectively. The OpenDP Library has a way to describe the domain of 2-dimensional NumPy arrays:

    ```
    # the domain of all 2-dimensional arrays with 4 columns
    domain = dp.np_array2_domain(num_columns=4, T=float)

    # arrays with 4 columns are in this domain, but 3 columns are not
    assert domain.member(np.random.normal(size=(1_000, 4)))
    assert not domain.member(np.random.normal(size=(1_000, 3)))
    ```

2. The *output space* consists of the domain of vectors, differing in terms of the L^1 (Manhattan) distance or L^2 (Euclidean) distance. With these choices of metrics, the sensitivity bounds the L^1 or L^2 distance between outputs of the transformation on adjacent data sets. The L^1 and L^2 metrics will be defined in the following section.

The following sections take a closer look at two variations of vector-valued transformations: statistics on data with bounded norms and statistics on grouped data.

Vector Norm, Distance, and Sensitivity

When studying the stability of transformations defined for vectors, you will typically work with the L^1 distance (also known as the *taxicab* or *Manhattan distance*) or L^2 distance (also known as the *Euclidean distance*).

The L^1 distance and L^2 distance are the L^1 norm and L^2 norm, respectively, of the difference between two vectors x and y:

$$d_{L1}(x, y) = \| x - y \|_1 \quad d_{L2}(x, y) = \| x - y \|_2$$

The L^1 and L^2 norms of $x = [x_1, x_2, ..., x_N]$, a vector of length N, are denoted:

$$\| x \|_1 = \sum_{i=1}^{N} |x_i| \quad \| x \|_2 = \sqrt{\sum_{i=1}^{N} x_i^2}$$

The definition of sensitivity (and stability) can be parameterized with these metrics. For instance:

L^1 sensitivity

The L^1 sensitivity of a transformation $T(\cdot)$ is $\max_{x \sim x'} d_{L1}(T(x), T(x'))$, where x and x' are b_{in}-neighboring data sets, i.e., $d_{IM}(x, x') \le b_{in}$ for some input metric IM.

The L^2 sensitivity can be defined similarly by substituting L^1 with L^2.

The absolute distance is a special case of both of these metrics when the dimensionality is one. Both metrics can be generalized to the L^p distance, for any real number $p \ge 1$, which uses the L^p norm:

$$d_{Lp}(x, y) = \| x - y \|_p \quad \| x \|_p = \left(\sum_{i=1}^{N} |x_i|^p \right)^{\frac{1}{p}}$$

In this setting, p denotes the order of the norm, which is separate and unrelated to the distance bounds b_{in} and b_{out}. This chapter only uses p with values of either 1 or 2. Whenever a result holds for both $p = 1$ and $p = 2$, it will be stated in terms of p, to avoid redundancy.

Aggregating Data with Bounded Norm

When trying to prove the stability of the sum, mean, and variance, it is natural to use L and U, descriptors for the lower and upper bound of each element in the data. You could equivalently use radius $R = (U - L)/2$ and origin $O = (U + L)/2$.

By a similar derivation, the sensitivity of the known-size sum works out to R, and the sensitivity of the unknown-size sum works out to $|O| + R$. To derive the latter, remember that $|x| = \max(x, -x)$, so $|O| + R = \max(R + O, R - O) = \max(|L|, U)$.

R, O, and p (1 or 2, denoting L^1 or L^2) are more natural descriptors for multidimensional data:

```
# the domain of all 2-dimensional arrays with row 1-norm at most 4
domain = dp.np_array2_domain(norm=4., p=1, origin=[0.] * 4)

# this data set is in the domain because the L1-norm of each row is at most 4
assert domain.member(np.array([
    [4.0,  0.0,  0.0, 0.0], # row 1 with L1-norm of 4.0
    [1.1, -2.7,  0.0, 0.0], # row 2 with L1-norm of 3.8
    [0.9,  0.2, -2.1, 0.5], # row 3 with L1-norm of 3.7
]))
```

The vector-valued sum transformation (denoted $\text{sum}(x)$) adds up all rows in a two-dimensional microdata data set x. If the p-norm of each row is bounded to at most R, centered at O, then you can prove that the sum is stable. Stability follows from the fact that the addition or removal of any one row will change the sum by at most $\| O \|_p + R$. In the following, x_i represents a row in the data set x.

Without loss of generality, let's assume x has N rows and x' has $N + 1$ rows. Moreover, the first N rows of x and x' are identical:

$$d_{Lp}(\text{sum}(x), \text{sum}(x')) \qquad \text{distance between transformation outputs}$$

$$= \; \left\| \sum_{i=1}^{N} x_i - \sum_{i=1}^{N+1} x'_i \right\|_p \qquad \text{substitute the function and metric}$$

$$= \; \left\| \sum_{i=1}^{N} x_i - \left(\sum_{i=1}^{N} x_i + x'_{N+1} \right) \right\|_p \qquad \text{rewriting the sum of } x'$$

$$= \; \left\| x'_{N+1} \right\|_p \qquad \text{all but the last term cancel}$$

$$\leq \; \| O \|_p + R \qquad \text{each row has bounded norm } R \text{ at } O$$

Just as in the scalar-valued version of this proof, this can be generalized to arbitrary input distance by employing the path property of the symmetric distance.

This derived bound is reflected in the following implementation of a vector-valued sum transformation:

```
def make_np_sum(norm, p, origin=None):
    dp.assert_features("contrib", "floating-point")
    assert norm >= 0, "norm must not be negative"

    # assume the origin is at zero if not specified
    origin = 0.0 if origin is None else origin

    #      C = ||O||_p                                    + R
    constant = np.linalg.norm(np.atleast_1d(origin), ord=p) + norm

    return dp.t.make_user_transformation(
```

```
            input_domain=dp.np_array2_domain(norm=norm, p=p, origin=origin),
            input_metric=dp.symmetric_distance(),
            output_domain=dp.vector_domain(dp.atom_domain(T=float)),
            output_metric={1: dp.l1_distance, 2: dp.l2_distance}[p](T=float),
            function=lambda data: data.sum(axis=0),
            stability_map=lambda b_in: b_in * constant)
```

Under the condition that the data set size is also known, then by a similar analysis, editing any one point may change the sum by at most $2 \cdot R$.

These transformations depend on a vector-valued clamp transformation. This transformation is still a row-by-row, but this time the row function f takes a vector x_i (one row) and returns a new vector whose norm R is bounded:

$$f(x_i) = x_i / \max\left(\frac{\|x_i\|_p}{\text{norm}}, 1\right)$$

For reference, this transformation is implemented in Python:

```
def make_np_clamp(norm, p, origin=None):
    dp.assert_features("contrib", "floating-point")
    assert norm >= 0., "norm must not be negative"

    # assume the origin is at zero if not specified
    origin = 0.0 if origin is None else origin

    def clamp_row_norms(data):
        data = data.copy()
        # shift the data around zero
        data -= origin

        # compute the p-norm of each row
        row_norms = np.linalg.norm(data, ord=p, axis=1, keepdims=True)
        # scale each row down to have norm at most 1
        data /= np.maximum(row_norms / norm, 1)

        # shift the normed data around zero back to `origin`
        data += origin
        return data

    return dp.t.make_user_transformation(
        input_domain=dp.np_array2_domain(T=float), # input data is unconstrained
        input_metric=dp.symmetric_distance(),
        output_domain=dp.np_array2_domain(norm=norm, p=p, origin=origin),
        output_metric=dp.symmetric_distance(),
        function=clamp_row_norms,
        stability_map=lambda b_in: b_in) # norm clamping is 1-stable row-by-row
```

The clamp, sum, and vector-valued Laplace mechanism come together:

```
meas = make_np_clamp(norm=4., p=1) >> \
       make_np_sum(norm=4., p=1) >> \
       dp.m.then_laplace(scale=4.)

meas(arg=np.ones((1_000, 4)))  # ~> [253.22, 245.95, 247.87, 246.22]
meas.map(1)                    # -> 1 = ε
```

The vector-valued Laplace mechanism is pulled from the OpenDP Library, and its privacy guarantees will be discussed in more detail in the next chapter.

This is the first time the `>>` has been used. The functional composition of two functions is a new function that runs them sequentially. Since functional composition and differentially private composition are easily confused, we instead call the functional composition *chaining*.[4] In the OpenDP Library, `>>` is shorthand for chaining. The output `meas` is a mechanism that, when run, runs each of the transformation functions sequentially on the data, and then the Laplace mechanism function.

 Take a moment to think about the sensitivity of queries for the vector-mean or vector-variance in the multidimensional case. How do they compare to their scalar analogs?

Grouped Data

Another example of vector-valued queries involves grouping data and querying each partition. Imagine you were asked to prepare a differentially private release of fitness data to show the effectiveness of a fitness app product.

You want to share counts of the number of unique individuals using your product, grouped by country of origin and birth decade. Given the structure of this query, it is safe to claim that any one individual may influence at most one partition, since any one individual cannot simultaneously have multiple countries of origin or birth decades. Adding or removing any one individual can influence at most one of the counts, so the L^1 sensitivity is one. This is shown in the following expression, where C is the set of all possible combinations of the grouping keys:

$$d_{L1}(T(x), T(x')) = \sum_{c \in C} |h_x(c) - h_{x'}(c)| \leq 1$$

---

4 There is a full section discussing chaining in "Chaining" on page 142.

A minor adjustment to the query can cause this very appealing property to degrade. When also binning by daily usage, on data that spans k days, the user may now influence the counts of up to k different days. Therefore, breaking the counts down by daily usage has caused the L^1 sensitivity to increase to k. Due to the higher sensitivity, more noise will need to be added to preserve the same level of privacy. In the following, all of the differences in histogram counts are zero, except for k bins that may differ by up to one:

$$d_{L1}(T(x), T(x')) = \sum_{c \in C} |h_x(c) - h_{x'}(c)| \le k$$

In this setting, where small differences are spread out over many different partitions, the L^2 sensitivity tends to grow in the square root of the L^1 sensitivity. In this case, as well, all of the differences in histogram counts are zero, except for k bins that may differ by up to one:

$$d_{L2}(T(x), T(x')) = \sqrt{\sum_{c \in C} (h_x(c) - h_{x'}(c))^2} \le \sqrt{k}$$

As you can see, this sensitivity is much smaller than before. Unfortunately, not all queries satisfy the constraint that an individual may influence each partition by at most one. For instance, count the number of days in which a user has actively worked out, grouped by country of origin and birth decade. In this setting, you would expect all differences in counts to be zero, except for one single histogram count that may differ by up to k.

$$d_{L2}(T(x), T(x')) = \sqrt{\sum_{c \in C} (h_x(c) - h_{x'}(c))^2} \le \sqrt{k^2} = k$$

When designing your queries, try to be mindful of these structures in your data. These structures are another form of domain descriptor that could help you significantly reduce the sensitivity, or answer more queries without increasing the sensitivity.

 Nearly every chapter will expand on vector-valued queries by discussing complementary transformations, compatible mechanisms, improvement of formalisms, or how to further applications.

In Practice

One of the first steps toward making a DP release is defining the initial metric space that your sensitive data set resides in. If you have made a DP release in the past, you may not have even recognized this step. Many DP libraries make an implicit assumption about the metric space. For the guarantees of any DP library to hold, the metric space of your data set must match the metric space the DP library uses. In this step, you should incorporate your public knowledge about the data set into the domain, choose a metric that characterizes the distance between neighboring data sets, and then set an upper bound on the distance b_{in}.

For instance, say your data set is a data frame—the data of individuals using your product. The data set resides in the domain of all data frames, where neighboring data sets differ by the symmetric distance. In many cases, the column names and data types are not considered sensitive, so you may restrict the domain to those data frames that match the expected schema. It is up to you to determine the bound on how many rows an individual may contribute.

Alternatively, say your data set is a single integer—the number of individuals in your household. The data set resides in the domain of integers, where neighboring data sets differ by the absolute distance. You know intuitively that any two neighboring data sets differ by at most one ($b_{in} = 1$).

Summary

This chapter has defined domains, metrics, and stable transformations that are commonly used in data analyses. Stable transformations provide the essential framework for transforming data in a way that preserves the closeness of adjacent data sets and makes it possible to modularize your data pipeline into self-contained, provably stable pieces.

We hope you have come to understand how this stability calculus can be applied so that you can go on to derive new stable transformations that suit the needs of your data analysis. Being able to reason about the stability of data transformations will allow you to translate existing data analysis techniques into stable transformations that can support your differentially private analyses.

Another goal of this chapter has been to familiarize you with the definition of stability, as it is a helpful stepping stone to understanding the definition of privacy. The next two chapters will extend this same mental model to cover various kinds of DP mechanisms.

Although this chapter focuses specifically on transformations, a very similar mental model also applies to mechanisms. Much like you say a transformation T is c-stable, you can also say that a mechanism M is ϵ-DP. This symmetry arises because the definition of privacy is a specialized kind of stability constraint.

A more thorough study of stable transformations was given before private mechanisms because private mechanisms need just a few more concepts beyond those used by transformations. As you will see, private mechanisms are the same as transformations, but the output metric space is replaced with a privacy measure, and the stability guarantee now qualifies as a privacy guarantee.

Now that you have an understanding of stability, metric spaces, metrics, and distances, you are well on your way to gaining a deep understanding of differential privacy.

Exercises

1. Write a program that takes as input two databases and returns whether they are adjacent.

2. According to the mathematical definition of a metric given in Appendix A, show that each of the metrics presented in this chapter are non-negative and symmetric, and obey the triangle inequality.

3. Identify the following transformations as either aggregates or general transformations. If they are not aggregates, specify their range. Construct a limitation on their input so that the stability is defined.

   a. $f(x) = \{x_i | x_i \in [L, U]\}$ (filter data to only elements in the range)

   b. $f(x) = \frac{1}{|x|} \Sigma_i x_i$

   c. $f(x) = x^2$

   d. $f(\vec{x}) = A\vec{x}$ where $A = \begin{pmatrix} 0 & 1 & 0 \\ 1 & 0 & 0 \\ 0 & 1 & 0 \end{pmatrix}$

4. Similar to def double discussed earlier in the chapter (see "Transformation: Double" on page 59), consider the following function that duplicates each record in a list:

   ```
   def duplicate(x: list):
       return x + x
   ```

   Under what metric could you argue that this is a stable function, and what would the stability of this transformation be?

5. Derive the sensitivity of the mean transformation, in the setting where the input data is bounded and the data set size is not known, but a lower bound M on the number of records in the data is known.

The following questions involve data set domains corresponding to other kinds of data sets, such as those consisting of text or graphs.

6. You have a graph data set where each individual can contribute one node. Show that the count of nodes in a graph is a stable transformation from the domain of graphs to the domain of integers.

7. You have a data set consisting of tweets and want to conduct sentiment analysis with a neural network that has been pretrained on a public data set. Can you claim that a transformation from the domain of tweets to a categorical domain of sentiments (where each individual is assigned one sentiment) is stable?

8. Recall that a data domain may consist of any medium of data. Take a moment to visualize the domains of data sets you may want to conduct a DP analysis over. What condition must there be on the data for it to be analyzed with differential privacy? What transformations would you want to apply to them? Are these transformations stable? Are there domain descriptors that would make them stable? If so, are there transformations that would establish these descriptors?

## CHAPTER 4

Private Mechanisms

A *mechanism* is a randomized function that takes a data set as input and returns a sample from a known probability distribution. The mechanism is considered private if it can be proven to satisfy differential privacy. Differentially private mechanisms are designed to convey useful information about the input data set.

This chapter formalizes and generalizes differentially private mechanisms. Private mechanisms build on concepts discussed in Chapter 3, like metric spaces, distance bounds, and stability. These concepts form the foundation of a mathematically rigorous, yet approachable, introduction to a variety of differentially private mechanisms.

Informally, differentially private mechanisms are similar in nature to transformations, in that they transform data in a way that keeps outputs "close." However, the kind of closeness for mechanism output is different: it is defined over the probabilities of the possible outputs. The unifying perspective is that differential privacy is a system for relating distances.

Each query decomposes into a series of functions: stable transformations followed by one *private mechanism* and then zero or more postprocessors. If you chain a transformation and mechanism, or a mechanism and postprocessor, you get a new mechanism (see Figure 4-1).

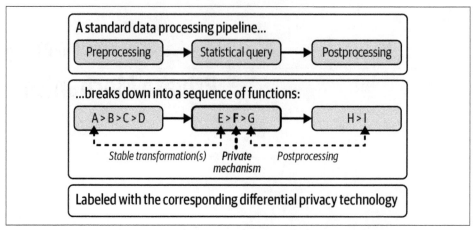

Figure 4-1. A data processing pipeline from both the non-DP perspective and DP perspective

This chapter will also walk through a series of examples to help familiarize you with mechanisms. Each example will demonstrate how to use the mechanism and how it satisfies differential privacy.

> Please be aware that code examples given in this chapter *do not satisfy privacy or stability guarantees*, because they do not account for finite-precision arithmetic.

Before diving into examples, you will need to become acquainted with two concepts: a *privacy measure* and the *definition of privacy*. A privacy measure is the key distinction between mechanisms and transformations, and the definition of privacy presented here is a more general definition of differential privacy that complements the definition of stability from Chapter 3.

Privacy Measure

Differentially private mechanisms return samples from a known probability distribution. Differential privacy limits how dissimilar, or distinguishable, these probability distributions can be when run on any two neighboring data sets.

The dissimilarity or distinguishability between distributions is precisely quantified by their *divergence*. Just as there are a variety of metrics to compute the distance between data sets, there are also a variety of divergences that can be used to measure the distance between distributions.

This chapter will only introduce one privacy measure: the *max-divergence*. The next chapter focuses on introducing other privacy measures.

Privacy Measure: Max-Divergence

Privacy loss parameters (like ϵ) represent an upper bound on the divergence between the output distributions on any two neighboring data sets.

There is a measure that corresponds to the kind of divergence used in pure ϵ-DP. To find this measure, first recall the definition of pure differential privacy from Chapter 2:

Pure differential privacy

A mechanism $M(\cdot)$ is ϵ-differentially private if for all possible neighboring data sets x and x', and every possible output y:

$$\Pr\left[M(x) = y\right] \le \Pr\left[M(x') = y\right] \cdot e^{\epsilon}$$

Recall how this definition was reworded to isolate ϵ:[1]

$$\max_{x \sim x'} \max_{z \in supp(M(\cdot))} \ln\left(\frac{\Pr\left[M(x) = z\right]}{\Pr\left[M(x') = z\right]}\right) \le \epsilon$$

You can rewrite this definition by substituting the *max-divergence*.

Max-divergence

The max-divergence between two probability distributions Y and Y' is:[2]

$$D_{\infty}(Y, Y') = \max_{y \in supp(Y)} \ln\left(\frac{\Pr\left[Y = y\right]}{\Pr\left[Y' = y\right]}\right)$$

---

1 This representation is useful when analyzing the randomized response mechanism.

2 Salil Vadhan, "Notes on the Definition of Differential Privacy," course notes from MIT 6.889, February 2013, *https://people.seas.harvard.edu/~salil/diffprivcourse/spring13/definition-notes.pdf*.

With the max-divergence, the definition of pure differential privacy simplifies:

Pure differential privacy
A mechanism M is ϵ-differentially private if:

$$\max_{x \sim x'} D_\infty(M(x), M(x')) \leq \epsilon$$

This representation of pure-differential privacy is appealing because it is directly interpretable: the privacy loss can be no greater than ϵ.

In this notation, $M(x)$ doesn't refer to the output of the mechanism but rather to a random variable. That is, the divergence is computing the distance between the distributions of the releases, not of the releases themselves.

Metric Versus Divergence Versus Privacy Measure

While metrics and divergences may feel very similar, they differ primarily in that divergences compute the distance between distributions, whereas metrics compute the distance between data sets.

The function that computes a divergence customarily uses a capital D instead of a lowercase d, as is used in metrics.

Divergences also don't satisfy two of the three requirements of metrics:

- Divergences are not symmetric; for any two distributions A and B, $D(A, B)$ is not necessarily equal to $D(B, A)$.
- Divergences do not satisfy the triangle inequality; for any three distributions A, B and C, $D(A, B) + D(B, C)$ may be less than $D(B, C)$.

Therefore, measures are categorically *not* metrics. You may even wonder how measures could be useful, given that they are not symmetric. It turns out that this is not particularly impactful in differential privacy, because you only care about the bigger of the two divergences (the case of the greatest distinguishability).

The key requirement for a divergence to qualify as a privacy measure is that it must be closed under postprocessing. That is, the divergence must have the property that you cannot postprocess a random variable in a way that will increase the divergence. Many types of divergence in probability theory do not satisfy this requirement, but this is an essential requirement for privacy: an adversary should never be able to process the outputs of a mechanism in a way that reveals more information about the sensitive data.

Now that you have some familiarity with privacy measures, you are ready for the definition of privacy.

Private Mechanisms

Private mechanisms share the same intuition and general structure as stable transformations but differ in that the output metric has been replaced with a privacy measure.

The definition of privacy here is more general than has been previously discussed, and is abstracted in the same way as transformations in Chapter 3.

Private mechanism

> A mechanism $M(\cdot)$ is (b_{in}, b_{out})-*private* with respect to an input metric IM and a *privacy measure* PM if, for any choice of data sets x and x' such that $d_{IM}(x, x') \leq b_{in}$, then $D_{PM}(M(x), M(x')) \leq b_{out}$.[3]

The input distance is a bound on how much an individual can influence a data set, and the output distance is a bound on how much an individual can influence the output distribution—in other words, how private the data release is.

Compared to the previous definition of privacy in Chapter 2, this definition of privacy better shows how the privacy loss parameter b_{out} complements b_{in}. This definition also clearly defines *how* two data sets may differ. Together, the input and output distance fully characterize the privacy guarantee of a differentially private algorithm.

Notice how similar this definition is to the definition of stability. The key change is the replacement of the output metric with a privacy measure.

Metric spaces are another concept that carries over from stable transformations. Transformations are a way to map data from one metric space to another metric space. Mechanisms are a way to map data from a metric space to a differentially private release. Metric spaces are essential for the input and output of transformations, and the input of mechanisms, but are not a good fit to model the output of mechanisms. There is no need to keep track of the output domain or find a suitable metric, as the output is already private and will remain that way due to closure under postprocessing.

---

3 Hay, Gaboardi, and Vadhan, "A Programming Framework for OpenDP."

You now have the framework in place to learn a vast collection of algorithms used in differential privacy. Just as was done in Chapter 3, this chapter will cover many examples of private mechanisms using the same proof technique: first, ask how much outputs can change (but this time under the privacy measure), and then simplify the resulting expression.

Now, let's revisit randomized response and the Laplace mechanism. While both were discussed in previous chapters, now you will study them in the context of this generalized definition.

Randomized Response

Randomized response was chosen for an introduction to differential privacy in Chapter 2 precisely because the input metric space is so simple as to be somewhat implicit. The input domain just consists of all booleans ($\{\top, \bot\}$), and the input metric is the *discrete distance*.

Discrete distance
   The discrete distance between two values x and x' is 0 if $x = x'$, otherwise 1.

Justified by the prior proof, you can claim that the randomized response mechanism is $(1, \ln(p/(1-p)))$-private under the discrete distance and pure-DP, because when $d_{\text{Discrete}}(u, v) \leq 1$, then $D_\infty(M(u), M(v)) \leq \ln(p/(1-p))$.

A common way to generalize the randomized response mechanism is to replace the input domain with some known discrete set, as exemplified in the following code:

```
import opendp.prelude as dp
from random import random, choice
import math

def make_randomized_response_multi(p: float, support: list):
    """
    :param p: probability of returning true answer
    :param support: all possible outcomes"""
    dp.assert_features("contrib", "floating-point")
    t = len(support)

    # CONDITIONS (see exercise 2)
    if t != len(set(support)):
        raise ValueError("elements in support must be distinct")
    if p < 1 / t or p > 1:
        raise ValueError(f"prob must be within [{1 / t}, 1.0]")

    def f_randomize_response(arg):
        lie = choice([x for x in support if arg != x])
        return arg if arg in support and random() < p else lie

    c = math.log(p / (1 - p) * (t - 1))
```

```
    return dp.m.make_user_measurement(
        input_domain=dp.atom_domain(T=type(support[0])),
        input_metric=dp.discrete_distance(),
        output_measure=dp.max_divergence(T=float),
        function=f_randomize_response,
        privacy_map=lambda b_in: min(max(b_in, 0), 1) * c,
        TO=type(support[0])
    )
```

You could use this measurement to privately release someone's multiple-choice answer:

```
rr_multi = make_randomized_response_multi(p=.4, support=["A", "B", "C", "D"])

print('privately release a response of "B":', rr_multi("B"))
print('privacy expenditure ε:',                rr_multi.map(1))  # ~0.288
```

The OpenDP Library contains a secure implementation of this mechanism.

It is left as an exercise to demonstrate that this generalization of randomized response is private under the discrete distance and pure DP.

The Vector Laplace Mechanism

Instead of just adapting the scalar-valued Laplace mechanism, as defined in Chapter 2, to the updated definition, this section also generalizes the Laplace to operate over vector aggregates with bounded L^1 sensitivity. In this case, the Laplace mechanism is applied to a k-dimensional vector $a = [a_1, a_2, ..., a_k]$, where a is a data set of aggregates that is typically output by a stable transformation, like a vector-valued sum transformation.

The vector-valued Laplace mechanism can be written in several equivalent ways. Each of these ways returns a sample from the Laplace distribution centered at a with scale r:

$$\begin{aligned} M(a) &= [a_1 + \text{Lap}(\mu = 0, r), & a_2 + \text{Lap}(\mu = 0, r), & \quad ..., & a_k + \text{Lap}(\mu = 0, r) \quad] \\ &= [\text{Lap}(\mu = a_1, r), & \text{Lap}(\mu = a_2, r), & \quad ..., & \text{Lap}(\mu = a_k, r) \quad] \\ &= \text{VLap}(\mu = a, r) & \text{equivalent representations} \end{aligned}$$

This mechanism satisfies pure differential privacy, where b_{out} corresponds to ϵ, and the privacy measure is the max-divergence:

$$\max_{a \sim a'} D_\infty(M(a), M(a'))$$

$$= \max_{a \sim a'} \max_{y \in supp(M(\cdot))} \ln\left(\frac{\Pr\left[M(a) = y\right]}{\Pr\left[M(a') = y\right]}\right) \qquad \text{substitute } D_\infty$$

$$= \max_{a \sim a'} \max_{y \in \mathbb{R}} \ln\left(\frac{\Pr\left[\text{VLap}(a, r) = y\right]}{\Pr\left[\text{VLap}(a', r) = y\right]}\right) \qquad \text{substitute } M(\cdot)$$

$$= \max_{a \sim a'} \max_{y \in \mathbb{R}} \ln\left(\frac{\Pi_{i=1}^{k} \frac{1}{2r} \exp\left(-\frac{|a_i - y_i|}{r}\right)}{\Pi_{i=1}^{k} \frac{1}{2r} \exp\left(-\frac{|a'_i - y_i|}{r}\right)}\right) \qquad \text{use pdf of multivariate Laplace}$$

$$= \max_{a \sim a'} \max_{y \in \mathbb{R}} \sum_{i=1}^{k} \ln\left(\frac{\exp\left(-\frac{|a_i - y_i|}{r}\right)}{\exp\left(-\frac{|a'_i - y_i|}{r}\right)}\right) \qquad \text{extract the sum by log rules}$$

$$= \max_{a \sim a'} \max_{y \in \mathbb{R}} \sum_{i=1}^{k} \frac{|a'_i - y_i| - |a_i - y_i|}{r} \qquad \text{exp and ln cancel}$$

$$\leq \max_{a \sim a'} \frac{\Sigma_{i=1}^{k} |a_i - a'_i|}{r} \qquad \text{by reverse triangle inequality}$$

$$= \frac{\max_{a \sim a'} \| a - a' \|_1}{r} \qquad \text{by definition of } L^1 \text{ distance}$$

Observe how the Laplace mechanism complements queries with known L^1 sensitivity: the L^1 sensitivity even appears directly in the formula. Substituting $\max_{x \sim x'} \| y - y' \|_1 = b_{in}$ gives the final bound, which holds for any possible pair of adjacent data sets:

$$max_{x \sim x'} D_\infty(M(x), M(x')) \leq \frac{b_{in}}{r}$$

Thus we can say the divergence between output distributions will never be greater than $\frac{b_{in}}{r}$, so the smallest upper bound on divergences ϵ is $\frac{b_{in}}{r}$.

In the overall scheme of relating distances, this function that samples Laplace noise is (b_{in}, b_{out})-private, where b_{out} is $\frac{b_{in}}{r}$, b_{in} is with respect to the L^1 distance, and b_{out} is in terms of ϵ pure-DP.

Many very common queries (like counts, sums, and means) are well-suited for the Laplace mechanism.

Discrete Laplace mechanism (geometric mechanism)

Some statistics are more naturally represented as integers, like the count. The Laplace mechanism has a variation supported on the integers: the discrete Laplace mechanism. The discrete Laplace mechanism has similar arguments as the Laplace mechanism, but its noise is sampled from the discrete Laplace distribution, which is supported on the integers $\mathbb{Z}$:

$$
\Pr\left[\mathrm{DLap}(\mu, r) = y\right] = \frac{\exp^{1/r} - 1}{\exp^{1/r} + 1} \cdot \exp\left(-\frac{|x - \mu|}{r}\right),
$$

where μ is the integer-valued shift, and r is the real-valued positive scale.

Another common name for the mechanism is the *geometric mechanism*, because the tails follow the geometric distribution, as shown in Figure 4-2.

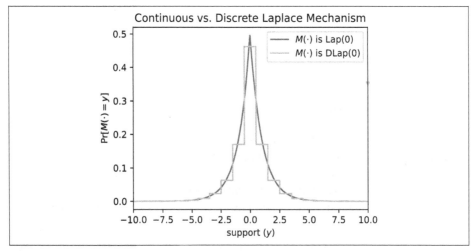

Figure 4-2. Laplace (Lap) versus geometric (DLap) distributions

An abridged proof is given for the privacy map on the scalar-valued discrete Laplace mechanism:

$$\max_{a \sim a'} D_\infty(M(a), M(a'))$$

$$= \max_{a \sim a'} \max_{y \in \mathbb{Z}} \ln \left(\frac{\Pr\left[\text{DLap}(a, r) = y\right]}{\Pr\left[\text{DLap}(a', r) = y\right]} \right) \quad \text{substitute } M_\infty \text{ and } M(\cdot)$$

$$= \max_{a \sim a'} \max_{y \in \mathbb{Z}} \frac{|a' - y| - |a - y|}{r} \quad \text{substitute pdf and simplify}$$

$$\leq \frac{\max_{a \sim a'} |a - a'|}{r} \quad \text{by reverse triangle inequality}$$

$$= \frac{b_{in}}{r} \quad \text{by definition of absolute distance}$$

The same can be shown for a vector-valued version of the mechanism (this is left as an exercise).

While the Laplace mechanism is an incredibly useful primitive, it is not always the best-suited algorithm to privatize your query. The Laplace mechanism can only privatize numbers, whereas some queries may involve private selection from a set or detection of the first anomaly in a sequence of events. Some numeric queries may also lose significant utility when the addition of noise perturbs the release beyond some unknown threshold.

Exponential Mechanism

As defined in Chapter 2, the exponential mechanism is used for private selection from a set of candidates.[4] In this setting, you know what the set of possible outputs can be (your candidate set), and you want to choose one (or more) candidates from that set that best answers a query on the private data set. The best candidate is defined according to a scoring function that assigns the score $s_c = \text{score}(x, c)$ to a candidate c for a data set x.

A motivating example (similar to the seminal paper) involves pricing: imagine that you have decided to sell off each of your baseball cards and want to choose the best price point to maximize profit. If you set the price too high, you will fail to find buyers, whereas setting the price too low will also mean losing money. This problem is not suitable for the Laplace mechanism, because a small perturbation to the chosen price may result in an extreme loss in realized profit, as there may be many buyers right at the edge. In this setting, assume that prospective buyers will tell you what they are willing to spend, so long as this information isn't leaked to other buyers.

To use the exponential mechanism, you must define a set of potential price points before conferring with the buyers. This set of potential price points forms the

---

4 Frank McSherry and Kunal Talwar, "Mechanism Design via Differential Privacy," in *Proceedings of the Annual IEEE Symposium on Foundations of Computer Science* (Piscataway, NJ: IEEE, 2007), 94-103.

candidate set. The exponential mechanism selects one of those candidates based on the private information from the buyers.

Just like many other DP mechanisms, you can break the algorithm into a stable transformation and a private mechanism. The stable transformation is the scoring function, which maps the private data set to a vector of scores. The private mechanism is the exponential mechanism, which selects one of the candidates based on the scores. A small postprocessor is then employed to index into the candidate set to retrieve the final selection.

You can think of the scoring as a data set aggregation, just like you might think of a data set sum as an aggregation. You can define a scoring transformation $T(\cdot)$ that aggregates a data set down to a vector of scores, where each score corresponds to a different candidate price point.

You can then use the infinity norm L^∞ to define a metric that computes the distance between adjacent score vectors. The sensitivity of this score vector is based on the greatest amount any one score may change.

L^∞ *distance*

The L^∞ distance between two vectors of scores and $s = [s_1, s_2, ..., s_k]$ and $s' = [s'_1, s'_2, ..., s'_k]$ is $d_{L\infty}(s, s') = \| s - s' \|_\infty = \max_i |s_i - s'_i|$.

The L^∞ metric is used on the output of the scorer and input to the exponential mechanism.

Quantile Score Transformation

An example of a useful scoring function is the *quantile score transformation*. This transformation assigns a score to each candidate in a vector c_i in a set of candidates C.[5]

The score function gives higher scores to candidates nearer the α-quantile in the data set x:

$$\text{score}(x, c) = -|(1 - \alpha) \cdot \#(x < c) - \alpha \cdot \#(x > c)|$$

The score function is based on the number of records in the data set that are less than c (denoted $\#(x < c)$) or greater than c (denoted $\#(x > c)$) for each candidate quantile c.

---

5 Adapted from Adam Smith, "Privacy-Preserving Statistical Estimation with Optimal Convergence Rates," in *Proceedings of the Forty-Third Annual ACM Symposium on Theory of Computing* (New York: ACM, 2011), 813–22. https://doi.org/10.1145/1993636.1993743.

If you'd like to find the median, let $\alpha = 0.5$. Candidates that evenly divide the data set will have the greatest possible score of zero, because the two terms will cancel each other out. The more unevenly that a candidate divides the data set, the more negative the score will become. It may help to think through how the scoring function will behave for other choices of α, like zero or one.

As written in Python, the score transformation executes this score function for each candidate, returning a vector of scores (one score for each candidate):

```python
def make_score_quantile_finite(candidates, alpha):
    dp.assert_features("contrib")
    assert 0 <= alpha <= 1, "alpha must be in [0, 1]"
    assert len(set(candidates)) == len(candidates), "candidates must be unique"
    def f_score_candidates(x):
        """Assuming `x` is sorted, scores every element in `candidates`
        according to rank distance from the `alpha`-quantile."""
        num_leq = (np.array(x)[None] <= candidates[:, None]).sum(axis=1)
        return -abs(num_leq - alpha * len(x))

    return dp.t.make_user_transformation(
        input_domain=dp.vector_domain(dp.atom_domain(T=type(candidates[0]))),
        input_metric=dp.symmetric_distance(),
        output_domain=dp.vector_domain(dp.atom_domain(T=float)),
        output_metric=dp.linf_distance(T=float),
        function=f_score_candidates,
        stability_map=lambda b_in: b_in * max(alpha, 1 - alpha))
```

The scoring transformation is stable because, when the distance between the input data sets is bounded, the distance between the output vectors is also bounded under the L^∞ distance:

$$\max_{x \sim x'} d_{L\infty}(x, x') = \max_{x \sim x'} \| \text{score}(x, c_i) - \text{score}(x', c_i) \|_\infty \le b_{in} \cdot \max(\alpha, 1 - \alpha)$$

This bound skips over many steps for brevity, but it would be good practice to fill in the gaps yourself. Start by substituting the definition of S, and then consider the cases of adding or removing a single record from the data set.

Finite support exponential mechanism

We are now ready to define the exponential mechanism when the input is a score vector x, containing one score for each candidate. The likelihood of selecting the ith candidate is proportional to the exponentiated score:

$$L(i) \sim \exp\left(\frac{x_i}{\tau}\right)$$

The τ parameter is the temperature. The temperature behaves in the same way as the scale parameter for additive noise distributions: higher temperatures result in more entropic sampling, which better masks the influence of individuals on the scores.

 Because of the exponential, better scores become exponentially more likely to be selected, which leads to nice utility guarantees.

You include a normalization term for the likelihoods to become probabilities:

$$\Pr\left[Y = i\right] = \frac{\exp\left(\frac{x_i}{\tau}\right)}{\Sigma_j \exp\left(\frac{x_j}{\tau}\right)}$$

To show the exponential mechanism is private, start by measuring the divergence between the two distributions:

$$\max_{s \sim s'} D_\infty(M(s), M(s'))$$

$$= \max_{s \sim s'} \ln\left(\frac{\exp\frac{s_i}{\tau}}{\Sigma_k \exp\frac{s_k}{\tau}} \Big/ \frac{\exp\frac{s_i'}{\tau}}{\Sigma_k \exp\frac{s_k'}{\tau}}\right) \qquad \text{substitute into } D_\infty \text{ definition}$$

$$= \max_{s \sim s'} \ln\left(\frac{\exp\frac{s_i}{\tau}}{\exp\frac{s_i'}{\tau}}\right) + \ln\left(\frac{\Sigma_k \exp\frac{s_k'}{\tau}}{\Sigma_k \exp\frac{s_k}{\tau}}\right) \qquad \text{break the ln}$$

$$= \max_{s \sim s'} \frac{s_i - s_i'}{\tau} + \ln\left(\frac{\Sigma_k \exp\frac{s_k' - s_k}{\tau}\exp\frac{s_k}{\tau}}{\Sigma_k \exp\frac{s_k}{\tau}}\right) \qquad \text{factor } s_i' = s_i' - s_i + s_i$$

$$\leq \max_{s \sim s'} \frac{\max_j\left(s_j - s_j'\right)}{\tau} + \frac{\max_j\left(s_j' - s_j\right)}{\tau} \qquad \text{take max of differences}$$

$$= \frac{2b_{in}}{\tau} \qquad \text{since } b_{in} = \max_{s \sim s'}\max_j\left(s_j - s_j'\right)$$

From this, we can say that for any possible choice of score data sets s and s', the divergence can never be greater than $\frac{2b_{in}}{\tau}$. Since ϵ is the maximum divergence over any pair of neighboring data sets, then $\epsilon = \frac{2b_{in}}{\tau}$.

Notice how this is the same as the relationship between ϵ, b_{in} and the scale (temperature) in the Laplace mechanism. The reason is that the exponential mechanism is a generalization of the Laplace mechanism. In fact, you can choose a scoring function that recovers the Laplace mechanism:

$$\text{score}(x, c) = -|x - c|$$

The sampling distribution of an exponential mechanism parameterized by this scoring function is a Laplace distribution:

$$\exp\left(\frac{-|x - c|}{\tau}\right)$$

A key difference between the two mechanisms is that the exponential is looser by a factor of 2. This is the price to pay for using a more general mechanism: the exponential mechanism can be used with scoring functions where a change in the underlying data set causes one score to increase and another score to decrease. You can avoid this penalty if the scoring function is monotonic (all scores will differ in the same direction on an adjacent data set). This can be captured mathematically with a metric extracted directly from the proof of the exponential:

Range distance
The range distance is $d_{\text{Range}}(x, x') = \max_i (x_i - x'_i) - \min_i (x_i - x'_i)$, where x and x' are numeric vectors.[6]

Continuing the previous derivation from right before this metric is used:

$$= \max_{s \sim s'} \frac{s_i - s'_i}{\tau} + \ln\left(\frac{\Sigma_k \exp \frac{s'_k - s_k}{\tau} \exp \frac{s_k}{\tau}}{\Sigma_k \exp \frac{s_k}{\tau}}\right) \qquad \text{continuing from above}$$

$$\leq \frac{\max_j \left(s_j - s'_j\right)}{\tau} - \frac{\min_j \left(s_j - s'_j\right)}{\tau} \qquad \text{take max of differences, flip sign}$$

$$= \frac{b_{in}}{\tau}$$

Where $b_{in} = \max_{s \sim s'} \max_j \left(s_j - s'_j\right) - \min_j \left(s_j - s'_j\right)$.

---

6 Section 2.1 of Jinshuo Dong et al., "Optimal Differential Privacy Composition for Exponential Mechanisms," in *Proceedings of the 37th International Conference on Machine Learning* (PMLR, 2020), 2597–606.

With this new metric, the exponential mechanism is no longer looser by a factor of two, but the sensitivity of the quantile score transformation gains a factor of two because it is not monotonic. Going forward, all mechanisms introduced for private selection will use the range metric.

The derived bound ($\tau = \frac{b_{in}}{\epsilon}$) is referred to as temperature in the following implementation. The intuition behind the naming is that particles have greater disorder, and more entropy, as the temperature rises. Similarly, the following implementation tends toward a maximally entropic, perfectly private, uniformly distributed output as the temperature parameter increases:

```
def make_finite_exponential_mechanism(temperature, monotonic=False):
    """Privately select the index of the best score from a vector of scores"""
    dp.assert_features("contrib", "floating-point")
    def f_select_index(scores):
        scores = np.array(scores)
        scores -= scores.max() # for numerical stability; doesn't affect probs

        likelihoods = np.exp(scores * temperature) # each candidate's likelihood
        probabilities = likelihoods / likelihoods.sum() # normalize
        # use inverse transform sampling from the cdf to select a candidate
        return np.argmax(probabilities.cumsum() >= np.random.uniform())

    return dp.m.make_user_measurement(
        input_domain=dp.vector_domain(dp.atom_domain(T=float)),
        input_metric=dp.linf_distance(T=float, monotonic=monotonic),
        output_measure=dp.max_divergence(T=float),
        function=f_select_index,
        privacy_map=lambda b_in: b_in / temperature * (1 if monotonic else 2))
```

As shown, this mechanism privately selects the single candidate with approximately the highest score. Together with the scorer transformation, since each function is stable, the entire function is stable. Starting from a bound on the distance between the input data sets, you can bound the distance between score vectors (sensitivity). Then, you can use this sensitivity to bound the distance between the probabilities of selecting each candidate. This gives the final bound on privacy.

To make use of this mechanism in practice, chain the scorer, mechanism, and finally postprocessor:

```
def make_private_quantile_in_candidates(candidates, alpha, scale):
    return make_score_quantile_finite(candidates, alpha=alpha) >> \
        make_finite_exponential_mechanism(scale) >> \
        (lambda idx: candidates[idx]) # postprocess: retrieve the candidate
```

The noisy score itself *cannot* be released. If you would like to release it, then prepare a separate query and use composition to release both. Since the score vector has bounded L^∞ sensitivity, then an index into the score vector can itself be seen as a data set transformation from a score vector to a score scalar with sensitivity measured via the absolute distance. You are already familiar with a mechanism on this metric space (Laplace)!

The previous example samples from a distribution with a finite number of possible outcomes. In general, the exponential mechanism samples from some scoring distribution, where values of the support with more utility are given higher scores, and are thus more likely to be selected. The exponential mechanism requires sampling from some distribution of scores, and in theory this scoring distribution could be *just about anything*. In practice, the exponential mechanism is only implemented for distributions from which finite computers can sample. Sometimes you can employ a clever trick to accomplish this sampling. The following variation of the exponential mechanism samples from a score distribution supported on an interval of real numbers.

Piecewise-Constant Support Exponential Mechanism

It can also be possible to efficiently implement the exponential mechanism when the support is a continuous interval. If the score distribution's density function is piecewise constant, then the sampling can be done in stages:[7]

1. Partition the interval by the data points
2. Privately select an interval using the finite-support exponential
3. Sample uniformly from the discretized interval

The following algorithm is a modification of the finite-support mechanism, where some key changes are marked "NEW" in comments:

```
def make_interval_exponential_mechanism(bounds, scorer, entropy):
    L, U = bounds; assert L < U, "bounds must be increasing"
    def f_select_from_interval(x):
        # NEW: sort, clip and bookend x with bounds
        x = np.concatenate(([L], np.clip(np.sort(x), *bounds), [U]))

        scores = np.array(scorer(x)) # score all intervals in x
        scores -= scores.max() # for numerical stability; doesn't affect probs
```

---

7 Adam Smith, "Privacy-Preserving Statistical Estimation with Optimal Convergence Rates," in *Proceedings of the Forty-Third Annual ACM Symposium on Theory of Computing* (New York: ACM, 2011), 813–22. *https:// doi.org/10.1145/1993636.1993743*.

```
# NEW: area = width     * height; gives each interval's likelihood
likelihoods = np.diff(x) * np.exp(scores * entropy)
probabilities = likelihoods / likelihoods.sum() # normalize

# use inverse transform sampling from the cdf to select an interval
index = np.argmax(probabilities.cumsum() >= np.random.uniform())
# NEW: sample uniformly from the selected interval
return np.random.uniform(low=x[index], high=x[index + 1])

    mono = 1 if "monotonic" in str(scorer.output_metric) else 2
    return dp.m.make_user_measurement(
        input_domain=scorer.input_domain,
        input_metric=scorer.input_metric,
        output_measure=dp.max_divergence(T=float),
        function=f_select_from_interval,
        privacy_map=lambda b_in: scorer.map(b_in) / entropy * mono)
```

The quantile score transformation is similarly modified:

```
def make_score_quantile_interval(alpha, T=float):
    assert 0 <= alpha <= 1, "alpha must be in [0, 1]"
    def f_score_quantile_interval(x):
        """Assuming `x` is sorted, scores each gap in `x`
        according to rank distance from the `alpha`-quantile."""
        ranks = np.arange(len(x) - 1)
        left, right = abs(ranks - alpha * len(x)), abs(ranks + 1 - alpha * len(x))
        return -np.minimum(left, right)

    return dp.t.make_user_transformation(
        input_domain=dp.vector_domain(dp.atom_domain(T=T)),
        input_metric=dp.symmetric_distance(),
        output_domain=dp.vector_domain(dp.atom_domain(T=float)),
        output_metric=dp.linf_distance(T=float),
        function=f_score_quantile_interval,
        stability_map=lambda b_in: b_in * max(alpha, 1 - alpha))
```

This time, the scoring function assumes the input data is sorted and returns a vector of ranks staggered around the expected alpha-quantile.

The exponential mechanism on an interval support uses the finite-support sampler to choose one interval (out of N + 1, since two boundary points were added):

```
def make_private_quantile_in_bounds(bounds, alpha, scale):
    scorer = make_score_quantile_interval(alpha)
    return make_interval_exponential_mechanism(bounds, scorer, scale)

meas = make_private_quantile_in_bounds(bounds=(0, 100.), alpha=.5, scale=1.)
print(meas(np.random.normal(22., scale=12, size=1000))) # ~> 21.37
print(meas.map(1)) # -> 1 = ε
```

Sampling from the distribution of the exponential mechanism is often computationally intractable, but sampling is possible for some well-behaved distributions, like finite and piecewise constant. Many more algorithms have been developed for sampling from other distributions, such as an infinite discrete support,[8] convex sets,[9] and spheres.[10]

Top-K

Both examples shown thus far are examples of selecting the top-1 candidate. However, in many common use cases, you instead want to select the top-k candidates.

The top-k can be released by *peeling*.[11] Repeatedly run the exponential mechanism on the data to select one candidate, and each time remove the selected candidate from the candidate set. The resulting output gives you a ranked ordering of the top-k candidates. The final privacy loss parameter is derived via the sequential composition of each of the mechanism invocations.

Unfortunately, this approach is computationally inefficient. You must run the mechanism k times, each time with one fewer candidate. There is an equivalent approach that resolves this while also bringing other convenient benefits: Report Noisy Max.

Report Noisy Max Mechanisms

Report Noisy Max (RNM) is a family of algorithms for private selection from a finite set of candidates.

To privately select the index of the best score from a vector of scores $S = [s_1, s_2, \ldots, s_k]$ in a way that satisfies ϵ-differential privacy, return $\text{argmax}_i\, s_i + z_i$, where z_i denotes the ith independent and identically distributed sample from an appropriate distribution. There are several possible distributions where this mechanism satisfies ϵ-differentially privacy.

For example, noisy max with noise sampled from a carefully calibrated *Gumbel distribution* is equivalent to the finite-support exponential mechanism. Since both approaches effectively sample an index from the same distribution, they can be used interchangeably.

---

8 Jeremiah Blocki, Anupam Datta, and Joseph Bonneau, "Differentially Private Password Frequency Lists." IACR Cryptology. ePrint Arch., 2016. *https://eprint.iacr.org/2016/153*.

9 Raef Bassily, Adam Smith, and Abhradeep Thakurta, "Private Empirical Risk Minimization: Efficient Algorithms and Tight Error Bounds," *IEEE 55th Annual Symposium on Foundations of Computer Science* (Piscataway, NJ: IEEE, 2014), 464–73.

10 Kareem Amin et al., "Differentially Private Covariance Estimation," in *Advances in Neural Information Processing Systems*, vol. 32 (Red Hook, NY: Curran Associates, 2019).

11 David Durfee and Ryan Rogers, "Practical Differentially Private Top-k Selection with Pay-What-You-Get Composition," in *Proceedings of the 33rd International Conference on Neural Information Processing Systems* (Red Hook, NY: Curran Associates, 2019), 3532–42.

The Gumbel distribution for a scale parameter β is defined by the following probability density function:

$$\Pr\left[Z = z\right] = \frac{1}{\beta} \cdot \exp\left(\frac{z}{\beta} - \exp\left(\frac{z}{\beta}\right)\right)$$

By sampling z_i from the Gumbel distribution with scale parameter $\beta = \frac{2\dot{b}_{in}}{\epsilon}$, the resulting noisy max mechanism is ϵ-differentially private.

This algorithm is much simpler than `make_finite_exponential_mechanism`: the scores are left as log-likelihoods, which avoids the numerical instability of exponentiating scores:

```python
def make_report_noisy_max_gumbel(scale, monotonic=False, T=float):
    dp.assert_features("contrib")
    assert scale >= 0, "scale must not be negative"
    return dp.m.make_user_measurement(
        input_domain=dp.vector_domain(dp.atom_domain(T=T)),
        input_metric=dp.linf_distance(T=T),
        output_measure=dp.max_divergence(T=float),
        # the value with the largest noisy score is the selected bin index
        function=lambda scores: np.argmax(np.random.gumbel(scores, scale=scale)),
        privacy_map=lambda b_in: b_in / scale * (1 if monotonic else 2))
```

Another nice computational benefit is that the algorithm can be adjusted to run on a data stream. In addition, the distribution of the top k indexes by noisy scores is equivalent to peeling the top k scores. Therefore, it is easy to adjust the algorithm to efficiently release the top k scores together in one shot.

A more careful analysis of the privacy proof *also* allows you to release the size of the gap between the score of the released index and the next smaller score, without any additional privacy cost.[12] This can help you get a sense of how confident the mechanism is in its selection.

Keep in mind that this noisy max approach is only useful when the support is finite, as it is clearly impossible to add noise to an infinite number of candidates.

---

12 Zeyu Ding et al., "Free Gap Information from the Differentially Private Sparse Vector and Noisy Max Mechanisms," in *Proceedings of the VLDB Endowment* 13, no. 3 (September 2019): 293–306.

Alternative distributions

The noise from several distributions can be added to scores to satisfy differential privacy in the noisy max mechanism. Noise from the Laplace and exponential distributions have seen common use in the noisy max as well. Laplace Noisy Max (LNM) also satisfies differential privacy and has been popularized in the literature, but it results in slightly less utility than Exponential Noisy Max (ENM).[13] For this reason, this section will just focus on the exponential distribution.

When the exponential report noisy max satisfies the same level of privacy as the Gumbel report noisy max, the utility of ENM can be better by up to a factor of 2 because it adds less noise overall. However, as of the time of this writing, there is no one-shot variation of ENM for releasing the top k noisy samples, nor has ENM been shown to satisfy a tighter zero-concentrated differential privacy guarantee like Gumbel report noisy max has (zCDP will be discussed in Chapter 5).

While the mechanisms discussed thus far in the book have been quite diverse, you can argue that all of them were in some way an instance of the exponential mechanism. The next mechanism is decidedly *not* representable via the exponential mechanism.

One way you can generalize the definition of privacy is to also allow for interactivity.

Interactivity

Private mechanisms can either be *interactive* or *non-interactive*. This distinction is based on how communication is modeled between the algorithm and the analyst. The Laplace and exponential mechanisms are both non-interactive, because communication is one-way from the algorithm to the analyst.

Realistically, analysts often expect more; it is more natural for analysts to want to ask questions interactively. This involves a strengthening of the definition of privacy. The privacy is measured not just over all choices of data sets x and x' but also all possible strategies an adversary may have. That is, the insights that an analyst/adversary gains into adjacent data sets will remain similar.[14]

---

13 The Exponential Noisy Max has also shown to be equivalent to the Permute-and-Flip mechanism; see Zeyu Ding et al., "The Permute-and-Flip Mechanism Is Identical to Report-Noisy-Max with Exponential Noise," arXiv, June 5, 2021. *https://arxiv.org/abs/2105.07260*.

14 Salil Vadhan and Tianhao Wang. "Concurrent Composition of Differential Privacy," in *Theory of Cryptography* (Berlin: Springer, 2021): 582–604.

More definitions of privacy will be discussed in Chapter 5. This distinction also generalizes the definition of privacy across all measures of privacy.

Some keywords to introduce in this context are *queries* and *queryables*: a query is a piece of communication from an analyst to a state machine, or queryable. One round of communication consists of the *query* sent to a queryable and the answer it returns.

There are many more interactive mechanisms in differential privacy, the first example of which will be the *above threshold* mechanism. The above threshold mechanism is an example of an interactive mechanism, and it satisfies this more general definition of privacy.

Above Threshold

The *above threshold* mechanism is used to find the identity of the first value in a stream above a threshold. The mechanism then terminates, refusing to answer any more queries.[15,16]

Before diving into the details of the mechanism, you should become familiar with the stream data type.

Streams

A *stream* is a sequence of values that are produced consecutively. The terminology is common in signal processing (where data is produced by a sensor) and in functional languages (where data is produced by a function).

Just as you can measure the distance between vectors, scalars, dataframes, and other forms of data, you can also measure the distance between streams. The same is true for the divergence between the distributions of randomized streams.

And similarly, just as you have many metrics to choose from when measuring the distance between vectors, you have many metrics to choose from when measuring the distance between streams. Instead of exploring the set of possible metrics, we'll just focus on the metric needed for the above threshold mechanism and introduce more as necessary.

15 From section 3.6 of Cynthia Dwork and Aaron Roth, *The Algorithmic Foundations of Differential Privacy* (Norwell, MA: Now Publishers, 2014).

16 Overview paper: Min Lyu, Dong Su, and Ninghui Li, "Understanding the Sparse Vector Technique for Differential Privacy," in *Proceedings of the VLDB Endowment* 10, no. 6 (February 1, 2017): 637–48.

The L^∞ distance between streams is very similar to the L^∞ distance for vectors. If a stream has bounded L^∞ sensitivity of d, then each element in a neighboring stream may differ by up to d. A similar extension can be made to the max-divergence.

In stream processing terminology, a *filter* processes a stream, producing another stream. A filter can even be proven to be a stable transformation or private mechanism and can be implemented via a queryable. Above threshold is an example of a stream filter: it is a private mechanism that returns a queryable.

Online Private Selection

You can think of "above threshold" as online private selection from a stream of candidates. The closest analogue to existing mechanisms is the Laplace Noisy Max (LNM) mechanism, but LNM still requires all candidates to be known up front.

The mechanism privatizes a stream with bounded L^∞ sensitivity:

```
def make_above_threshold(threshold, scale, monotonic=False):
    """Privately find the first item above `threshold` in a stream."""
    dp.assert_features("contrib", "floating-point")

    def f_above_threshold(stream):
        found, threshold_p = False, laplace(loc=threshold, scale=scale)
        def transition(query):
            nonlocal found # the state of the queryable
            assert not found, "queryable is exhausted"

            value = laplace(loc=stream(query), scale=2 * scale)
            if value >= threshold_p:
                found = True
            return found
        return dp.new_queryable(transition, Q=query_type(stream), A=bool)

    return dp.m.make_user_measurement(
        input_domain=queryable_domain(dp.atom_domain(T=type(threshold))),
        input_metric=dp.linf_distance(T=type(threshold), monotonic=monotonic),
        output_measure=dp.max_divergence(T=float),
        function=f_above_threshold,
        privacy_map=lambda b_in: b_in / scale * (1 if monotonic else 2),
    )
```

In the case of above_threshold, the state of the queryable simply consists of the found boolean.

When you invoke above_threshold, you get a queryable. The queryable implements a private filter on the input stream, emitting a private output stream:

```
meas = make_above_threshold(threshold=4, scale=1.)
# since the measurement privatizes a stream, initialize with a dummy stream
qbl = meas(lambda x: x)
```

```
qbl(2) # very likely to emit False
qbl(3) # likely to emit False
qbl(6) # likely to emit True for the first time
qbl(4) # expected to throw an assertion error
```

There are more connections between the above threshold mechanism and noisy max:

- The gap between the noisy threshold and noisy query can also be released *without* additional privacy consumption.
- You can apply another private mechanism to release an estimate of the score *with* additional privacy consumption.
- You can tighten the analysis with the range distance.

Differentially private stream processing algorithms share the modularity of other DP algorithms.

Stable Transformations on Streams

You may now be wondering what you can do with the above threshold mechanism: under what conditions are your analyses best served by privatizing a stream?

Consider a situation where you want to know the first query on a data set that returns a value above a threshold. To accomplish this, first construct a stable transformation from a sensitive data set to a stable filter, and then chain this transformation and the above threshold mechanism together:

```
def make_query_stream(input_domain, input_metric, b_in, b_out):
    """Return a stream for asking queries about a data set"""
    dp.assert_features("contrib")
    T = type(b_out)
    input_space = input_domain, input_metric
    output_space = dp.atom_domain(T=T), dp.absolute_distance(T=T)
    stream_space = queryable_domain(output_space[0]), dp.linf_distance(T=T)

    def f_query_stream(data):
        def transition(trans):
            assert trans.input_space == input_space
            assert trans.output_space == output_space
            assert trans.map(b_in) <= b_out, "query is too sensitive"
            return trans(data)
        return dp.new_queryable(transition, A=T)

    return dp.t.make_user_transformation(
        *input_space, *stream_space, f_query_stream,
        stability_map=lambda b_in_p: b_in_p / b_in * b_out
    )
```

The `query_stream` function takes a data set x and returns a queryable, upon which you may submit a stream of transformations. Since each transformation has bounded sensitivity, the resulting stream has bounded L^∞ sensitivity and can be privatized by the preceding threshold mechanism:

```
space = dp.vector_domain(dp.atom_domain(T=int)), dp.symmetric_distance()
meas = make_query_stream(*space, b_in=1, b_out=1) >> \
        make_above_threshold(threshold=4, scale=1.)
```

The algorithm now searches for the first query above a threshold in a stream of queries. This example submits a sensitivity-1 unique count first (which is likely below the threshold) and then a sensitivity-1 count (which is likely above the threshold):

```
qbl = meas([1, 2, 2, 2, 3])
print(qbl(dp.t.make_count_distinct(*space))) # likely to emit False
print(qbl(dp.t.make_count(*space))) # likely to emit True
```

There are many stable transformations on streams that can be used with the above threshold mechanism. It is your responsibility to ensure that the stream processing transformations you use satisfy the necessary stability properties of the mechanism you want to use them with. Luckily, stable or differentially private primitives are completely encapsulated to be easily composable and provably correct in isolation.

Summary

You are now familiar with the core primitives of pure-differential privacy. At this point, you should be comfortable reasoning about privacy measures and understanding how privacy can be defined relative to the max-divergence. Given a mechanism like randomized response, you should be able to demonstrate the mechanism is private. Further, you should understand the difference between the interactive and non-interactive models of privacy.

Pure differential privacy enables a wide variety of useful algorithms, but it is not the only way to satisfy differential privacy. There are relaxations of differential privacy that enable another suite of useful differentially private algorithms. You can think of these as different kinds of divergence—different ways to measure the distance between distributions.

The next chapter will focus on these relaxations to the definition of privacy, and the mechanisms that become possible when you use them.

Exercises

1. Use the randomized response mechanism to construct a local-DP mechanism for estimating the mean. Hint: use lower and upper extreme values as the mechanism's support.

2. Imagine you are an adversary who is trying to violate privacy. How would you attack `make_randomized_response_multi` if it were missing either of its two CONDITIONS?

3. Create a central-DP mechanism for releasing the precision metric: the number of true positives divided by the total number of positive examples. Assume all data is boolean, expected values are not private, and predicted values are private.

4. A list of sales arrives once a day. Assume you know customers make at most one purchase per day and that the most expensive sale is 10.

   a. Write an $\epsilon = 1$ reporting tool that alerts you the first day sales are above 100. A starter script is provided:

```
from ch04_stream import make_above_threshold, queryable_domain
import opendp.prelude as dp
TODO = "fix usages of this variable"


def make_sum_stream(bounds):
    dp.assert_features("contrib")
    T, L, U = type(bounds[0]), *bounds
    def f_sum_stream(stream):
        transition = lambda b_in: TODO # implement the new stream
        return dp.new_queryable(transition, Q=dp.Vec[T], A=T)

    stream_output_domain = dp.vector_domain(dp.atom_domain(bounds=bounds))
    return dp.t.make_user_transformation(
        input_domain=queryable_domain(stream_output_domain),
        # technically l-infty of sym dists
        input_metric=dp.symmetric_distance(),
        output_domain=queryable_domain(dp.atom_domain(T=float)),
        output_metric=dp.linf_distance(T=T, monotonic=True),
        function=f_sum_stream,
        stability_map=TODO # what is the stability of the new stream?
    )

meas = TODO # construct the complete measurement
assert meas.map(1) <= 1, "ε should be at most 1"
qbl = meas(lambda x: x) # `meas` will privatize the identity stream

#        Day 1,      Day 2,     DAY 3 (BIG), Day 4 (likely never seen)
sales = [[9.27, 9.32], [1.34] * 3, [8.92] * 30, [12.73, 8.34, 7.32], ...]
# scan the sales data stream until the mechanism detects high sales
print("high sales on day:",
        next(i + 1 for i, s in enumerate(sales) if qbl(s)))
```

   b. How would you modify the reporting tool to detect low sales?

## CHAPTER 5

Definitions of Privacy

So far in this book, you have become familiar with how the privacy parameter ϵ bounds the privacy loss of a data release. However, pure-differential privacy (or ϵ-differential privacy) can be overly restrictive, resulting in a privacy analysis that adds more noise than is practically necessary. This chapter presents other definitions of differential privacy that are widely used in practice, as well as the mechanisms they enable.

You learned in Chapter 4 that the key criteria of a privacy measure is that it possesses immunity against postprocessing. This means that for a mechanism $M(\cdot)$ to satisfy differential privacy, it is impossible to manipulate a data release in a way that will increase the divergence between the probability distributions $M(x)$ and $M(x')$, where x and x' are adjacent data sets.

This chapter introduces the privacy measures behind other variants of differential privacy. These variants of differential privacy also improve utility or interpretability and preserve robustness against auxiliary information and support for composition.

This chapter discusses the following variants of differential privacy, which meet these criteria and are in popular use:

- Approximate differential privacy: (ϵ, δ) or $\epsilon(\delta)$
- Rényi differential privacy: $\bar{\epsilon}(\alpha)$
- Zero-concentrated differential privacy: ρ
- Bounded range: η
- Characteristic functions: $\phi(t)$
- f-differential privacy: $\beta(\alpha)$

This chapter also introduces probabilistic differential privacy, which, while *not* closed under postprocessing, still proves to be a useful tool.

The δ parameter, in particular, makes a whole new class of mechanisms possible. All of these variants of differential privacy provide new ways to improve utility while preserving a meaningful level of privacy. For each of the variants of differential privacy discussed in this chapter you will learn:

- A motivation, mathematical definition, and interpretation of its meaning
- How to convert to the privacy loss parameters of other variants of differential privacy
- How to compose privacy loss parameters
- Example mechanisms

Before getting started, let's define a baseline that can be used to compare measures of privacy.

The Privacy Loss Random Variable

Recall the earlier discussion of privacy loss in "Privacy Loss" on page 28. The advantage an adversary gains from observing a DP release varies depending on the specific outcome of the release. One release may happen to reveal very little sensitive information, because the sampled value is in a region of the support where the log ratio of probabilities is small. Another release (from the same mechanism) may sample from a region of the support that maximizes the log-ratio at ϵ.

Take, for instance, the Laplace mechanism, as shown in Figure 5-1.

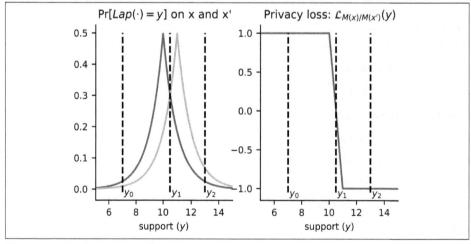

Figure 5-1. Laplace privacy loss

The left plot shows the distribution of releases on adjacent data sets x and x'. Three potential releases are highlighted at $y_1 = 7$, $y_2 = 10.5$, and $y_3 = 13$. The corresponding privacy losses are graphed on the right plot.

When an adversary wants to determine which data set an individual is in (either x or x'), they only have one release to work with:

- If the mechanism released y_1, then the adversary is as confident as they could be that the true data set is x, resulting in the worst-case privacy loss of ϵ.

- If the mechanism released y_2, then the adversary gains no useful information to help them decide which data set is the true data set, resulting in a privacy loss of zero.

- If the mechanism released y_3, then the adversary is misled into thinking the true data set is x', resulting in a privacy loss of $-\epsilon$.

The *privacy loss random variable* (PLRV, denoted Z) captures how this privacy loss varies over different runs of the mechanism. You can sample a privacy loss $z \sim Z$ by first simulating the mechanism (sample $y \sim Y$) and then using the release y to calculate the privacy loss.

The PLRV is defined as follows:

$$Z = \ln \left(\frac{\Pr \left[M(x) = y \right]}{\Pr \left[M(x') = y \right]} \right)$$

where Z denotes the privacy loss incurred by observing y, and x and x' are adjacent data sets.

The PLRV quantifies the advantage an adversary gains from observing a DP release y. The advantage varies depending on the specific outcome of the release.

ϵ-differential privacy ensures that, for all adjacent data sets x and x', the privacy loss is bounded by ϵ. Therefore, $\Pr \left[|Z| > \epsilon \right] = 0$, for any choice of adjacent data sets. You can see this constraint reflected in the right image in Figure 5-1.

The PLRV and ϵ are closely related but are not the same.

The parameter ϵ is the maximum privacy loss over any choice of adjacent data sets x, x' and any outcome y. ϵ describes a property of the PLRV.

As this chapter continues, the conditions under which Z is bounded will be relaxed, but the definition of Z will remain the same. In all cases, it will be possible to translate the bounds placed on Z to either an ϵ or (ϵ, δ) bound on Z.

Approximate Differential Privacy

Where ϵ allows a multiplicative difference between distributions, δ (delta) allows an additive difference, or *slack*. The δ parameter *smooths* the max-divergence measure, allowing the relative difference between distributions to be large, so long as the absolute difference remains small.

δ is used in conjunction with another privacy parameter, like ϵ. It is recommended to set δ to be *cryptographically small*, such as 10^{-9} or smaller. δ should also be *much less* than $1/N$ (where N is the size of your data set),[1] and never any greater than 10^{-6}.[2]

This is because approximate-DP allows for catastrophic privacy failure, in that the adversary may sometimes gain unlimited advantage (even $Z = \infty$). An example of this is the *name-and-shame* mechanism,[3] which publishes each individual's data in the clear with probability δ (this mechanism is not used in practice).

Approximate-DP mechanisms used in practice can still provide a meaningful privacy guarantee if they *fail gracefully*. This additional criterion means that, even if the divergence exceeds ϵ, the adversary still won't gain much of an advantage. Approximate-DP mechanisms used in practice have a justification for why the algorithm fails gracefully. This chapter includes these justifications when applicable.

δ-approximate differential privacy
A mechanism $M(\cdot)$ is (ϵ, δ)-approximately differentially private if for all possible neighboring data sets x and x', and any subset S of the possible outputs:

$$\Pr\left[M(x) \in S\right] \le \Pr\left[M(x') \in S\right] \cdot e^{\epsilon} + \delta$$

---

1 Mark Bun and Thomas Steinke, "Concentrated Differential Privacy: Simplifications, Extensions, and Lower Bounds," in *Theory of Cryptography* 9985 (Berlin: Springer, 2016).

2 Another illustrative example is Frank McSherry, "How Many Secrets Do You Have?" GitHub, *https://oreil.ly/orXYW*.

3 Adam Smith and Jonathan Ullman, "Privacy in Statistics and Machine Learning Lecture 10: Advanced Composition," course notes for BU CS591 S1/NEU CS 7880, Spring 2021.

Pure differential privacy is a special case when $\delta = 0$. Just like with pure-DP, you can still isolate ϵ in this definition:

$$\max_{x \sim x'} \max_{S \subseteq supp(M(x))} \ln\left(\frac{\Pr\left[M(x) \in S\right] + \delta}{\Pr\left[M(x') \in S\right]}\right) \leq \epsilon$$

The privacy measure can be extracted from within this inequality.

δ-approximate max-divergence
The smoothed max-divergence between two probability distributions Y and Y' is:

$$D_\infty^\delta(Y, Y') = \max_{S \subseteq supp(Y)} \ln\left(\frac{\Pr\left[Y \in S\right] + \delta}{\Pr\left[Y' \in S\right]}\right)$$

Now that you have the approximate max-divergence, the definition of approximate differential privacy simplifies.

δ-Approximate differential privacy (via divergence)
A mechanism M is (ϵ, δ)-differentially private if for all possible neighboring data sets x and x':

$$\max_{x \sim x'} D_\infty^\delta(M(x), M(x')) \leq \epsilon$$

A relatively simple approach to show that a mechanism satisfies approximate-DP is to instead show that the mechanism satisfies probabilistic-DP, which implies approximate-DP.[4] Probabilistic-DP requires that the PLRV Z will only ever exceed ϵ with probability at most δ (that is, $\Pr\left[|Z| > \epsilon\right] \leq \delta$).[5] For this reason, the δ term is often likened to the probability that the mechanism will fail to be ϵ-DP.

Probabilistic-DP is not a generally suitable measure of privacy because it is not closed under postprocessing, but it remains useful because it carries a simple and intuitive interpretation and because (ϵ, δ)-probabilistic-DP implies (ϵ, δ)-approximate-DP. The following two classes of mechanisms (truncated noise and PTR) rely on this intuition.

---

4 Sebastian Meiser, "Approximate and Probabilistic Differential Privacy Definitions." IACR Cryptology. ePrint Arch., 2018, *https://eprint.iacr.org/2018/277.pdf*.

5 The precise requirement that approximate-DP places on the PLRV is more complicated; a derivation can be found in Lemma 9 of Clement L. Canonne, Gautam Kamath, and Thomas Steinke, "The Discrete Gaussian for Differential Privacy," in *Advances in Neural Information Processing Systems*, vol. 33 (Red Hook, NY: Curran Associates, 2020): 15676-88.

Truncated Noise Mechanisms

Truncated noise mechanisms are a simple example of a mechanism that uses a delta parameter. The mechanism introduced here is a Laplace mechanism but with the tails cut off: releases cannot differ from the true value by more than r (radius).

This kind of mechanism can be used to privately estimate the true data set size with non-negative error. Such an estimate can then be used as a domain descriptor to help privately estimate the mean, variance, or covariance (see "Transformation: Unknown-Size Mean" on page 73). The following implementation samples from the truncated Laplace distribution via rejection sampling:

```python
def make_truncated_laplace(scale, radius):
    dp.assert_features("contrib", "floating-point") # not floating-point-safe!

    def f_add_tlap(arg):
        while True: # rejection sampling
            noise = np.random.laplace(scale=scale)
            if abs(noise) <= radius:
                return arg + noise

    def privacy_map(b_in):
        epsilon = b_in / scale
        delta = np.expm1(epsilon) / (np.expm1(radius / scale) * 2)
        return epsilon, delta

    return dp.m.make_user_measurement(
        input_domain=dp.atom_domain(T=float),
        input_metric=dp.absolute_distance(T=float),
        output_measure=dp.fixed_smoothed_max_divergence(T=float),
        function=f_add_tlap,
        privacy_map=privacy_map)
```

Let b represent the noise scale, and r the radius. The values returned from the function have probability density:[6]

$$\Pr\left[M(x) = y\right] = \begin{cases} 0 & |x| > r \\ \dfrac{B}{2b} \exp\left(-\dfrac{|x - y|}{b}\right) & |x| \le r \end{cases}$$

In this function, B is a correction factor to compensate for the removed tails. In the derivation of ϵ, the factors in the numerator/denominator of the odds-ratio cancel each other, so epsilon remains unchanged ($\epsilon = b_{in}/b$).

---

6 Quan Geng et al., "Tight Analysis of Privacy and Uility Tradeoff in Approximate Differential Privacy," in *Proceedings of the International Conference on Artificial Intelligence and Statistics* (PMLR, 2020): 89-99.

In the case of the truncated noise mechanism, shown in Figure 5-2, δ corresponds to the probability of releasing a value in a region of the support that is completely unreachable on a neighboring data set, due to the noise truncation. This constitutes a *distinguishing event* because the PLRV does not just exceed ϵ; it is infinite: an adversary can definitively distinguish, based on the release, whether the input data set was x or x'.

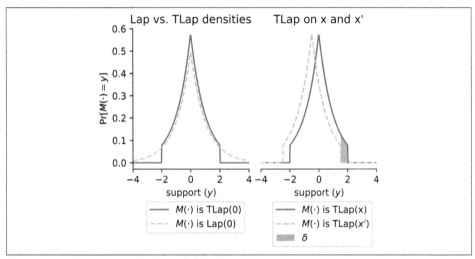

Figure 5-2. Overview of the truncated Laplace mechanism

For the truncated noise mechanism, this region is the last b_{in} of *one* of the tails, since only one tail is ever distinguishing for a fixed choice of adjacent data sets. Integrating this region gives the following expression:

$$\delta = \frac{1}{2} \frac{\exp(\epsilon) - 1}{\exp(r/b) - 1}$$

In this case, the probability that the PLRV exceeds ϵ is bounded to at most δ. This probabilistic-DP guarantee then implies approximate-DP.

The truncated noise mechanism guarantees that the magnitude of noise added will be no greater than r. Returning to the example of estimating an upper bound on data set size, simply add r to the release. This will give you a biased estimate that will slightly inflate the sensitivity but otherwise enable interesting new analyses.

Propose-Test-Release

Propose-test-release (PTR) is another commonly used mechanism that takes advantage of the local sensitivity.[7] On nicely behaved data sets, much less noise can be added than when analyzed with global sensitivity, and *stable values* can even be released in the clear.[8] Propose-test-release is named after the general flow of the algorithm:

1. Propose an upper bound on the local sensitivity.

2. Test a private release of the sensitivity to see if it is less than the bound.

3. Release the statistic if the test passed.

The local sensitivity was defined narrowly for the mean in Chapter 1, and you are now ready to learn the more general definition.

Local stability

A function $f(\cdot)$ is (b_{in}, b_{out})-*locally stable* at data set x with respect to input metric MI and output metric MO if, for any choice of data set x' such that $d_{MI}(x, x') \leq b_{in}$, then $d_{MO}(f(x), f(x')) \leq b_{out}$.

This definition is nearly the same as the definition of stability, but the max is only computed over data sets that are neighboring to x (your data set). This can result in a much smaller sensitivity but also makes the sensitivity data-dependent. An adversary could infer additional information about the data set based on the noise magnitude, which is why it is not used directly. Now that you have a δ term, it is possible to take advantage of the local sensitivity.

A motivating example is finding the most frequently visited URL in a data set of URLs. Assuming you don't know the set of possible URLs beforehand, it can be difficult to answer this query with the exponential mechanism because the set of possible URLs is so large.

1. You could instead only release the most frequently visited URL if your data set is *far away* from any other data set whose most frequent URL is different. If you know the answer never changes in the neighborhood of data sets around your data set, the local sensitivity is zero (with regard to the discrete metric). If the sensitivity is zero, then the URL could be released in the clear. Therefore, *propose* that the local sensitivity is zero.

---

7 Cynthia Dwork and Jing Lei, "Differential Privacy and Robust Statistics," in *Proceedings of the Forty-First Annual ACM Symposium on Theory of Computing* (New York: ACM, 2009): 371–80, *https://doi.org/10.1145/1536414.1536466*.

8 Adam Smith and Abhradeep Thakurta, "Differentially Private Model Selection via Stability Arguments and the Robustness of the Lasso," *Journal of Machine Learning Research* 30 (2013): 819-850.

Before you can conduct the test, first privately estimate the distance to instability. This is the distance to the nearest data set where the local sensitivity is greater than the proposal. For the most frequent URL query, the distance to the nearest unstable data set is the difference between the number of hits for the most frequent URL and the second-most frequent URL. You can release this distance privately: use a mechanism that you are familiar with to privatize it. The Laplace mechanism is an obvious choice; add noise with scale $1/\epsilon_1$.

2. Now *test* that the proposed sensitivity is no smaller than the local sensitivity. Since you only have the noisy estimate of the distance to instability to work with, the best you can do is give a probabilistic bound: the local sensitivity is no greater than the proposed sensitivity with probability $1 - \delta$. You can test this by checking that the distance to instability is sufficiently large that the noise is unlikely to cause a false positive.

   For the most frequent item example, Laplace noise was added, so you can integrate the right tail: a sample can only be drawn from beyond $\ln(1/\delta)/\epsilon_1$ with probability δ. Therefore, if the noisy estimate of the distance to instability is greater than $\lceil \ln(1/\delta)/\epsilon_1 \rceil$, you know the local sensitivity is no greater than the proposed sensitivity with probability $1 - \delta$.[9]

3. Now that you have a high probability bound, you are ready to *release*. If the distance to instability is smaller than the threshold, then refuse to answer the query at a total privacy loss of (ϵ_1, δ). Otherwise, release your query on the data for a total privacy loss of $(\epsilon_1 + \epsilon_2, \delta)$. For the frequent item example, the query we wanted to run has a sensitivity of zero, so ϵ_2 is zero, and the total privacy spend is just (ϵ_1, δ).

Propose-test-release is a general framework that can be used for any privacy analysis. PTR is another case where, when the privacy loss exceeds ϵ, the privacy loss is infinite, causing a distinguishing event. Nevertheless, the PTR framework is very commonly used to release histograms where the key sets are unknown. The reason why the mechanism fails gracefully is that a release is only made if the sensitive data set is far from instability: the data of many individuals would have to change to cause a change in the release.

Approximate-DP guarantees are commonly represented with a *privacy profile*.[10] A privacy profile is a function, or curve, relating ϵ and δ. A privacy profile can tell you a mechanism is $(\epsilon(\delta), \delta)$-DP or $(\epsilon, \delta(\epsilon))$-DP when given functions to compute ϵ or

9 Salil Vadhan, "The Complexity of Differential Privacy," in *Tutorials on the Foundations of Cryptography*, ed. Yehuda Lindell (Berlin: Springer, 2017): 347–450. *https://doi.org/10.1007/978-3-319-57048-8_7*.

10 Borja Balle et al., "Privacy Profiles and Amplification by Subsampling," *Journal of Privacy and Confidentiality*, 10, no. 1 (January 1, 2020), *https://doi.org/10.29012/jpc.726*.

δ, respectively. For the mechanisms you've seen thus far, the privacy profile is simple: for any choice of δ greater than the failure probability, ϵ is fixed.

In the following mechanisms, the privacy profiles will vary; as δ increases, ϵ decreases.

(Advanced) Composition

Just as epsilon parameters add up when you compose mechanisms, so too do the delta parameters.

δ-approximate differentially private composition
    If M_1 is (ϵ_1, δ_1)-DP and M_2 is (ϵ_2, δ_2)-DP, then the composition M_C, defined as $M_C(x) = (M_1(x), M_2(x))$, is $(\epsilon_1 + \epsilon_2, \delta_1 + \delta_2)$-DP.

The proof of this composition is similar to the proof of the composition of epsilon parameters:[11]

You want to know the greatest distance between distributions.

$$\max_{x \sim x'} D^{\delta}_{\infty}(M_C(x), M_C(x'))$$

Now substitute the divergence: $D^{\delta}_{\infty}(\cdot, \cdot)$

$$= \max_{x \sim x'} \max_{S \subseteq supp(M(x))} \ln\left(\frac{\Pr\left[M_C(x) \in S\right] + \delta}{\Pr\left[M_C(x') \in S\right]}\right)$$

M_1 and M_2 are independent from each other, so they can be separated.

S_1 and S_2 are subsets of possible outcomes from M_1 and M_2 respectively.

$$= \max_{x \sim x'} \max_{S_1, S_2} \ln\left(\frac{\Pr\left[M_1(x) \in S_1\right] \cdot \Pr\left[M_2(x) \in S_2\right] + \delta_1 + \delta_2}{\Pr\left[M_1(x') \in S_1\right] \cdot \Pr\left[M_2(x') \in S_2\right]}\right)$$

Use log rules. This is larger because product terms are added.

$$\leq \max_{x \sim x'} \max_{S_1, S_2} \ln\left(\frac{\Pr\left[M_1(x) \in S_1\right] + \delta_1}{\Pr\left[M_1(x') \in S_1\right]}\right) + \ln\left(\frac{\Pr\left[M_2(x) \in S_2\right] + \delta_2}{\Pr\left[M_2(x') \in S_2\right]}\right)$$

Substitute divergences back in.

$$= \max_{x \sim x'} D^{\delta_1}_{\infty}(M_1(x), M_1(x')) + D^{\delta_2}_{\infty}(M_2(x), M_2(x'))$$

$$\leq \epsilon_1(\delta_1) + \epsilon_2(\delta_2)$$

---

11 Cynthia Dwork et al., "Our Data, Ourselves: Privacy Via Distributed Noise Generation," in *Advances in Cryptology—EUROCRYPT 2006*, ed. Serge Vaudenay, vol. 4004, (Berlin: Springer, 2006): 486–503, *https://doi.org/10.1007/11761679_29*.

You can repeatedly apply this theorem to compose n mechanisms. Then, for a sequence of mechanisms M_i, each satisfying (ϵ_i, δ_i)-DP, their composition satisfies $(\Sigma_i \epsilon_i, \Sigma_i \delta_i)$-DP. That is, the epsilons and deltas simply "add up."

When you have a large number of queries (typically at least around 30), *advanced composition* can make the composed ϵ smaller, asymptotically in the number of queries, by a square root.[12] Advanced composition accomplishes this by adding δ' (a small number you choose) to the total privacy spend.

Advanced composition

For a sequence of mechanisms M_i, each satisfying (ϵ_0, δ_0)-DP, then their composition satisfies $\left(\epsilon_0 \cdot \left(\sqrt{2k \ln (1/\delta')} + k\left(e^{\epsilon_0} - 1\right)\right), k\delta_0 + \delta'\right)$-DP.

The intuition behind this composition result is that it is exceedingly unlikely that the PLRV for each release in the composition takes on the worst case, ϵ_0. In fact, many releases likely have *negative* privacy loss. A negative privacy loss means that the release actually *misinforms* the adversary. Advanced composition takes advantage of a result in probability theory (specifically the Azuma inequality), to derive a smaller, high-probability bound for the privacy loss of the composition. Therefore, the probability that the composed PLRV exceeds ϵ is only increased by δ'. This mechanism fails gracefully because, even if the PLRV were to exceed ϵ, the PLRV still can't exceed $k \cdot \epsilon_0$, because of basic composition.

To get a better understanding of how composition works, lets implement advanced composition. First, it is necessary to ensure that the supporting elements (input domain, input metric, and privacy measure) match:

```
def get_elements(mechanisms):
    # ensure that all mechanisms have homogeneous...
    input_domain, = {m.input_domain for m in mechanisms} # ...input domain,
    input_metric, = {m.input_metric for m in mechanisms} # ...input metric,
    output_measure, = {m.output_measure for m in mechanisms} # ...and measure

    return input_domain, input_metric, output_measure
```

If the supporting elements don't match, the function raises an exception:

```
get_elements([ # create a sequence of k=2 mechanisms with different domains
    make_randomized_response_multi(p=.7, support=["A", "B", "C"]),
    make_truncated_laplace(scale=1., radius=10.)
])
```

---

12 Cynthia Dwork, Guy N. Rothblum, and Salil Vadhan, "Boosting and Differential Privacy," in *2010 IEEE 51st Annual Symposium on Foundations of Computer Science* (Piscataway, NJ: IEEE, 2010): 51–60, *https://doi.org/10.1109/FOCS.2010.12.*

You can now define the mechanism with the aid of this utility. The function on the compositor simply evaluates each mechanism on the input data. The privacy map exactly implements the bound in the definition of advanced composition:

```
def make_advanced_composition(mechanisms, delta_p):
    """construct an advanced composition mechanism"""
    dp.assert_features("contrib", "floating-point")

    input_domain, input_metric, output_measure = get_elements(mechanisms)

    # ensure that the privacy measure is approx-DP
    assert output_measure == dp.fixed_smoothed_max_divergence(T=float)

    def privacy_map(b_in):
        epsilons, deltas = zip(*(M.map(b_in) for M in mechanisms))
        # respect the assumption that epsilons and deltas are homogeneous
        #     (this is very loose when ε_i, δ_i are heterogeneous)
        eps_0, del_0, k = max(epsilons), max(deltas), len(mechanisms)

        # t =  sqrt(2 * k *     ln(1 / δ'     )) + k * (   exp( ε_0 ) - 1)
        t = np.sqrt(2 * k * np.log(1 / delta_p)) + k * (np.exp(eps_0) - 1)

        #      (ε_0   * t, δ_0   * k + δ')
        return eps_0 * t, del_0 * k + delta_p

    return dp.m.make_user_measurement(
        input_domain, input_metric, output_measure,
        function=lambda arg: [M(arg) for M in mechanisms],
        privacy_map=privacy_map)
```

Now think about the asymptotics: basic composition bounds the final loss to $k\epsilon$, whereas advanced composition asymptotically bounds it to $O(\sqrt{k}\epsilon)$. Advanced composition will result in much smaller privacy guarantees for ϵ when the number of queries k is large. However, keep in mind that the advanced composition gives looser privacy guarantees than the basic composition when k is small, due to the constants involved:

```
domain = dp.vector_domain(dp.atom_domain(T=float), size=10_000)
t_clamp = (domain, dp.symmetric_distance()) >> dp.t.then_clamp((0., 10.))

M_i = [ # create a sequence of k=2 mechanisms
    t_clamp >> dp.t.then_mean() >> make_truncated_laplace(scale=.1,
            radius=1.),
    t_clamp >> dp.t.then_variance() >> make_truncated_laplace(scale=1.,
            radius=10.)
]

m_ac = make_advanced_composition(M_i, delta_p = 1e-7)
print(m_ac.map(2)) # -> (0.08, 5.5629e-07) = (ε, δ)
```

```
m_bc = dp.c.make_basic_composition(M_i)
print(m_bc.map(2)) # -> (0.02, 4.5629e-07) = (ε, δ)
```

Counterintuitively, in this case the resulting ϵ is *smaller* when using basic composition.

Advanced composition is the most natural to use with the mechanisms discussed thus far, such as pure-DP mechanisms, truncated noise distributions, and PTR. The Gaussian mechanism, to be discussed next, is an example of a mechanism that has better alternatives for composition, based on a tailored privacy analysis.

The Gaussian Mechanism

The Gaussian mechanism is central to differential privacy, mainly due to its tighter composition results when compared to the Laplace mechanism. The Gaussian mechanism perturbs outputs just like the Laplace mechanism, but samples from the Gaussian distribution instead.

The Gaussian distribution with mean μ and variance σ^2 is defined by the following probability density function:

$$\Pr\left[M(x) = y\right] = \frac{1}{\sigma\sqrt{2\pi}} e^{\frac{-1}{2}\left(\frac{x-y}{\sigma}\right)^2}$$

The Gaussian mechanism makes several trade-offs compared to the Laplace mechanism. The Gaussian mechanism expects inputs with bounded L^2 sensitivity. This is a significant benefit, since the L^2 sensitivity can be *much* smaller than the L^1 sensitivity.[13]

The Gaussian mechanism has relatively thin tails, which results in significantly improved composition. This is the greatest advantage of the Gaussian mechanism: when answering a large number of queries, it tends to require much less noise for the same level of privacy, compared to the Laplace mechanism with advanced composition.

Observe how the tails of the Gaussian mechanism in Figure 5-3 are lighter than those of the Laplace.

---

13 Under the right conditions, the L^2 sensitivity can be smaller by a square root. Refer back to Chapter 3 for more on the L^2-distance.

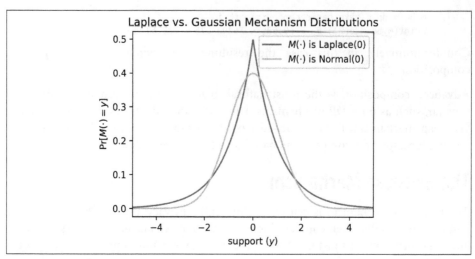

Figure 5-3. Laplace versus Gaussian

The thin tails also account for the greatest downside of the Gaussian mechanism: it does not satisfy pure differential privacy. In Figure 5-4, some outcomes of the PLRV (the log ratio of probabilities, or divergence) are shown in vertical lines for the output distributions of the Gaussian mechanism on adjacent data sets.

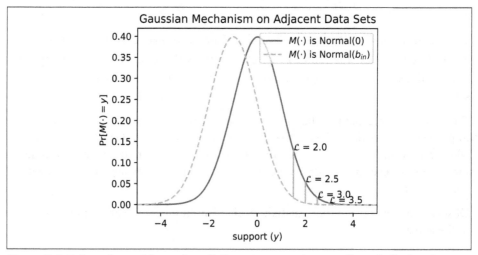

Figure 5-4. Privacy losses (shown in red) for outcomes y increase linearly farther from the origin

Since epsilon is the maximum divergence over any possible outcome, and the divergences increase without limit as you get farther from the origin, the Gaussian mechanism cannot satisfy pure-DP.

On the other hand, far from the origin, the absolute distance between the probabilities on adjacent data sets becomes cryptographically small because the probability densities are small. You can see this in the plot: the tails of the distribution are mashed together. The δ term allows for a small absolute distance between the distributions, which resolves the issue with the multiplicative distance (ϵ) in the tails.

Under the assumption that ϵ is no greater than one (a necessary condition from the derivation that is too often missed when used in practice) and that b_{in} is the sensitivity of x in terms of the L^2 distance, the Gaussian mechanism is private if the following inequality holds:[14]

$$\sqrt{2 \cdot \ln{(1.25/\delta)}} \cdot b_{in}/\sigma \le \epsilon$$

This privacy curve/profile $\epsilon(\delta)$ quantifies the distance between distributions in the same sense that ϵ or (ϵ, δ) does. The curve bounds ϵ for every choice of δ within $[0, 1]$.

You might naively implement the Gaussian mechanism using standard libraries, like NumPy:

```
def make_naive_gaussian_mechanism(scale, delta):
    dp.assert_features("contrib", "floating-point") # not floating-point-safe!
    assert scale >= 0 and 0 < delta < 1

    def privacy_map(b_in): # takes in l2-sensitivity
        assert b_in >= 0, "sensitivity must be non-negative"

        epsilon = np.sqrt(2 * np.log(1.25 / delta)) * b_in / scale
        assert epsilon <= 1., "this proof requires ε <= 1"

        return epsilon, delta

    return dp.m.make_user_measurement(
        input_domain=dp.vector_domain(dp.atom_domain(T=float)),
        input_metric=dp.l2_distance(T=float),
        output_measure=dp.fixed_smoothed_max_divergence(T=float),
        function=lambda data: np.random.gaussian(shift=data, scale=scale),
        privacy_map=privacy_map)
```

Unfortunately, this naive implementation does not technically satisfy differential privacy because of complications in the inner workings of the sampling algorithm.[15]

---

14 Dwork et al., "Our Data, Ourselves: Privacy Via Distributed Noise Generation," 486–503.

15 Jiankai Jin et al,. "Are We There Yet? Timing and Floating-Point Attacks on Differential Privacy Systems," *2022 IEEE Symposium on Security and Privacy (SP)* (New York: IEEE, 2022): 473–88.

The OpenDP Library has a hardened implementation of the Gaussian mechanism:

```
import opendp.prelude as dp
# define the space of floating-point vectors that differ in L2 distance
space = dp.vector_domain(dp.atom_domain(T=float)), dp.l2_distance(T=float)
# apply the mechanism over the space
gaussian_mechanism = space >> dp.m.then_gaussian(scale=1.)
```

Notice how this mechanism doesn't take a δ term: this is because the Gaussian mechanism is typically not analyzed directly under approx-DP. The OpenDP Library defaults to analyzing the Gaussian mechanism under a different privacy measure, which will be introduced later. The reason is that you must choose a specific δ_i for each mechanism when trying to compose multiple instances of the Gaussian mechanism under approx-DP. If you are using advanced composition, you also must choose a δ' for the composition itself. These choices of δ parameters are arbitrary, and incorrectly allocating δ among your queries leads to an overestimated privacy loss.

For this reason, even though the Gaussian mechanism satisfies $\epsilon(\delta)$-DP, it is typically not directly analyzed under approx-DP. Under approximate differential privacy, the benefits of composition are mostly wasted: the PLRV exceeds ϵ in a structured way that δ doesn't capture, meaning useful information about the PLRV is lost.

In the next several sections, you will learn about measures of privacy that are better suited to capturing this information about the PLRV.

Rényi Differential Privacy

Where pure differential privacy bounds the maximum privacy loss, Rényi differential privacy bounds the average privacy loss (with two clarifications):[16]

1. Rényi differential privacy (RDP) is named after the Rényi divergence, which generalizes the mean to have an order α. The generalized mean becomes more sensitive to extreme values as the order α increases. For example, the arithmetic mean corresponds to when α is two, and the maximum (which is most sensitive to extreme values) corresponds to when α is infinity.

2. Rényi differential privacy bounds the generalized mean of the exponentiated privacy loss (the probability ratio). That is, Rényi differential privacy guarantees that $\mathbb{E}\left[e^{(\alpha-1)\cdot Z}\right] \leq \bar{\epsilon}$ (as opposed to $\Pr\left[|Z| > \epsilon\right] = 0$ for pure-DP).

These two clarifications imply an interesting property of RDP: it is equivalent to pure-DP when α is infinity.

---

16 Ilya Mironov, "Renyi Differential Privacy," in *2017 IEEE 30th Computer Security Foundations Symposium (CSF)* (Piscataway, NJ: IEEE, 2017): 63–75, *https://doi.org/10.1109/CSF.2017.11*.

Rényi divergence

Given two probability distributions Y and Y', the *Rényi divergence of order* α is:

$$D_\alpha(Y, Y') = \frac{1}{\alpha - 1} \ln \mathbb{E}_{y \sim Y'} \left(\frac{\Pr[Y = y]}{\Pr[Y' = y]} \right)^\alpha$$

This divergence is directly used to define RDP:

Rényi differential privacy

A mechanism M is $(\alpha, \bar{\epsilon})$ RDP if for some order $\alpha > 1$, and for all possible neighboring data sets x and x':

$$\max_{x \sim x'} D_\alpha(M(x), M(x')) \leq \bar{\epsilon}(\alpha)$$

Notationally, the bar distinguishes RDP epsilon ($\bar{\epsilon}$) from DP epsilon (ϵ). This signifies how RDP bounds the generalized mean privacy loss instead of the max privacy loss.

The primary motivation for RDP is its simple and tight characterization of the Gaussian mechanism $M(\cdot)$. If you are feeling overwhelmed with the math, just focus on understanding the first line, the direction of (in)equalities, and the result in the last line:

$$\max_{x \sim x'} D_\alpha(M(x), M(x'))$$

$$= \max_{x \sim x'} \frac{1}{\alpha - 1} \ln \mathbb{E}_{z \sim M(x')} \left(\frac{\Pr[M(x) = z]}{\Pr[M(x') = z]} \right)^\alpha \qquad \text{substitute the divergence}$$

$$\leq \frac{1}{\alpha - 1} \ln \mathbb{E}_{z \sim M(x')} \left(\frac{\Pr[M(0) = z]}{\Pr[M(\mu) = z]} \right)^\alpha \qquad \text{where } \|\mu\|_2 = b_{in}$$

$$= \frac{1}{\alpha - 1} \ln \int_d \Pr[M(0) = z]^\alpha \cdot \Pr[M(\mu) = z]^{1 - \alpha} dz \qquad \text{since } \mathbb{E}[X] = \int x \cdot f(x) \, dx$$

$$= \frac{1}{\alpha - 1} \ln \frac{1}{\sigma\sqrt{2\pi}} \int_{\mathbb{R}} \frac{\exp\left(-\alpha z^2/(2\sigma^2)\right)}{\exp\left(-(1 - \alpha)(z - b_{in})^2/(2\sigma^2)\right)} dz \qquad \text{rotated to one dimension}$$

$$= \frac{1}{\alpha - 1} \ln \left[\frac{\sigma\sqrt{2\pi}}{\sigma\sqrt{2\pi}} (\alpha^2 - \alpha) b_{in}^2/(2\sigma^2) \right]$$

$$= \alpha b_{in}^2/(2\sigma^2) \leq \bar{\epsilon}(\alpha)$$

Therefore, the Gaussian mechanism satisfies $\left(\alpha, \alpha b_{in}^2/(2\sigma^2)\right)$-RDP, where b_{in} is in terms of the L^2 distance. RDP also supports basic (linear) composition, just like pure- and approx-DP.

Rényi differentially private composition

If M_1 is $(\alpha, \bar{\epsilon}_1)$-RDP and M_2 is $(\alpha, \bar{\epsilon}_2)$-RDP, then $M_1 \circ M_2$ is $(\alpha, \bar{\epsilon}_1 + \bar{\epsilon}_2)$-DP.

Even though RDP is a relaxation of (weaker than) pure-DP, it is still stronger than approximate-DP, and thus can always be transformed into an (ϵ, δ)-DP guarantee. RDP is considered stronger than approx-DP because it does not allow for distinguishing events. This means that even though the PLRV may probabilistically exceed ϵ, it can never be infinity.

RDP to approximate-DP

Any mechanism that is $(\alpha, \bar{\epsilon})$-RDP also satisfies $\left(\bar{\epsilon} + \ln\left(\delta^{-1}\right)/(\alpha - 1), \delta\right)$-DP.[17]

This translates an RDP bound on the mean privacy loss to an $\epsilon(\delta)$ guarantee: when the mean loss is bounded, you can find a bound on the maximum privacy loss (ϵ) with high probability $(1 - \delta)$.

In practice, RDP guarantees often come in the form of an $\bar{\epsilon}(\alpha)$ curve. This way, when converting to approximate-DP, you can choose the α that admits the smallest ϵ for a given δ:

$$\epsilon(\delta) = \min_{\alpha > 1} \bar{\epsilon}(\alpha) + \frac{\ln\left(\delta^{-1}\right)}{\alpha - 1}$$

This can easily be done by just checking all integer α's between 1 and 200, as it is unlikely for the best choice of α to be larger. If the minimizing choice of α is larger, then you still get a valid *over*estimate of ϵ.

The conversion from RDP to approx-DP is somewhat lossy, so it is generally the most efficient use of budget to try to wait to convert to approx-DP until as late as possible.

Mechanisms can also satisfy δ-approximate RDP, which can be used to express mechanisms with distinguishing events, like truncated noise or PTR. This is compatible with the conversion to privacy profiles: δ is split, for example, between the probability of a false positive on the PTR test and the privacy profile of the Gaussian.

The next section discusses a closely related privacy measure: zero-concentrated differential privacy.

---

17 A tighter bound can be found in Borja Balle et al., "Hypothesis Testing Interpretations and Rényi Differential Privacy," in *Proceedings of the Twenty-Third International Conference on Artificial Intelligence and Statistics* (PMLR, 2020): 2496-2506.

Zero-Concentrated Differential Privacy (zCDP)

zCDP is very similar to RDP but restricts the divergence of all possible α, not just one.[18] zCDP is popular because it abstracts α: you need only manage a single privacy parameter ρ, instead of a privacy curve $\bar{\epsilon}(\alpha)$. This is why zCDP is the default privacy measure for the Gaussian mechanism in the OpenDP Library and in many common DP deployments.

zero-concentrated differential privacy
> A mechanism M is ρ-zero concentrated differentially private (zCDP) if for all $\alpha > 1$, and for all possible neighboring data sets x and x':

$$\max_{x \sim x'} D_\alpha(M(x), M(x')) \leq \alpha \cdot \rho$$

You can think of zCDP as an infinite number of Rényi differential privacy guarantees, one for each possible choice of α. This admits a simple relationship between zCDP and RDP: for any choice of the α parameter, ρ-zCDP implies $(\alpha, \alpha \cdot \rho)$-RDP The converse is not true; thus zCDP is a *stronger* requirement for privacy than RDP.

For example, the Gaussian mechanism can be shown to satisfy $b_{in}^2/(2\sigma^2)$-zCDP. This implies that the Gaussian mechanism satisfies $\left(\alpha, \alpha b_{in}^2/(2\sigma^2)\right)$-RDP, as expected.

Just like the discrete Laplace mechanism, there is also a discrete Gaussian mechanism, and an instance of it can also be constructed via the OpenDP Library.[19] The code to instantiate one is nearly identical to the Gaussian mechanism, but this time the input domain consists of single integers:

```
# define the space of floating-point vectors that differ in L2 distance
space = dp.vector_domain(dp.atom_domain(T=int)), dp.l2_distance(T=float)
# apply the mechanism over the space
gaussian_mechanism = space >> dp.m.then_gaussian(scale=1.)
```

Strength of Moments-Based Privacy Measures

Now that you've become acquainted with moments-based accounting, let's take a moment to compare the utility against basic and advanced composition. Assuming a global privacy budget of $(1, 10^{-6})$-DP, allocated evenly among k instances of the Gaussian mechanism (on the x-axis), the effective per-query privacy parameters are shown in Figure 5-5.

---

18 Bun and Steinke, "Concentrated Differential Privacy: Simplifications, Extensions, and Lower Bounds."

19 Canonne, Kamath, and Steinke, "The Discrete Gaussian for Differential Privacy."

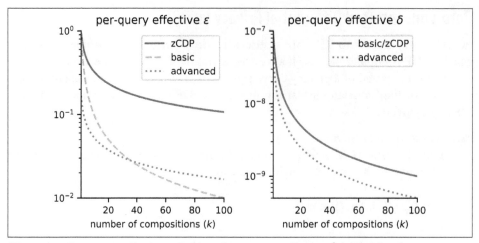

Figure 5-5. Per-query effective ϵ (left) and per-query effective δ (right) for the same overall privacy guarantee

While advanced composition starts to outperform basic composition at around 30 mechanisms, the moments-based accountants (zCDP and RDP) significantly outperform both.

Keep in mind that moments-based accounting is not as general: it provides a tailored analysis suitable for composition of the Gaussian mechanism and its variants.

Rényi- and zero-concentrated-DP are both *stronger* than approximate differential privacy in that they do not allow distinguishing events (δ is always finite). They are also both *weaker* than pure differential privacy, because the PLRV is bounded probabilistically (δ is always nonzero).

Since pure-DP is stronger than zCDP, you can translate: ϵ-DP implies $\frac{\epsilon^2}{2}$-zCDP.

This property makes it possible to use mechanisms that satisfy DP alongside mechanisms that satisfy zCDP. The exponential mechanism in particular has a much tighter conversion to zCDP, via another new measure of privacy: *bounded range*.

Bounded Range

Bounded range is another example of a tailored privacy analysis that benefits a class of mechanisms—in particular, the exponential mechanism.

Bounded range

A mechanism M is η-bounded range (BR) if for all possible neighboring data sets x and x', and any two outcomes y, y':

$$\frac{\Pr\left[M(x) = y\right]}{\Pr\left[M(x') = y\right]} \leq \frac{\Pr\left[M(x) = y'\right]}{\Pr\left[M(x') = y'\right]} \cdot e^{\eta}$$

BR restricts the PLRV Z to an ϵ-wide interval that overlaps zero. This means BR is an even *stronger* definition of privacy than pure differential privacy. Where pure differential privacy bounds the PLRV Z to $[-\epsilon, \epsilon]$, BR instead bounds Z to range $t - \epsilon \leq Z \leq t$ for some $t \in [0, \epsilon]$.

The x-axis in Figure 5-6 corresponds to the support of the PLRV (the distribution of privacy loss probabilities).

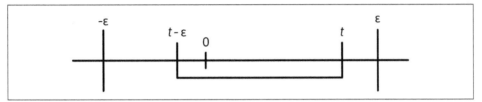

Figure 5-6. A bounded-range window with width ϵ, shifted by $t = .757$

Under this intuition, any mechanism that satisfies ϵ-DP satisfies 2ϵ-BR. The exponential mechanism is better: it already satisfies ϵ-bounded-range.[20] You'll find a proof of this in Appendix C.

Utilizing the fact that BR is a stronger measure of privacy, it can be shown that η-BR implies $\frac{\eta^2}{8}$-zCDP. Together with the fact that the exponential mechanism is already ϵ-BR, this means that the exponential mechanism satisfies $\frac{\epsilon^2}{8}$-zCDP (not just $\frac{\epsilon^2}{2}$-zCDP, like other mechanisms).

This is a powerful result; you can answer far more queries under the same measure of privacy as used by the Gaussian mechanism, all with the benefits of zCDP's tighter composition of mechanisms.

---

20 Durfee and Rogers, "Practical Differentially Private Top-k Selection," 3532–42.

Privacy Loss Distributions

It is important to remember that every DP mechanism has a PLRV, including mechanisms consisting of the composition of other mechanisms. Say you have two mechanisms $M_1(\cdot)$ and $M_2(\cdot)$; then you can construct a new mechanism representing their composition $M_C(x) = (M_1(x), M_2(x))$. If M_1, M_2 and M_C have PLRVs of Z_1, Z_2, and Z_C, respectively, then Z_C is the sum of random variables Z_1 and Z_2.

You can show this by plugging M_C into the definition of the PLRV. You know the release from the composition consists of the constituent releases from M_1 and M_2, so $y_C = (y_1, y_2)$:

$$
\begin{aligned}
Z_C &= \ln\left(\frac{\Pr\left[M_C(x) = (y_1, y_2)\right]}{\Pr\left[M_C(x') = (y_1, y_2)\right]}\right) \\
&= \ln\left(\frac{\Pr\left[M_1(x) = y_1\right]\Pr\left[M_2(x) = y_2\right]}{\Pr\left[M_1(x') = y_1\right]\Pr\left[M_2(x') = y_2\right]}\right) \\
&= Z_1 + Z_2
\end{aligned}
$$

Intuitively, when an adversary sees the outcomes of two mechanisms, they net the sum of the privacy losses, because they benefit from the information from both releases.

The distribution of the PLRV, which is called the privacy loss distribution (PLD), gives the probabilities of occurrence of each possible realized privacy loss.[21] For example, the PLD for the Gaussian mechanism is also Gaussian: $N(\eta, 2 \cdot \eta)$, where $\eta = \frac{\Delta^2}{2 \cdot \sigma^2}$, and Δ and σ represent the sensitivity and noise scale, respectively.[22]

Figure 5-7 shows the PLD of an instance of the Gaussian mechanism with a sensitivity and noise scale of one, for a *dominating pair* of input data sets x and x' (two adjacent data sets with maximal distance). When you make a differentially private release with the Gaussian mechanism, the privacy loss, or divergence between output distributions, is a sample from/follows this PLD.

---

21 David M. Sommer et al., "Privacy Loss Classes: The Central Limit Theorem in Differential Privacy," in *Proceedings on Privacy Enhancing Technologies*, 2019, no. 2 (April 2019): 245–69, *https://doi.org/10.2478/popets-2019-0029*.

22 Borja Balle and Yu-Xiang Wang, "Improving the Gaussian Mechanism for Differential Privacy: Analytical Calibration and Optimal Denoising," in *International Conference on Machine Learning* (PMLR, 2018): 394-403.

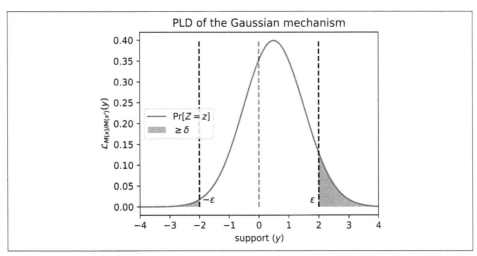

Figure 5-7. Gaussian PLD

There are intuitive connections here: the Gaussian mechanism's PLD has infinite support, which is consistent with the privacy loss being unbounded under pure-DP. The distribution is biased positive, as each release does leak some information. Samples from the PLD can be negative, which corresponds to the sampled noise value drowning out the difference between input data sets. The volume under the curve for privacy losses z that exceed ϵ is an upper bound for δ, corresponding to the probabilistic-DP requirement that $\Pr\left[|Z| > \epsilon\right] \le \delta$.[23]

If you have the PLD, you can also convert it into ϵ: take the maximum absolute value from the support that has nonzero probability. You can similarly convert into (ϵ, δ) by finding the point ϵ for which the probability mass in the tails is at most δ.

In probability theory, the probability distribution of the sum of two random variables Z_1 and Z_2, distributed according to probability density functions $z_1(x)$ and $z_2(x)$, is given by the convolution of their probability density functions, defined as:

$$(z_1 * z_2)(x) = \int_{-\infty}^{+\infty} z_1(\tau)z_2(x - \tau)d\tau$$

This is the fundamental perspective needed to understand composition in differential privacy:

> Composition in differential privacy is the sum of PLRVs, or equivalently, the convolution of PLDs.

---

23 δ can be made smaller by using the approx-DP requirement that $\mathbb{E}_Z\left[\max\left(0, 1 - e^{\epsilon - Z}\right)\right] \le \delta$.

The various measures of privacy we've discussed until now have described properties of the PLRV, such as which member of the support has the greatest magnitude (ϵ) or the PLRV's generalized mean ($\bar{\epsilon}(\alpha)$). You've also seen how to derive similar properties about the sum of other PLRVs through composition results, like basic composition ($\epsilon_1 + \epsilon_2$-DP and $\rho_1 + \rho_2$-zCDP).

The following sections discuss techniques that take a different approach: they try to directly represent the PLD itself, either through numerical or analytic methods.

 The following sections on numerical composition and characteristic functions give high-level overviews of advanced topics in differential privacy. The purpose of these sections is *not* to give you a comprehensive understanding of their mechanics. They are discussed to enrich your conceptual understanding of PLDs and to help you gain an understanding of their trade-offs compared to prior compositors.

Numerical Composition

By this point, you have encountered a variety of approaches for bounding the PLRV, but there are still a couple of drawbacks:

- Mixing measures of privacy is lossy. It is natural to want to use an adaptive sequence of mechanisms, where each mechanism's privacy loss is best characterized by the measure of privacy most natural for it. Converting between measures of privacy many times is very lossy and inefficiently consumes your budget.

- While each measure of privacy has *improved* composition in its own way, they have all had incomplete information about the PLRV. Having complete knowledge of the PLRV can be used to derive smaller privacy parameters.

Numerical composition resolves these issues at the expense of an increase in implementation complexity. Instead of bounding the PLRV with privacy loss parameters, you could instead store the PLD itself (the probability of each possible privacy loss). In practice, to handle the continuous support of the PLD on finite computers, the PLD is represented with a discrete approximation (the probability masses of each possible privacy loss interval).[24]

Under the numerical composition approach, each mechanism is tasked with preparing a discretized PLD describing the PLRV, instead of privacy loss parameters. Each time you compose any two mechanisms, make sure to derive the PLD of

---

24 Sivakanth Gopi, Yin Tat Lee, and Lukas Wutschitz, "Numerical Composition of Differential Privacy," *Advances in Neural Information Processing Systems* 34 (2021): 11631–42.

the composition by convolving the constituent PLDs together. The convolution is typically handled via an application of the discrete Fourier transform. Finally, when you are ready to characterize the final privacy loss, convert the composed PLD back out into privacy parameters.

To maintain accurate privacy guarantees, this approach must incorporate errors introduced in the discretization and numerical inaccuracy into the final estimation of the privacy parameters. It has been found that, in practice, the privacy loss parameters derived from numerical composition can be made arbitrarily close to the optimal privacy loss parameters under very reasonable computational requirements.

Nevertheless, the implementation is complex; it involves deriving discretized privacy loss distributions for each mechanism in a way that can be convolved with the Fourier transform efficiently (where a coarser approximation is better), and yet with as little error as possible (where a finer approximation is better).

It can help to reassess. The purpose of the discretization is to make it possible to numerically approximate the PLD. Might there be another method to characterize the PLD that doesn't require numerical approximations?

Characteristic Functions

The *moment-generating function* (MGF) and *characteristic function* are alternative ways to specify probability distributions. Both of these functions have been a subtext in this chapter. While they were never explicitly discussed, they have still been quietly influencing our trajectory.

The MGF of a random variable Z is $\mathbb{E}\left[e^{t \cdot Z}\right]$. Interestingly, Rényi differential privacy already bounds $\mathbb{E}\left[e^{(\alpha - 1) \cdot Z}\right] \le \bar{\epsilon}$. Therefore, RDP implies a bound on the MGF of order $t = \alpha - 1$. There are some downsides to the MGF: not all distributions have an MGF, and RDP still turns out to be a lossy representation of the PLRV.

The characteristic function of a random variable Z is $\mathbb{E}\left[e^{i \cdot t \cdot Z}\right]$, denoted $\phi(t)$. The numerical compositor implies a bound on the characteristic function; characteristic functions fill the same conceptual role as the discretized approximation to the PLD in numerical composition. Characteristic functions improve on MGFs in the same ways that numerical composition improves on the RDP MGF-based privacy accounting: the characteristic function always exists (so all mechanisms can be represented, even mechanisms with distinguishing events), and composition with characteristic functions is tight.[25]

---

25 Yuqing Zhu, Jinshuo Dong, and Yu-Xiang Wang, "Optimal Accounting of Differential Privacy via Characteristic Function," in *Proceedings of the 25th International Conference on Artificial Intelligence and Statistics* 151 (PMLR, 2022): 4782–4817.

Under the characteristic function approach, each mechanism is tasked with preparing a characteristic function $\phi(t)$ that represents the privacy loss distribution. You can now take advantage of a general property of characteristic functions; the characteristic function of the sum of two random variables is the product of their characteristic functions. This is simpler than you might think.

If $M_C(x) = (M_1(x), M_2(x))$, and the characteristic functions of the PLRVs of $M_1(\cdot)$ and $M_2(\cdot)$ are $\phi_1(t)$ and $\phi_2(t)$, respectively, then $\phi_C(t) = \phi_1(t) \cdot \phi_2(t)$. This incredibly simple approach is called the *analytical Fourier accountant*; it accomplishes the Fourier convolution of PLDs analytically (by direct computation, instead of numerical approximation).

While this approach is conceptually simple, it is also not without trade-offs; it can be nontrivial to derive a suitable characteristic function for new mechanisms, and the conversion of a characteristic function $\phi(t)$ to (ϵ, δ) does still involve a numerical algorithm. Nevertheless, characteristic functions provide an elegant conceptual framing to the problem of differentially private composition—that differentially private composition is the convolution of PLDs.

Hypothesis Testing Interpretation

Differential privacy can also be interpreted in terms of hypothesis testing.

In this formulation, differential privacy assumes an adversary has unbounded auxiliary information and constructs two hypothetical data sets x and x'. There is one data set with Alice (who is being targeted), and one without her. The adversary wants to determine which data set is more like the actual data, which will allow them to infer if Alice is in the data.

This is expressed through *null* (H_0) and *alternative* (H_1) hypotheses:[26]

H_0: underlying data is x H_1: underlying data is x'

In standard statistical terminology, you "fail to reject" H_0 when a test statistic falls into an *acceptance region*. In the context of differential privacy, the test statistic is the data release, and the acceptance region is the set of possible outcomes that indicate Alice is in the data.

There are two ways the acceptance region can be wrong, which would cause an adversary to arrive at the wrong conclusion:

---

26 Larry Wasserman and Shuheng Zhou, "A Statistical Framework for Differential Privacy," *Journal of the American Statistical Association* 105, no. 489 (March 2010): 375–89.

1. Type I: Alice is in the data, but H_0 is rejected (α).

2. Type II: Alice is not in the data, but H_0 is not rejected (β).

If you are familiar with hypothesis testing, this may feel strange; you want higher error rates because higher error rates correspond to better privacy. When the acceptance region shrinks, Type I errors become more likely (higher α), and Type II errors become less likely (lower β). The converse is true when the acceptance region grows.

f-differential privacy

The f in f-differential privacy describes the relationship between α and β as the acceptance region varies. f may be represented with a $\beta(\alpha)$ trade-off curve: at any given choice of α (Type I error rate), the trade-off curve tells you the smallest possible β (Type II error rate) among all possible acceptance regions.[27]

Perfect privacy is attained when $\beta(\alpha) = 1 - \alpha$. Take, for example, $\alpha = 0.5$, meaning $\beta = 0.5$. Any determination you may make about Alice's inclusion in the data set has a 50% chance of being wrong (see Figure 5-8).

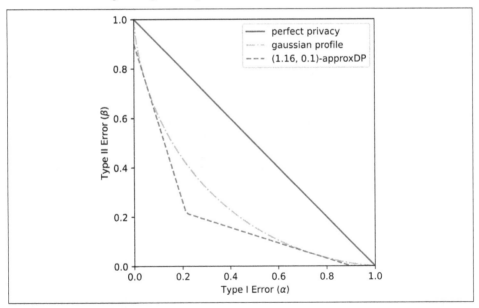

Figure 5-8. f-DP trade-off curves

27 Jinshuo Dong, Aaron Roth, and Weijie J. Su, "Gaussian Differential Privacy," *Journal of the Royal Statistical Society Series B: Statistical Methodology* 84, no. 1 (2022): 3-37.

Figure 5-8 shows three privacy curves, corresponding to perfect privacy, a smooth trade-off curve for the Gaussian, and a trade-off curve derived from a single (ϵ, δ) pair. The (ϵ, δ) corresponds to $\left(1, 10^{-6}\right)$-approximate DP through the following relationship:

$$\beta_{\epsilon, \delta}(\alpha) = \max\left(0, 1 - \delta - e^\epsilon \alpha, e^{-\epsilon}(1 - \delta - \alpha)\right)$$

This function allows you to represent approx-DP guarantees as trade-off curves. Privacy profiles (like $\epsilon(\delta)$) are an equivalent, alternative representation of trade-off functions (like $\beta(\alpha)$).

An approximation of a $\beta(\alpha)$ curve from an $\epsilon(\delta)$ curve is shown in Figure 5-9 by discretizing the curve to a finite number of (ϵ, δ) pairs.

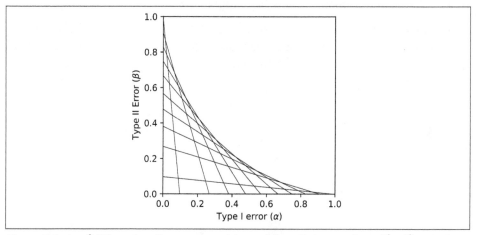

Figure 5-9. An f-DP trade-off curve approximated by a finite number of (ϵ, δ) pairs/ linear supporting functions

In this way, the hypothesis testing interpretation of DP can provide a new perspective on the privacy parameters.

Summary

Differential privacy has many measures of privacy, and knowing which one to use can significantly improve the utility and interpretability of your analysis. A common thread through these new privacy measures is the addition of a δ term, either directly (δ-approximate variations of other privacy measures) or indirectly (through RDP or zCDP).

As you apply mechanisms to your data, try to keep the PLRV in mind. Whether the mechanism fails gracefully when the privacy loss exceeds the expected bound (be it $\epsilon, \bar{\epsilon}, \rho$, or something else) should factor into your decision on what δ is acceptable for your use case. Mechanisms that admit distinguishing events, like PTR or truncated noise, should be considered carefully.

On the other hand, the δ slack term enables analyses otherwise impossible with pure-DP. For instance, PTR can be used to release statistics supported by an unknown key set (applications in SQL can be found in Chapter 7). In addition, the Gaussian mechanism, which needs this relaxation, is a fundamental primitive that appears in countless differentially private mechanisms. Examples of this will continue to appear throughout the rest of this book. Of particular interest, Gaussian noise is used to build DP machine learning models. This will be discussed in greater detail in Chapter 9.

Exercises

1. An adversary may record how much time it takes to execute a mechanism to infer additional information about a data set. This is called a *timing attack*. Assume you know that the execution time of a mechanism may differ by no more than t on any adjacent data set. Can you construct a function that modifies any given mechanism to protect against timing side-channels by also making the elapsed time a differentially private release?

    a. Hint: try using the truncated Laplace mechanism. To simplify this question, you can ignore timing side-channels introduced by the truncated Laplace mechanism itself.[28]

2. Recall the visualization of the realized privacy loss of the Laplace mechanism over its support seen in Figure 5-1. Create the same visualization but for the Gaussian mechanism. Once you are done, consider why the visualization looks so simple, and interpret why the y-axis is unbounded.

3. Write a Gaussian mechanism compositor that convolves privacy loss distributions. Keep in mind two key simplifications:

    a. The PLD of the Gaussian mechanism is $N(\eta, 2 \cdot \eta)$, where $\eta = \Delta^2 / (2 \cdot \sigma^2)$.

    b. The convolution of two Gaussians is Gaussian. That is, if $X \sim N(\mu_1, \sigma_1^2)$ and $Y \sim N(\mu_2, \sigma_2^2)$, then $X + Y \sim N(\mu_1 + \mu_2, \sigma_1^2 + \sigma_2^2)$.

---

28 A Framework for Differential Privacy Against Timing Attacks, TPDP 2023, Poster session.

4. Create a directed graph of the strength of privacy guarantees for pure-DP, approx-DP, BR, zCDP, RDP, and f-DP. In your graph, you should always be able to convert from stronger definitions of privacy to weaker definitions of privacy.

5. Write a function to convert an (ϵ, δ) guarantee into a (α, β) guarantee. What is the Type II error of a (1., 1e-6)-approxDP privacy guarantee, when the Type I error is at most .2? Interpret the meaning of this guarantee.

## CHAPTER 6

Fearless Combinators

In the context of DP, the term *combinators* encompasses algorithms that build new stable transformations and private mechanisms from other functions. Many algorithms in differential privacy can be expressed this way, making it a useful qualifier to describe a class of DP algorithms. While the name *combinator* may seem complex at first, the concept is completely approachable. You are already familiar with chaining and composition, which are two examples of combinators. The main topics discussed in this chapter are:

- Chaining
- Privacy measure conversion
- Generalized composition
- Privacy amplification
- Sample and aggregate
- Private selection from private candidates

Along the way, you'll learn about some new mechanisms that can be built up from previous mechanisms, through the use of these combinators:

- Bounds estimation (chaining/postprocessing)
- B-Trees (chaining/postprocessing)
- Sparse vector technique (adaptive composition)
- Multi-quantiles (parallel composition)
- Shuffle-DP (amplification)
- k-means (private selection from private candidates)

Chaining

Chaining is another word for *functional composition*, where a new function is constructed that iteratively applies two functions to an input:[1]

$$f_c(x) = f_2(f_1(x))$$

The combinator representation doesn't fix the initial argument x, instead opting to delay application:

```python
def make_chain_mt(f_2, f_1):
    """Construct a new measurement representing f_c(x) = f_2(f_1(x))"""
    # check that f_1 is a transformation and f_2 is a measurement
    assert isinstance(f_2, dp.Measurement) and isinstance(f_1, dp.Transformation)

    # transformation's output space must conform with measurement's input space
    assert f_2.input_domain == f_1.output_domain
    assert f_2.input_metric == f_1.output_metric

    # construct a new measurement representing the functional composition
    return dp.m.make_user_measurement(
        input_domain=f_1.input_domain,
        input_metric=f_1.input_metric,
        output_measure=f_2.output_measure,
        function=lambda x: f_2(f_1(x)),
        privacy_map=lambda b_in: f_2.map(f_1.map(b_in)))
```

This is the approach used to build up differentially private algorithms. Depending on what you are chaining, you need to employ either metric spaces, presented in Chapter 3, or the postprocessing property.

For instance, say you have a stable transformation and a private mechanism. If the stable transformation emits data in the same metric space that the private mechanism expects, then you can construct a new private mechanism that is a functional composition.

This concept can be illustrated with the OpenDP Library. In this example, since the sum's output space and Laplace mechanism's input space match, the chaining of the two components is successful:

```python
# call a constructor to produce a transformation
stable_trans = dp.t.make_sum(
    dp.vector_domain(dp.atom_domain(bounds=(0, 1))),
    dp.symmetric_distance())

# call a constructor to produce a measurement
```

---

1 Hay, Gaboardi, and Vadhan, "A Programming Framework for OpenDP."

```
private_mech = dp.m.make_laplace(
    stable_trans.output_domain,
    stable_trans.output_metric,
    scale=1.0)

new_mech = dp.c.make_chain_mt(private_mech, stable_trans)

# investigate the privacy relation
symmetric_distance = 1
epsilon = 1.0
assert new_mech.map(symmetric_distance) <= epsilon

# invoke the chained measurement's function
mock_data = [0, 0, 1, 1, 0, 1, 1, 1]
release = new_mech(mock_data)
```

The privacy guarantee of the resulting mechanism is automatically derived, as the new mechanism expects data and distance bounds with respect to the input metric space of the original transformation. A similar logic follows for chaining two stable transformations together: the interior metric spaces must match, and the resulting transformation relates between the outer metric spaces.

Finally, postprocessing can be seen as another kind of chaining. Since differentially private guarantees are closed under postprocessing, any arbitrary function can be applied to the output of a mechanism. Therefore, a new private mechanism can be constructed by chaining a private mechanism with an arbitrary postprocessing function.

This kind of chaining arises in a simple but popular bounds estimation algorithm.

Example: Bounds Estimation

Many differentially private estimators expect bounded data, but it is not always clear what bounds to use. The ideal approach is to choose clipping bounds based on prior knowledge you have of the problem domain. For instance, if you have data on individuals' heights, you are much better off choosing clipping bounds based on other, non-private data sources. For example, you could reference publicly available aggregate statistics on heights to estimate your expected range.

However, if this is not possible, there are techniques to estimate bounds privately. Note that privately estimating bounds will require spending part of your privacy budget. This leads to a rule of thumb: privately estimating bounds only tends to help improve utility when your best guess of clipping bounds is likely off by more than an order of magnitude.

There is no clear-cut best approach for bounds estimation, but we'll cover an approach based on postprocessing a noisy histogram. The approach is to first group the data into bins that get exponentially larger, privately count the number of elements in each bin, and then try to identify the first bin from negative infinity and the first bin from positive infinity where the private count is statistically significant:[2]

```
def make_private_bounds_via_histogram(scale, alpha=1e-9):
    return (
        make_logarithmic_binning() >>
        dp.t.then_count_by_categories(np.arange(-2099, 2100), False) >>
        dp.m.then_laplace(scale) >>
        make_find_bounds(scale, alpha)
    )
```

Assuming you are already familiar with private counting (make_count_by_cate gories and make_laplace), only make_logarithmic_binning and make_find_bounds are new.

The following code snippet defines a new 1-stable transformation for binning floating-point numbers. This implementation is tailored to 64-bit floating-point numbers. It assigns a bin label to each number in your data set, corresponding to Figure 6-1:

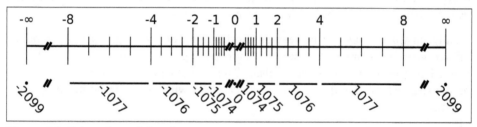

Figure 6-1. Private bounds bands

```
def make_logarithmic_binning():
    """bin each datum into a floating-point band"""
    dp.assert_features("contrib")
    input_domain = dp.vector_domain(dp.atom_domain(T=float))
    output_domain = dp.vector_domain(dp.atom_domain(T=int))
    metric = dp.symmetric_distance()

    def f_bin_by_band(arg):
        arg = np.array(arg)
        band = np.log2(abs(arg)) # bands grow exponentially
        band[~np.isfinite(arg)] = 1025 # infinities get their own band
        return ((arg >= 0) * 2 - 1) * (band.astype(int) + 1074) # sign * band

    return dp.t.make_user_transformation(
        input_domain, metric, output_domain, metric,
        f_bin_by_band, lambda b_in: b_in)  # 1-stable
```

2 Royce J. Wilson et al., "Differentially Private SQL with Bounded User Contribution," in *Proceedings on Privacy Enhancing Technologies 2020* (2019): 230–250.

Behind the cuts in the number line, the bins continue to decrease in size as they approach zero and increase in size as they approach infinity, up to the largest representable finite floating point number.

The purpose of the postprocessor is to choose the first bin from the left (`lower_idx`), and the first bin from the right (`upper_idx`), where the noisy count is large enough that it is unlikely to be explained solely by random noise. Once these bins are identified, the function returns the lower edge of the lower bin and the upper edge of the upper bin:

```
def make_find_bounds(scale, alpha=1e-9):
    """makes a postprocessor that finds bounds from a vector of noisy counts"""
    n_bands = 2099 + 1 + 2099 # negative bands, zero, positive bands
    threshold = -scale * np.log(2 - 2 * (1 - alpha) ** (1 / (n_bands - 1)))

    def f_find_bounds_from_bin_counts(counts):
        assert len(counts) == n_bands, "expected one count per-band"
        lower_idx = (counts > threshold).argmax() - 1
        upper_idx = n_bands - (counts > threshold)[::-1].argmax()
        idx = np.array([lower_idx, upper_idx]) - 2099

        with np.errstate(over="ignore"):
            return ((idx >= 0) * 2 - 1) * 2. ** (abs(idx) - 1075)

    return f_find_bounds_from_bin_counts
```

When these primitives are used together, they constitute a measurement that privately estimates the lower and upper bounds of a data set:

```
meas = make_private_bounds_via_histogram(scale=3., alpha=1e-9)
print(meas(np.random.normal(size=1000, scale=10))) # ~> [-8.0, 8.0]
print(meas.map(1)) # -> .333 = ε
```

Together, the transformations, measurement, and postprocessor constitute a new measurement used for private bounds estimation.

Another very popular mechanism in DP practice is the B-Tree mechanism, which can also be broken down into simpler, chainable primitives.

Example: B-Tree

A naturally arising, commonly recurring type of data release involves releasing count statistics at multiple levels of aggregation. For example, the US Census Bureau may want to release counts of the number of people per state, county, tract, and block. The US Census Bureau refers to this as the *geographic spine*. One approach you could take is to only release the data at the finest level of aggregation, per block, and then sum the noisy block level counts to estimate the per-tract, per-county, and per-state counts (see Figure 6-2).

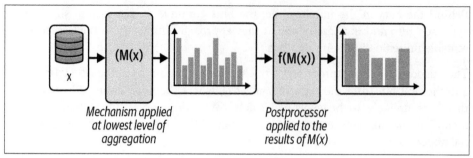

Figure 6-2. Chaining with postprocessor

While this does provide a valid estimate of the higher-level counts, these estimates are quite noisy. For instance, the estimate of the number of people in a state would have noise added separately for each block. When you care about accurate counts at multiple levels of aggregation, it makes more sense to split your budget among the levels (see Figure 6-3). Assuming you split your budget evenly among the four levels, then four times as much noise would be added to the per-block counts (leaf nodes), but many orders of magnitude less noise would be added to the per-state counts (root nodes).

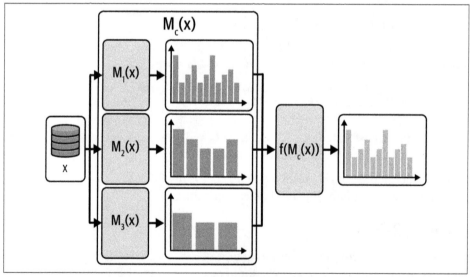

Figure 6-3. Composition with consistency postprocessor

Unfortunately, this introduces a new issue. Since noise is added separately at each level of aggregation, the sums of noisy per-block counts will not be equal to the per-tract counts, and likewise up the spine. From a statistical perspective, this is a problem of deriving the minimum variance estimate from multiple statistical measurements.[3] Since the noise scale and distribution are public information, you can use inverse variance weighting:

$$\bar{y} = \frac{\frac{y_p}{\sigma_p^2} + \Sigma_i^b \frac{y_i}{n\sigma_c^2}}{\frac{1}{\sigma_p^2} + \frac{1}{n\sigma_c^2}}$$

In this equation:

- y_p: parent count
- y_i: i^{th} child count
- σ_p: parent standard deviation (for the discrete Laplace, just use the $\sqrt{2} \cdot$ scale)
- σ_c: child standard deviation

The algorithm applies this weighting from the leaf nodes, iteratively up to the root of the tree. It iterates through pairs of child and parent layers, reassigning the parent counts to $\bar{y}$, and down-weights the respective variances.

It then does a second pass from the root to the leaves, making all layers consistent with one another. The function takes in the noise scale used at each layer and returns the consistent leaf node counts. This consistency algorithm assumes a dense rectangular structure:

```
def postprocess_tree_histogramdd(hists, std):
    """Make a set of noisy hypercubes of successive summations
    consistent with each other.
    See 4.1: https://arxiv.org/pdf/0904.0942.pdf

    :param hists: A dict of {axes: hist},
        where each hist is a `len(axes)`-dimensional counts array.
    :returns the leaf layer histogram
    """
    # sort the keys by number of axes
    hists = dict(sorted(hists.items(), key=lambda p: len(p[0])))
    # ensure all hists are float
    hists = {k: v.astype(float) for k, v in hists.items()}

    axes = list(hists)

    # find shape of each axis. Last histogram holds all axis lengths
    category_lengths = np.array(hists[axes[-1]].shape)
```

---

3 Michael Hay et al., "Boosting the Accuracy of Differentially-Private Histograms Through Consistency," in *Proceedings of the VLDB Endowment* 3, no. 1–2 (2010): 1021–32.

```
# variance of postprocessed current layer. Starting at leaves,
# which are not postprocessed
var = std[axes[-1]] ** 2
# ...
```

This postprocessor starts by initializing the necessary variables. The histograms are organized in a manner that makes them hierarchical: one-way marginal counts are placed before two-way marginals, and so on.

The following algorithm will sweep from the leaf nodes (where there are the most axes) to the root. To get things started, the variance of the current layer is stored in var and will be updated iteratively as the algorithm sweeps up through the layers.

The sweep works by iterating through each pair of parent and child layers:

```
# ...
# bottom-up scan to compute z
for parent, child in zip(axes[::-1][1:], axes[::-1][:-1]):
    axes_to_sum = _axes_to_sum(child=child, parent=parent)
    b = _branching_factor(category_lengths, axes_to_sum)

    # derive overall variance of parent after weighted averaging
    var = 1 / (1 / std[parent]**2 + 1 / (b * var))

    # weight parent contribution based on its proportion of inverse variance
    alpha = var / std[parent]**2

    # hists[parent] has not been overriden because traversal order
    # is bottom to top
    term1 = alpha * hists[parent]

    # hists[child] has been overwritten by previous loop
    term2 = (1 - alpha) * hists[child].sum(axis=axes_to_sum)

    hists[parent] = term1 + term2
# ...
```

At the end of this section, the parent counts are updated to the average of the direct estimate and a secondary estimate gained by summing the counts in the child layer. The average is weighted based on the expected variance; estimates of the parents collected by summing up children are down-weighted because they tend to be noisier.

A second set of counts h_b is necessary for the return trip. On the return trip, children are updated so that they sum exactly to their parents, further reducing the error of the children:

```
# ...
h_b = {a: h.copy() for a, h in hists.items()}

# top down scan to compute h
for parent, child in zip(axes[:-1], axes[1:]):
```

```
        axes_to_sum = _axes_to_sum(child=child, parent=parent)
        b = _branching_factor(category_lengths, axes_to_sum)

        correction = (h_b[parent] - hists[child].sum(axis=axes_to_sum)) / b
        h_b[child] += np.expand_dims(correction, axes_to_sum)

    # entire tree is consistent, so only the bottom layer is needed
    return h_b[axes[-1]]
```

Once the algorithm makes its linear pass up and down the tree, all layers are consistent with one another. You only need to keep the leaf nodes, since summing the child nodes of any one layer will exactly match the layer above it.

This algorithm *only* handles the postprocessing of a set of private k-way marginals. To use it, you'll need to release statistics at multiple levels of aggregation. It chains with a sequential compositor mechanism that releases hists, where each mechanism being composed releases a multidimensional histogram.

Postprocessing based on inverse variance weighting is a broadly applicable approach for combining multiple noisy estimates for the same quantity. In the setting of hierarchical k-way marginals, you can exploit this in a structured way to reduce the variance at all levels of aggregation.

Privacy Measure Conversion

In Chapter 5, each new measure of privacy was accompanied by a bound that could be used to convert to a previous measure of privacy. This kind of conversion can also be represented with combinators.

The following example shows a simple combinator that can be used to convert a pure-DP mechanism to an approx-DP mechanism by adding a zero-delta term:

```
import opendp.prelude as dp
space = dp.atom_domain(T=float), dp.absolute_distance(T=float)
meas_pureDP = space >> dp.m.then_base_laplace(scale=10.)

# convert the output measure to `FixedSmoothedMaxDivergence`
meas_fixed_approxDP = dp.c.make_pureDP_to_fixed_approxDP(meas_pureDP)

# FixedSmoothedMaxDivergence distances are (ε, δ) tuples
meas_fixed_approxDP.map(1.) # -> (0.1, 0.0)
```

This is a useful mental model to carry with you; even if a mechanism does not satisfy the definition of privacy you need for your overall computation, you can always convert to the definition of privacy you need, so long as the definition of privacy you need is not stronger.

For example, recalling "Rényi Differential Privacy" on page 126, a ρ-zCDP guarantee implies an $(\alpha, \rho \cdot \alpha)$-RDP guarantee:[4]

```python
def make_zCDP_to_RDP(meas):
    """Convert a zCDP mechanism to an RDP mechanism"""
    dp.assert_features("contrib")
    assert meas.output_measure == dp.zero_concentrated_divergence(T=float)

    def privacy_map(b_in):
        # ρ-zCDP implies (α, ρ * α)-RDP
        def rdp_curve(alpha):
            assert alpha > 1, "RDP order (alpha) must be greater than one"
            return meas.map(b_in) * alpha
        return rdp_curve

    return dp.m.make_user_measurement(
        meas.input_domain, meas.input_metric, renyi_divergence(),
        function=meas.function, privacy_map=privacy_map)
```

The following example demonstrates using a combinator to convert a zCDP mechanism to an approx-DP mechanism by directly using the OpenDP Library:[5]

```python
meas_zCDP = space >> dp.m.then_base_gaussian(scale=0.5)

# convert the output measure to approx-DP
meas_approxDP = dp.c.make_zCDP_to_approxDP(meas_zCDP)

# this distance in approx-DP is represented with an ε(δ) curve
εδ_curve = meas_approxDP.map(1.)
```

While the conversion from zCDP to RDP is *lossless*, other conversions between privacy measures can be *lossy*. A conversion is considered lossy when the resulting privacy parameters are larger than they would be if the optimal conversion was based on complete information about the PLRV.

In particular, the conversion from moments-based accounting under RDP or zCDP to approx-DP is lossy.

Since conversions between privacy measures can be lossy, it is recommended to compose within the same measure of privacy when possible and delay conversion into a weaker privacy measure (like approx-DP) until the end of your analysis.

---

4 Mironov, "Renyi Differential Privacy," 263–75.

5 A tighter conversion is used from: Canonne, Kamath, and Steinke, "The Discrete Gaussian for Differential Privacy."

Composition

Composition is a kind of mechanism built up from other mechanisms. From the perspective of combinators, composition is a combinator over mechanisms.

Composition has several axes of variation:

- Sequential or parallel (see Chapter 2)
- Measure of privacy (see Chapter 5)
- Non-adaptive, adaptive, or concurrent (query interactivity)
- Compositor, odometer, or filter (parameter interactivity)

Each combination admits a different kind of composition. Composition theorems thus far have been non-adaptive. This is the most restrictive setting, where all of the queries and their privacy parameters must be fixed before ever making a release.

You can generalize composition with respect to queries and with respect to privacy parameters. First, let's explore *adaptivity*, or how queries may vary.

Adaptivity

Adaptive composition allows you to adaptively choose the next query after releasing the previous query. Interestingly, adaptive composition does not assume query independence, which means that privacy guarantees remain intact even when a query incorporates results from previous queries.

Adaptive composition
> For a sequence of k adaptively chosen differentially private queries $M_i(x)$, each satisfying ϵ_i-DP, the adaptive composition satisfies $\sum_i^k \epsilon_i$-differential privacy.[6]

Similar relaxations have been proven for essentially all measures of privacy, including approx-DP, RDP, zCDP, and f-DP.

Unfortunately, adaptive composition doesn't allow for *interleaving* queries to multiple mechanisms. When you have an interactive mechanism, like the above threshold algorithm introduced in "Above Threshold" on page 105, then this becomes somewhat limiting. For instance, you cannot run two instances of above threshold concurrently; as soon as you spawn a second above threshold queryable, the first one must refuse to answer any more queries, lest it violate the sequentiality constraint of the adaptive compositor.

---

6 Dwork et al., "Our Data, Ourselves: Privacy Via Distributed Noise Generation," 486–503.

To address this, there is a second relaxation to allow for the *concurrent* composition of interactive mechanisms. At the time of writing this book, concurrent composition is still an ongoing area of research.[7] However, it has been demonstrated that concurrent composition is just as tight as the adaptive composition under approximate, Rényi, and f-differential privacy.

The adaptive/concurrent compositor is the first example of interactive composition; when you invoke this compositor on your data set, you get a queryable. This compositor queryable expects private mechanisms to be passed as queries:

```
m_rr = dp.m.make_randomized_response_bool(prob=.55)
m_sc = dp.c.make_sequential_composition(
    m_rr.input_domain, m_rr.input_metric, m_rr.output_measure,
    1, [1., 1.]
)
# spawns an instance of the compositor that you can interact with
qbl = m_sc(True)
# consume the first privacy parameter (of 2) by releasing a randomized response
qbl(m_rr) # ~> True

# The compositor now has one remaining query that may consume ε = 1.
# Can nest a second compositor to sub-divide the remaining budget:
m_sc2 = dp.c.make_sequential_composition(
    m_rr.input_domain, m_rr.input_metric, m_rr.output_measure,
    1, [0.6, 0.4]
)
qbl2 = qbl(m_sc2)
# the sub-compositor is now exhausted:
qbl2(m_rr) # ~> True
qbl2(m_rr) # ~> False
```

In this example, the compositor mediates access to the data and enforces privacy guarantees, assuming that the queries satisfy the promised guarantees. The internals of the compositor look like the following:

```
def make_sequential_composition(
    input_domain, input_metric, output_measure, b_in, b_mids):
    """When invoked with some data, spawns a compositor queryable."""
    dp.assert_features("contrib")
    # this example implementation assumes the privacy measure is pure-DP
    assert output_measure == dp.max_divergence(T=float)

    # when data is passed to the measurement...
    def f_data_to_compositor_queryable(data):
        # ...a new queryable is spawned that tracks the privacy expenditure
        d_mids_p = list(b_mids)

        # this function will be called each time a query is passed
```

---

7 Vadhan and Wang, "Concurrent Composition of Differential Privacy."

```
def transition(query):
    # ensure that the query (a measurement) can be applied to the data
    assert query.input_domain == input_domain
    assert query.input_metric == input_metric
    assert query.output_measure == output_measure
    assert query.map(b_in) <= d_mids_p[0], "insufficient budget for query"

    release = query(data)
    d_mids_p.pop(0) # consume the budget if the release is successful
    return release

return dp.new_queryable(transition)

def privacy_map(b_in_p):
    assert b_in_p <= b_in
    return b_in * sum(b_mids)

return dp.m.make_user_measurement(
    input_domain, input_metric, output_measure,
    function=f_data_to_compositor_queryable,
    privacy_map=privacy_map)
```

As shown in the privacy map, if you fix your privacy parameters ahead of time, then the adaptive composition enjoys the same linear sum behavior as in the sequential composition.

The *sparse vector technique* (SVT) is an example of a popular mechanism used to identify the first k events above a threshold. SVT can be assembled from the above threshold mechanism ("Above Threshold" on page 105) and adaptive composition; use the sequential composition of k above threshold mechanisms.

 While gluing these mechanisms together is "simple and easy," SVT can be made tighter when one noisy threshold is shared among all instances of the above threshold mechanism. This is a case where a careful, global analysis can admit tighter guarantees.[8]

Notice that while the compositors can be made more flexible in terms of choosing mechanisms, they still don't allow you to adaptively choose privacy parameters.

---

8 Lyu et al., "Understanding the Sparse Vector Technique for Differential Privacy."

Odometers and Filters

Privacy odometers and *privacy filters* allow you to adaptively specify the privacy loss parameters, with the downside that they tend to charge a bit more (in terms of privacy loss) for each query.[9]

In some cases, having the flexibility to adaptively choose privacy parameters may be worth the increased privacy spend. Odometers and filters contrast to the previously discussed compositors, where all future privacy loss parameters must be fixed before making the first DP release.

A *privacy odometer* keeps track of the privacy spend of an adaptively chosen sequence of queries. Privacy odometers have two interfaces: you can either query a privacy odometer with a mechanism you'd like to run on the data, or ask the privacy odometer for its current privacy loss consumption:

```
import opendp.prelude as dp
dp.enable_features("contrib", "honest-but-curious")

# for simplicity, consider a metric space consisting of {T, F}
domain, metric = dp.atom_domain(T=bool), dp.discrete_distance()

odometer = make_sequential_odometer(
    domain, metric, output_measure=dp.max_divergence(T=float))

data = True # a very simple data set
qbl = odometer(arg=data)

# the privacy consumption of the odometer starts at zero
assert qbl(Map(b_in=1)) == 0

# query the odometer queryable and release the output
print(qbl(dp.m.make_randomized_response_bool(prob=0.75)))

# the privacy consumption of the odometer has now increased to ln(3)
assert qbl(Map(b_in=1)) == 1.0986122886681098
```

A *privacy filter* can be viewed as a privacy odometer with a fixed upper bound on the total privacy consumption. This fixed upper bound is enforced by a *continuation rule*, which is a function that determines if the filter is allowed to answer each incoming query. If the hypothetical privacy spend is greater than the bound, the continuation rule rejects the incoming query:

---

9 Ryan Rogers et al., "Privacy Odometers and Filters: Pay-as-You-Go Composition," in *Proceedings of the 30th International Conference on Neural Information Processing Systems (NIPS'16)* (Red Hook: Curran Associates Inc., 2016): 1929–37.

```
# enforce a (b_in, b_out)-closeness continuation rule
m_filter = make_odometer_to_filter(
    odometer=odometer, b_in=1, b_out=1.1)

data = True # a very simple data set
qbl = m_filter(arg=data)

# accepted, because the total privacy spend would be less than 1.1
qbl(dp.m.make_randomized_response_bool(prob=0.75))

# rejected, because the total privacy spend would now exceed 1.1
qbl(dp.m.make_randomized_response_bool(prob=0.75))
```

Privacy filters can be employed within a compositor with fixed privacy parameters to allow adaptive selection of privacy parameters in an otherwise static analysis. This code example first creates a top-level compositor, then spawns a privacy filter with the first query:

```
top_level_compositor_meas = dp.c.make_sequential_composition(
    domain, metric,
    dp.max_divergence(T=float), # privacy measure
    1, [1.1, 1.1] # b_in, b_out
)

data = True # a very simple data set
qbl = top_level_compositor_meas(arg=data)

# compositor queryable accepts the privacy filter because it is (1, 1.1)-DP
qbl_filter = qbl(m_filter)

# filter queryable now accepts an adaptively chosen sequence of privacy losses
qbl_filter(dp.m.make_randomized_response_bool(prob=0.6))

# even when the top-level compositor becomes exhausted...
qbl(dp.m.make_randomized_response_bool(prob=0.75))

# ...the filter queryable still accepts queries,
# because the top-level compositor allows concurrent composition
qbl_filter(dp.m.make_randomized_response_bool(prob=0.55))

# rejects any query that violates the continuation rule
qbl_filter(dp.m.make_randomized_response_bool(prob=0.75))
```

Privacy odometers and filters are flexible primitives that enable interactive data analysis. giving you the flexibility to submit multiple rounds of queries, each taking advantage of information gained in the previous rounds. More generally, compositors, odometers, and filters can interoperate with one another via nesting; compositors and filters can themselves be nested under other compositors, odometers, and filters. It is also possible to use compositors, odometers, and filters with other combinators for chaining and converting the privacy measure.

Partitioned Data

This section introduces a unified perspective for reasoning about the stability of partitioned data (either randomly, by grouping, or other means). This is possible via a metric that computes distances between partitioned data sets. The metric connects data splitting operations with vectorized operations (like aggregations, parallel composition, and sample and aggregate).

The stability or privacy of computations on partitioned data tends to make use of three pieces of information:

1. The number of partitions an individual may influence

2. The total influence an individual has over all partitions

3. The greatest amount an individual may influence any one partition

These three pieces of information can be represented by a metric that first computes a vector of per-partition distances (the symmetric distance between each respective partition) and then computes the L^0, L^1, and L^∞ norms:

```
def d_Partition(x, x_p, d=d_Sym):
    """L0, L1 and L∞ norms of the distances between neighboring partitions"""
    dists = abs(np.array([d(x_i, y_i) for x_i, y_i in zip(x, x_p)]))
    #       |d(x, x')|_0    , |d(x, x')|_1, |d(x, x')|_∞
    return (dists != 0).sum(), dists.sum(), dists.max()
```

This is a natural choice of output metric for a grouping transformation or a partitioning transformation:

```
def make_partition_randomly(input_domain, num_partitions):
    dp.assert_features("contrib")
    assert can_be_partitioned(input_domain) # like vectors, arrays

    def f_partition_randomly(data):
        data = np.array(data, copy=True)
        # randomly partition data into `num_partitions` data sets
        np.random.shuffle(data)
        return np.array_split(data, num_partitions)

    return dp.t.make_user_transformation(
        input_domain=input_domain,
        input_metric=dp.symmetric_distance(),
        output_domain=dp.vector_domain(input_domain, size=num_partitions),
        output_metric=partition_distance(dp.symmetric_distance()),
        function=f_partition_randomly,
        # TODO: what kind of domain descriptors can you use to improve this?
        # TODO: how might you modify the function to improve this?
        stability_map=lambda b_in: (b_in, b_in, b_in))
```

In this code example, the data is randomly shuffled. Then, in the worst case for the L^0 norm, an individual may spread their influence across b_{in} partitions. The total influence an individual has (corresponding to the L^1 norm) doesn't change when you partition the data. The worst case for the third value, the L^∞ norm, is when all contributions from an individual are made to a single partition.

Example: Grouping on Asylum Seeker Data

It is more natural to incorporate prior knowledge when grouping. Consider a data set of asylum seeker logs, where each record contains the applicant's home country and a year under which they received asylum.

You may have prior knowledge that all data from an asylee would fall into one partition, which tightens the L^0 norm to one. This is the case when the data is split by home country. Alternatively, you may have prior knowledge that all contributions fall into different partitions. Since the data is yearly, then partitioning the data by year will admit an L^∞ norm of one.

This prior knowledge is encoded as descriptors on the input domain:

```
# when grouped by "Home Country"
# an individual may contribute to at most one partition
max_partitions={"Home Country": 1},
# when grouped by "Year"
# each partition has at most one contribution from each individual
max_per_partition={"Year": 1})
```

The grouping transformation then exploits this information, when applicable:

```
def make_groupby(input_domain, by):
    dp.assert_features("contrib")
    # prior knowledge about l0 and l∞ norm are inherent to the data frame's domain
    l0, linf = extract_prior_knowledge(input_domain, by)

    return dp.t.make_user_transformation(
        input_domain=input_domain,
        input_metric=partition_distance(),
        output_domain=groupby_domain(),
        output_metric=partition_distance(),
        function=lambda df: df.groupby(by),
        stability_map=lambda b_in: (min(l0, b_in), b_in, min(linf, b_in)))
```

This was the underlying structure for "Grouped Data" on page 80. Knowing these bounds on the L^0, L^1, and L^∞ norms can result in vector-valued queries with significantly lower L^1 and L^2 sensitivities. The following count transformation takes advantage of this information when deriving the L^2 sensitivity:

```
def make_group_size():
    """make a transformation that computes the size of each group"""
    dp.assert_features("contrib")
    return dp.t.make_user_transformation(
        input_domain=groupby_domain(),
        input_metric=partition_distance(),
        output_domain=series_domain(),
        output_metric=dp.l2_distance(T=float),
        function=lambda groupby: groupby.size(),
        stability_map=lambda l0_l1_li: np.sqrt(l0_l1_li[0]) * l0_l1_li[2])
```

In this case, if per-partition contributions are at most one (according to L^∞), then the sensitivity grows only in the square root of the number of affected partitions (according to L^0).

The final piece is extending the Gaussian mechanism to privatize pandas series:

```
def make_pd_gaussian(scale):
    """Make a gaussian noise mechanism that privatizes a series.
    Assumes the index is public information."""
    dp.assert_features("contrib")

    space = dp.vector_domain(dp.atom_domain(T=float)), dp.l2_distance(T=float)
    m_gauss = dp.m.make_gaussian(*space, scale)

    return dp.m.make_user_measurement(
        input_domain=series_domain(),  # assuming that the index is public info
        input_metric=m_gauss.input_domain,
        output_measure=m_gauss.output_measure,
        function=lambda s: pd.Series(m_gauss(s.to_numpy()), index=s.index),
        privacy_map=m_gauss.map)
```

When chained together, you can release a differentially private count of the number of asylum-seekers per year and per country:

```
m_gb = (
    make_groupby(input_domain, by=["Home Country", "Year"])
    >> make_group_size()
    >> make_pd_gaussian(scale=1.0)
)

print(m_gb(df))
print(m_gb.map(1))
```

Observe that the L^0 constraint on year implies the same constraint when grouped with other factors.

Parallel Composition

Parallel composition is a combinator that applies mechanisms to data partitions.[10]

```
def make_parallel_composition(mechanisms):
    dp.assert_features("contrib")

    input_domain, input_metric, output_measure = get_elements(mechanisms)

    assert input_metric == dp.symmetric_distance(), "expected microdata input"

    def privacy_map(b_in):
        l0, _l1, linf = b_in
        return l0 * max(m.map(linf) for m in mechanisms)

    return dp.m.make_user_measurement(
        input_domain=dp.vector_domain(input_domain, size=len(mechanisms)),
        input_metric=partition_distance(dp.symmetric_distance()),
        output_measure=output_measure,
        # apply the ith mechanism to the ith partition
        function=lambda parts: [m_i(p_i) for m_i, p_i in zip(mechanisms, parts)],
        # privacy loss is the max among partitions
        privacy_map=privacy_map)
```

This implementation of the mechanism makes use of bounds on both the L^0 and L^∞ norms. The total privacy loss is the greatest privacy loss in any one partition, multiplied by the number of partitions an individual may influence.

This partition distance will reappear for other varieties of combinators, but let's first cover an example algorithm that employs careful use of composition results to create a more complex algorithm. The following section shows an algorithm for estimating multiple quantiles using both adaptive composition and parallel composition.

Example: Multi-Quantiles

Say you want to release multiple quantile estimates, one for each α in {0.1, 0.25, 0.4, 0.5, 0.6, 0.75, 0.9}.

Instead of estimating each quantile independently, you can exploit the structure of the query and use parallel composition.[11] Start by privately estimating the middle, 0.5-quantile. You can now use adaptive composition to estimate the next pair of quantiles.

---

10 Frank McSherry, "Privacy Integrated Queries: An Extensible Platform for Privacy-Preserving Data Analysis," in *Proceedings of the 2009 ACM SIGMOD International Conference on Management of Data* (New York: ACM, 2009), 19–30, *https://doi.org/10.1145/1559845.1559850*.

11 Haim Kaplan et al., "Differentially Private Approximate Quantiles," in *Proceedings of the International Conference on Machine Learning* (2022).

Now, partition the data by the released quantile. Observe that the median of the lower partition corresponds to the 0.25-quantile of the entire data set, and the median of the upper partition corresponds to the 0.75-quantile of the entire data set. Assuming each partition is disjoint, parallel composition allows you to release both of these quantiles for the price of one.

The algorithm can be applied recursively. The three released quantiles partition the data into four subsets, upon which you independently release the 0.1-, 0.4-, 0.6-, and 0.9-quantiles. This algorithm exploits previous answers to recursively break the problem into smaller, parallel queries over disjoint subsets of the domain.

You can view this as a binary tree: each node in the tree is a release, and the height of the tree is the number of rounds the algorithm must run. Therefore, the total privacy expenditure only grows according to the $\log_2$ in the number of quantiles to be released.

The following mechanism employs the quantile mechanism (from Chapter 4) to estimate each quantile:

```python
def make_private_multi_quantile_in_bounds(bounds, alphas, scale):
    dp.assert_features("contrib")
    def f_recursive_quantiles(x, alphas, bounds, epsilon):
        # base cases
        if len(alphas) == 0:
            return [] # for when the tree is not full

        if len(alphas) == 1:
            return [make_private_quantile_in_bounds(bounds, alphas[0], scale)(x)]

        # always estimate the middle quantile
        mid = (len(alphas) + 1) // 2
        p = alphas[mid]
        v = make_private_quantile_in_bounds(bounds, p, scale)(x)

        # split x and alphas apart into sub-problems (while rescaling alphas)
        x_l, x_u = x[x < v], x[x > v]
        alphas_l, alphas_u = alphas[:mid] / p, (alphas[mid + 1 :] - p) / (1 - p)

        # recurse down left and right partitions
        return [
            *f_recursive_quantiles(x_l, alphas_l, (bounds[0], v), epsilon),
            v,
            *f_recursive_quantiles(x_u, alphas_u, (v, bounds[1]), epsilon),
        ]
    # ...
```

This function recursively calls itself on finer and finer partitions, until all quantiles have been estimated. This algorithm doesn't directly use make_parallel_composition, as it has a much simpler recursive representation.

Due to the recursive nature of this algorithm, the corresponding privacy expenditure is analyzed globally:

```
# ...
def privacy_map(b_in):
    # the per-partition loss is maximized when alpha is 1
    per_part_loss = make_private_quantile_in_bounds(bounds, 1.,
                                                     scale).map(b_in)
    # by parallel composition up to b_in partitions can be
    # influenced per-layer
    per_layer_loss = b_in * per_part_loss
    # the recursion depth/number of layers is ceil(log_2(|alphas|))
    num_layers = len(alphas).bit_length()
    # by sequential composition over the releases of each layer
    return float(per_layer_loss * num_layers)

return dp.m.make_user_measurement(
    input_domain=dp.vector_domain(dp.atom_domain(T=float)),
    input_metric=dp.symmetric_distance(),
    output_measure=dp.max_divergence(T=float),
    function=lambda x: f_recursive_quantiles(np.array(x), alphas, bounds,
    scale),
    privacy_map=privacy_map)
```

Due to the clever use of composition combinators, to estimate seven quantiles, the privacy budget only has to be split three ways:

```
alphas = np.array([0.1, 0.25, 0.4, 0.5, 0.6, 0.75, 0.9])
bounds = (0., 100.)
scale = 100.
m_mq = make_private_multi_quantile_in_bounds(bounds, alphas, scale)

data = np.random.uniform(0, 100, size=10_000)
print(m_mq(data)) # ~> [9.735, 25.518, 40.292, 50.388, 59.679, 74.757, 89.544]
print(m_mq.map(1)) # -> 0.06 = ε
```

The resulting quantile estimates look accurate while only consuming $\epsilon = 0.06$.

Privacy Amplification

This section discusses two techniques to amplify the privacy of your analysis:

- Privacy amplification by *subsampling*[12]
- Privacy amplification by *shuffling*[13]

When the specific assumptions of these techniques are met, they can be used to reduce the overall privacy spend without impacting utility.

Subsampling amplifies privacy because any potential adversary can no longer know *who* is present in the sample, even if they know who is present in the population. Amplification by subsampling is applied under one of two perspectives. If your data set is a sample from a larger population, then privacy amplification gives a tighter accounting of the actual privacy spend. On the other hand, you may choose to actively sample down from a larger data set, under the expectation that sampling won't significantly damage the utility of the analysis.

The privacy analysis differs depending on the sampling procedure. The two sampling procedures of interest are simple random sampling and Poisson sampling.

Privacy Amplification by Simple Random Sampling

A simple random sample uniformly selects n items from a population of size N without replacement. If you know your data set is a simple random sample from a larger population, and you know the sampling proportion n/N, then you can employ privacy amplification. A downside to this approach is that it is based on knowing both a lower bound on the population size N and an upper bound on the sample size n.

The OpenDP Library has a combinator that implements this result:

```
dp.enable_features("honest-but-curious")

space = dp.vector_domain(dp.atom_domain(T=float, size=10)),
        dp.symmetric_distance()
meas = (
    space >>
    dp.t.then_clamp((0., 10.)) >>
    dp.t.then_mean() >>
    dp.m.then_laplace(scale=0.5)
```

---

12 Kaplan et al., "Differentially Private Approximate Quantiles."

13 Vitaly Feldman et al., "Hiding Among the Clones: A Simple and Nearly Optimal Analysis of Privacy Amplification by Shuffling," in *2021 IEEE 62nd Annual Symposium on Foundations of Computer Science (FOCS)* (Piscataway, NJ: IEEE, 2022) 954–64.

```
)

amplified = dp.c.make_population_amplification(meas, population_size=100)

# Where we once had a privacy utilization of ~2 epsilon...
assert meas.map(2) <= 2. + 1e-6

# ...we now have a privacy utilization of ~.4941 epsilon.
assert amplified.map(2) <= .4941
```

In practice, you don't typically have access to the full data set, so the combinator does not perform the sampling itself; it is up to you to verify that the data set is a simple sample and that the population size is correct. This is why the honest-but-curious flag is required.

Sometimes you don't know the population size and/or sample size but do know the sampling *rate*.

Privacy Amplification by Poisson Sampling

To take a Poisson sample, iterate through each record in your data set, and with probability λ, include it in the mini-batch.

Since each row in the data set only has a λ chance of being used in the release, the privacy loss is amplified by a factor roughly proportional to λ. Privacy amplification via Poisson sampling is used frequently in differentially private machine learning, to be discussed in Chapter 9.

Privacy Amplification by Shuffling

In the local-DP model, an adversary can distinguish which response came from which individual. Intuitively, you'd expect a lower privacy consumption if the answers are shuffled so that an adversary can't directly trace each answer back to an individual. Shuffling also doesn't impact the utility of most statistical estimators, which makes it generally applicable.

This observation leads to shuffle-DP, a model of privacy that is stronger than central-DP but weaker than local-DP. In this model, local-DP responses are first sent to a shuffler before being sent on to an analyst.

Individuals who release data in this model enjoy a privacy guarantee with smaller parameters than would be necessary for the same analysis without shuffling. Even if the shuffler were compromised, individuals are still protected by the local DP guarantee (although with larger privacy parameters).

Sample and Aggregate

Sample and aggregate bounds the stability of an arbitrary black-box function $f(\cdot)$. The technique first partitions your sensitive data and then maps $f(\cdot)$ over each partition to produce a vector of aggregates.[14] You can apply existing differentially private methods to the resulting vector of aggregates.

The technique can be extremely convenient when $f(\cdot)$ is complicated. On the other hand, you pay for this convenience via reduced utility. The sample and aggregate technique tends to have much less utility than a private estimator based on a tailored white-box function (like a DP-sum).

The utility is further impacted if $f(x)$ is poorly approximated by $f(s)$, where s is a random subset of the data set x. A function like $\min(x)$ is a prime example of this. If the subset s does not contain the minimum of the data set, then $f(s)$ can be an arbitrarily poor approximation of $f(x)$. Fortunately, many estimates are approximated well by subsets.

The data set of aggregates has bounded Hamming distance: if you know individuals may contribute at most b_{in} records to a data set, then you know they can influence up to b_{in} partitions:

```
def make_sample_and_aggregate(
        input_domain, output_domain, num_partitions, black_box):
    dp.assert_features("contrib", "honest-but-curious")

    # SAMPLE: randomly partition data into `num_partitions` data sets
    trans_subsample = make_partition_randomly(input_domain, num_partitions)

    # AGGREGATE: apply `black_box` function to each partition
    trans_aggregate = dp.t.make_user_transformation(
        input_domain=dp.vector_domain(input_domain, size=num_partitions),
        output_domain=dp.vector_domain(output_domain, size=num_partitions),
        input_metric=dp.symmetric_distance(),
        output_metric=dp.hamming_distance(),
        function=lambda parts: [black_box(part) for part in parts],
        stability_map=lambda b_in: b_in) # 1-stable

    return trans_subsample >> trans_aggregate
```

This implementation reuses the partitioning transformation from "Partitioned Data" on page 156. However, only the L^0 norm is used in this setting. In the resulting data set of aggregates, an individual can only influence as many rows as the number of partitions they were located in.

---

14 Kobbi Nissim et al., "Smooth Sensitivity and Sampling in Private Data Analysis," in *Proceedings of the Thirty-Ninth Annual ACM Symposium on Theory of Computing* (New York: ACM, 2007): 75–84.

You can view sample and aggregate as a 1-stable transformation from microdata to a data set of aggregates.

 If, when you partition, you enforce that each person may influence at most *one* partition, then the stability map becomes constant. Regardless of b_{in}, only at most one partition may differ, so the resulting vector of aggregates has stability of at most one.

One popular approach in common practice is to use sample and aggregate to release predictions from an ensemble of machine learning algorithms. This will be discussed in more detail in "Private Aggregations of Teacher Ensembles" on page 230.

Private Selection from Private Candidates

If you've ever found yourself in a situation where you need more utility, you may have been tempted to run your mechanism multiple times and only use the best result. However, cherry-picking results from multiple runs of a mechanism biases the output distribution, which breaks the privacy guarantee.

Private selection from private candidates (PSPC) offers the next best thing: you can choose the mechanism output that has the best noisy utility, in exchange for a factor-of-three increase to your privacy budget.[15] This approach is also a form of private selection, just like the exponential mechanism, but differs in that the set of potential outputs does not need to be known to the analyst.

The algorithm repeatedly invokes a mechanism until a randomly selected number of trials is exhausted:

```
def make_pspc_geometric(meas, p):
    """implements pure-DP private selection from private candidates"""
    dp.assert_features("contrib", "floating-point")
    assert 0 < p < 1, "p is the probability of stopping"
    assert meas.output_measure == dp.max_divergence(T=float)

    def f_choose_best_run(data):
        # sample the geometric distribution- conditioned on not being zero!
        k = np.random.geometric(p) + 1 # geometric is memoryless

        # evaluate the measurement k times
        candidates = (meas(data) for _ in range(k))
        # select the candidate with the highest score
        return max(candidates, key=lambda c: c[0])
```

---

15 Jingcheng Liu and Kunal Talwar, "Private Selection from Private Candidates," in *Proceedings of the 51st Annual ACM SIGACT Symposium on Theory of Computing* (2019): 298–309.

```
return dp.m.make_user_measurement(
    *meas.input_space, dp.max_divergence(T=float),
    f_choose_best_run, privacy_map=lambda b_in: meas.map(b_in) * 3)
```

When it costs ϵ to invoke the mechanism, this algorithm costs 3ϵ to run. Although this approach does incur a factor-of-3 penalty on the privacy budget, it may be worth paying this penalty for the benefit of selecting the best candidate from a pool of samples.

This technique is particularly applicable when you don't have useful prior information on how to set a parameter for a DP algorithm. Take, for example, private k-means clustering.

Example: k-Means

There are many approaches for DP k-means, the most naive and straightforward of which is based on *Lloyd's algorithm*,[16] which involves these steps:

1. Sample k initial points, called *centroids*, denoted c_i (must be data-independent).

2. Assign each member of the data set to a partition C_i based on its nearest centroid (parallel composition).

3. For each partition, calculate the mean value of its points. This becomes the new centroid for the partition (DP vector-valued mean).

4. Return to step 2 until the centroids stop changing (sequential composition).

The notes in parentheses give the gist on how to do this privately. Observe that this k-means clustering algorithm requires you to fix k, the number of clusters, before running the algorithm. A poor initial choice of k will significantly reduce the utility, but refitting the algorithm with different choices of k will significantly increase the privacy loss.

This is an ideal situation for PSPC, but you need a way to measure utility: the Calinski-Harabasz index gives the ratio of between-cluster separation (BCSS) over within-cluster separation (WCSS). Higher scores represent better separated, more tightly packed clusters:

$$\text{CH} = \frac{\text{BCSS} \cdot (n - k)}{\text{WCSS} \cdot (k - 1)}$$

In the following definition, n_i denotes the number of records in partition C_i:

---

16 Avrin Blum et al., "Practical Privacy: The SuLQ Framework," in *Proceedings of the Twenty-Fourth ACM SIGMOD-SIGACT-SIGART Symposium on Principles of Database Systems*, (New York: ACM, 2005): 128–38.

$$\text{BCSS} = \sum_{i=1}^{k} n_i \parallel c_i - \bar{x} \parallel_2^2 \quad \text{WCSS} = \sum_{i=1}^{k} \sum_{x \in C_i}^{k} \parallel x - c_i \parallel_2^2$$

Notice that BCSS can be estimated by postprocessing statistics released by the DP Lloyd algorithm. A DP sum can be used to estimate WCSS. Altogether, by sequential composition, you can construct a mechanism that releases a DP CH score and DP centroids with a randomly selected number of clusters k and random initial centroids.

PSPC then maximizes the CH utility score. Given that PSPC will fit k-means multiple times, PSPC also provides some level of robustness against poor initialization of starting centroids, which is a common problem encountered when clustering.

A more general version of PSPC is used for DP machine learning, as you will see in "Private selection from private candidates" on page 228. In that setting, the measurement satisfies RDP instead.

Summary

The theory of differential privacy allows for modularity; complex algorithms can be broken down into granular stable transformations and mechanisms that are glued together with combinators. This property of differential privacy makes it possible to implement complex algorithms by isolating their pieces and then tackling each piece one at a time. First, prove the stability or privacy properties of an algorithm, then write and test an implementation and build up.

The next chapters apply this framework of stable transformations, private mechanisms, and combinators to several problem domains: data sets with unbounded contribution, statistical modeling, machine learning, and synthetic data.

Exercises

1. Construct a measurement that implements the sparse vector technique by composing k above threshold mechanisms.

   a. Use your SVT measurement to extend the reporting tool from Exercise 4 in "Exercises" on page 108 to alert you up to 4 times.

2. Generate an array of 1,000 random floats from the standard normal distribution.

   a. Calculate the mean of the data.

   b. Make $\epsilon = \frac{1}{10}$-DP releases for the 5th and 95th percentiles for the data.

   c. Clip the data according to the released percentiles.

d. Recompute the mean—how has it changed? Could clipping in this manner introduce bias?

e. How can choosing clipping bounds by calculating non-private 5th and 95th percentiles break privacy guarantees?

3. Write a new mechanism named `make_private_bounds_via_quantile` that makes use of existing combinators (for composition) and mechanisms (for releasing the quantile). The purpose of this mechanism is to tighten a *very* loose guess on the data bounds to reduce the sensitivity in subsequent analyses.

4. Prove that DP observes parallel composition.

Differential Privacy in Practice

## CHAPTER 7

Eyes on the Privacy Unit

Your choice of privacy unit is at least as important as the choice of privacy loss parameters themselves. The privacy unit governs what you are protecting, which directly affects the strength of the privacy guarantee. Privacy units in real-world deployments often contain some nuance; they may not correspond to individuals, and this obscures the interpretation of the privacy guarantee.

In addition, you must be able to identify the privacy unit of your data set before you can even begin to chain together stable transformations and private mechanisms. Unfortunately, you have not yet been given the necessary tools to characterize the privacy unit on a very common class of real-world data sets: data with unbounded user contributions.

These are the two primary motifs in this chapter—helping you understand the implications of your choice of privacy unit and providing you with more tools to characterize your privacy unit. It is your responsibility, as a practitioner of differential privacy, to correctly characterize the unit of privacy in your DP analyses and to choose units of privacy that will give meaningful privacy guarantees.

This chapter will present you with scenarios where you will need to define the unit of privacy. Although the scenarios are illustrative, the projects presented here share similar characteristics to important data releases that are currently being conducted in the technology space. One example of such a data release is happening today at LinkedIn.

LinkedIn is a professional networking platform with over one billion users. The *Audience Engagement* project is one of its most notable data sharing initiatives. This project uses differential privacy to share engagement statistics and marketing analytics with analysts. The LinkedIn Audience Engagements API is interactive;

analysts are given a monthly privacy allowance and may submit more queries over time.[1]

The LinkedIn data release involves the two factors that affect how the unit of privacy is defined and protected. These are of central importance in this chapter. First, the privacy unit LinkedIn uses is a person-month, which is more narrow than an individual. This means that the privacy budget allotted for each analyst is refreshed each month. In your own DP analyses, your privacy unit must be meaningful for the DP guarantee to be meaningful.

Second, individuals in the LinkedIn data may make unbounded contributions to the data set. What happens when a data set contains an unknown/unlimited amount of data that corresponds to each instance of your privacy unit? This situation commonly arises in many practical use cases of differential privacy, like the LinkedIn scenario, hospital visit databases, and network log databases. In such cases, the sensitivity of many statistics becomes infinite, which fails to provide meaningful differential privacy guarantees. This chapter explores transformations that bound the influence of individuals on the data set, and private mechanisms that work on data sets with unbounded user contribution.

Finally, this chapter discusses how differential privacy maps onto relational database operations in both the settings of bounded and unbounded contributions. Through the use of identifiers, transformations can still be applied to data sets that do not have bounded contributions. This is also where joins and unions, in particular, are first discussed.

By the end of this chapter, you should be able to do the following:

- Distinguish between and contrast user-level privacy and other choices of privacy units
- Define data set adjacency in the presence of unbounded contributions
- Understand the process of data set truncation to bound contributions using reservoir sampling
- Optimize data set truncation to improve the utility of DP estimates or improve runtime
- Understand τ-thresholding, which can enable DP analysis of data sets with unknown domains
- Reason about the stability of common relational data operations, including joins

---

1 Ryan Rogers et al., "LinkedIn's Audience Engagements API: A Privacy Preserving Data Analytics System at Scale," *Journal of Privacy and Confidentiality* 11, no. 3 (2021).

Before introducing these new topics, let's first ground the terminology for the unit of privacy you have become familiar with so far.

Levels of Privacy

The first step of any differentially private analysis is to identify what you are trying to protect: the *unit of privacy* or *privacy unit*. A natural choice of privacy unit is a person.

User-level privacy
> A user-level privacy guarantee is a privacy guarantee that applies when any single user/individual/person may differ.

For example, the student database from "Case Study: Applying DP in a Classroom" on page 8 is an example of a user-level privacy guarantee, where the unit of privacy is a student. A user-level privacy guarantee can be achieved even when each row in the data set corresponds to a test taken by a student and a student may take multiple tests. In such a situation, you may claim that neighboring data sets differ by only at most k rows, because each student has taken only at most k tests. This factor of k will influence the sensitivity of your queries and, in turn, the derived privacy parameters.

Unit-level privacy
> A unit-level privacy guarantee is a privacy guarantee that applies when any single unit may differ.

A tempting adjustment to the classroom example is to instead advertise a test-level privacy guarantee. The immediate result is a k-fold reduction in total privacy loss, which is very exciting. However, the strength of the privacy guarantee weakens commensurately— the privacy guarantee only accounts for the influence any one test may have on the resulting release.

Notice that you may shift your perspective without affecting any of the details of the analysis. A user-level differential privacy guarantee can imply a stronger privacy guarantee for a finer privacy unit. For instance, the student-level privacy guarantee implies a k-fold stronger test-level privacy guarantee, assuming each student may only take k tests.

The same can hold in the other direction: imagine the US Census Bureau releasing statistics with person-level privacy. If you know a limit on the number of persons in a household, then you can imply a weaker household-level privacy guarantee.

Your choice of privacy unit is of essential importance when you publish a differentially private release. Publishing student test scores at test-level privacy only provides the advertised privacy protection for any one of a student's test scores. Arguably, test-level privacy is not a meaningful guarantee, and students are left with a k-fold weaker implied privacy guarantee.

User-Level Privacy in Practice

Your use case may introduce factors that make it impractical to achieve user-level privacy. If you cannot practically obtain user-level privacy, you need to decide if a finer privacy unit still lends meaningful privacy guarantees.

For instance, if an individual is able to create multiple LinkedIn accounts under different emails, then trying to distinguish which accounts were created by the same user (to bound user contributions) is impractical and somewhat self-defeating. Therefore, weakening the guarantee to account-level privacy may be a suitable trade-off if you can realistically expect each of the accounts to behave independently. In principle, under these conditions, an account-level guarantee wouldn't significantly underestimate a user-level guarantee.

This captures the primary argument that making the privacy unit more granular can be an acceptable compromise. If data across finer groupings remains independent, then an adversary cannot coordinate information learned about individuals across the groupings.[2]

By contrast, in the classroom example, you could argue that test-level privacy would not provide a meaningful privacy guarantee to students because a student's performance across exams is dependent; for example, a student who earns a high score on an exam is more likely to earn a high score on the next exam. Therefore, calibrating a differentially private release to provide "adequate" test-level privacy would in truth subject students to a k-fold weaker student-level privacy guarantee.

Choosing a more granular privacy unit to reduce privacy consumption differs from the purely quantitative methods employed in differential privacy theory because data dependence is not easy to quantify. Misattributing independence can make you vulnerable to providing privacy guarantees that are not meaningful. If accounts, tests, or any other distinction you use to narrow the unit of privacy are not truly independent, then the user will suffer the full privacy loss of each and every release on their data. Nevertheless, narrowing the unit of privacy may be necessary to practically apply differential privacy to your use case.

Many deployments of differential privacy have used more granular privacy units. Often data curators want to make releases at a regular cadence, data releases become

---

2 Elbert Du and Cynthia Dwork, "Improved Generalization Guarantees in Restricted Data Models," in *3rd Symposium on Foundations of Responsible Computing (FORC 2022)* (Schloss Dagstuhl: Leibniz-Zentrum fur Informatik, 2022).

outdated over time, and the preparation of one differentially private release on your data generally makes it easier to run again in the future. This is how DP releases are conducted for the Census Bureau (user-decade) (*https://oreil.ly/0VPp2*), LinkedIn Audience Engagements (user-month) (*https://oreil.ly/Z2v3-*), and Wikipedia page views (user-day) (*https://oreil.ly/1RMZr*).

Browser Logs Example: A Naive Event-Level Guarantee

Let's see an example of an analyst unwittingly providing an event-level DP guarantee. In this example, differential privacy will be satisfied, despite not providing a meaningful guarantee. This example should help you understand the importance of understanding the nature of your data sets.

Consider a data set of browser logs, where each row represents an event described by the following fields:

- Employee ID
- Date of the event
- Time the event occurred
- The address of the domain visited

Suppose an analyst wants to release the visit count for four websites. They have access to the following data set (Table 7-1) that contains browser logs of 1,234 employees of a company, from August to December 2020.

Table 7-1. Database of browser logs

Employee Id	Date	Time	Domain
872	08-01-2020	12:00	mail.com
867	10-01-2020	11:00	games.com
934	11-01-2020	08:00	social.com
872	09-15-2020	17:00	social.com
867	11-13-2020	05:00	mail.com
014	10-27-2020	13:00	social.com

The analyst computes a differentially private count of visits to each of these websites:

- *mail.com*
- *bank.com*
- *social.com*
- *games.com*

across each of the following months:

- August
- September
- October
- November
- December

To proceed with the task, the analyst naively sets the sensitivity of the COUNT query to 1, since adding or removing one row will influence the count by one. They then use the Laplace mechanism to privatize the count with what appears to be a very conservative budget of $\epsilon = 0.1$.

The analyst feels confident that this data release will not violate the privacy of individuals in the data, instead only revealing high-level browsing patterns, and prepares a release of the data in Table 7-2.

Table 7-2. Site visit counts

	August	September	October	November	December
bank.com	32465	32687	32495	32406	32879
games.com	346	398	412	32	41
mail.com	70567	73640	72857	71948	71954
social.com	2305	1726	2126	0	0

A closer inspection of the outputs reveals a significant drop in the number of visits from October to November for *games.com* and *social.com*. If you knew your coworker took a leave of absence during this time, then you could surmise your coworker's browsing habits even though the data scientist made a release utilizing differential privacy.

Let's understand why this happened. According to the definition of ϵ-differential privacy, the likelihood of observing any given output of the mechanism $M(x)$ is nearly the same as observing $M(x')$, where x and x' are neighboring data sets. When $\epsilon = 0.1$, the definition of ϵ-differential privacy ensures that for any set of possible outcomes S:

$$\frac{Pr[M(x) \in S]}{Pr[M(x') \in S]} \leq e^{0.1} \approx 1$$

The problem is that the data analyst calibrated sensitivity in a way that will provide an event-level privacy guarantee when a user-level privacy guarantee is more appropriate. If the analyst knows that each coworker may only generate 1,000 browser log entries, then the implied user-level privacy guarantee is more like $1{,}000 \cdot 0.1 = 100 = \epsilon$. Clearly, this privacy guarantee is far too weak and explains why your coworker's influence was not masked.

In practice, it is highly unlikely that each user is limited to only generating 1,000 log entries. This raises a new problem: the distance between neighboring data sets is unbounded.

 We now return to assuming the individual is the unit of privacy, for presentational convenience.

Data Sets with Unbounded Contributions

When any given individual may contribute an unbounded number of rows to a data set, then adjacent data sets may differ by an infinite number of rows. This means the sensitivity of many statistics also becomes infinite, because the sensitivity tends to scale linearly according to the data set distance.

Differentially private methods can be applied to data sets with unbounded contribution as long as each row in the data contains an identifier that ties it back to your unit of privacy. For instance, in user-level privacy, each record in the data set must contain a user ID.

You can even take advantage of this property to define a metric that captures how these data sets remain neighbors:

Identifier distance
    The identifier distance between data sets is the number of identifiers appearing in either x or x', but not both. That is, the identifier distance between data sets x and x' is the cardinality of the symmetric difference of the identifiers: $d_{\text{ident}}(x, x') = |\text{identifiers}(x) \triangle \text{identifiers}(x')|$.[3]

The identifier distance is similar to the symmetric distance, but the difference is only computed across identifiers. Assuming each individual in your data has one unique identifier, then two data sets that differ in the addition or removal of at most one individual remain 1-neighboring under the identifier distance. This remains true even though each individual may have unbounded row contributions:

```
def d_Id(x, x_p, identifiers):
    """compute the identifier distance"""
    return d_Sym(identifiers(x), identifiers(x_p))
```

---

3 Adapted from Wilson et al., "Differentially Private SQL with Bounded User Contribution."

For instance, when `bl` is a pandas data frame of browser logs, and `bl_p` is one possible adjacent data set with employee ID 867 removed, the data set distance works out to be one, even though employee 867 may make an unbounded number of data set contributions:

```
print(d_Id(bl, bl_p, identifiers=lambda x: set(x["Employee Id"]))) # -> 1
```

Approaches for privatizing data sets with unbounded user contribution employ a transformation that has constant stability per identifier:

- Certain statistics have constant sensitivity regardless of user contribution.
- Data set truncation transformations summarize each user's data within a constant number of rows.

Statistics with Constant Sensitivity

The count of distinct identifiers is insensitive to the number of data set contributions. Therefore, you can construct a 1-stable transformation that relates an identifier distance to an absolute distance (sensitivity). Concretely, the addition or removal of the data corresponding to up to k individual IDs will result in a change in the output of at most k.

This transformation can be extended to hierarchical counting queries. The count of the number of unique individuals within each data partition is also insensitive to the number of contributions. The sensitivity of such a query is based on the number of partitions an individual may influence, which follows the L^1 and L^2 sensitivity derivations previously discussed in Chapter 3.

Let's return to the browser logs example ("Browser Logs Example: A Naive Event-Level Guarantee" on page 175) for a moment. Instead of releasing a count of the number of *visits* to each category, you could release a count of the number of *unique individuals* who have visited each category. The L^1 sensitivity works out to the number of unique categories.

Similarly, in LinkedIn's case, the top-K articles that have the largest number of unique page views have constant sensitivity. This is true for more general scenarios, such as a DP mean or quantile of the number of records a user contributes to a data set.

Many such queries decompose further into a data set preprocessing transformation and a DP count query. For instance, in the case of the count of distinct individuals, you could transform a data set with unbounded contribution to a data set of unique user identifiers before applying the traditional DP count mechanism. This kind of transformation is a special case of a data set truncation transformation.

Data Set Truncation

A general approach to bound user contribution is called *data set truncation*, which involves grouping by the user ID and then aggregating.[4] Data set truncation transformations are k-stable, where k is the maximum number of records emitted by the aggregation. Such transformations are more broadly applicable than relying on constant sensitivity, but they can require greater computational overhead.

The summarizer can be essentially any black-box function that takes the data behind a single identifier and emits at most k records. Here are three examples:

Only keep aggregate statistics about the records associated with each user.
Data associated with each user can be aggregated down to a single record via computing summary statistics like means, quantiles, modes, and frequency sampling. The goal is to leverage simple statistics to obtain a representative record. A truncation transformation that employs this aggregation approach is 1-stable when only one record is returned per identifier.

Keep first (or last) k records associated with each user based on timestamp.
Using the timestamp as a filtering condition is a simple and efficient method of summarizing a user. However, this approach may induce bias in downstream releases. In the browser logs database, suppose a data scientist wants to limit the number of events per user and decides to keep only the first five events that happen in each day. Suppose further that there is a common behavioral pattern at the company where for 95% of employees, the first four browser visits are always to *mail.com*. Choosing events based on the time stamp would create a bias toward *mail.com*, and most likely, a data analysis made using the data could lead to incorrect conclusions.

Sample k records using the reservoir sampling algorithm.
Reservoir sampling is a randomized algorithm for selecting k samples from n items that is commonly used in differential privacy deployments to obtain a representative sample. Applications of reservoir sampling often deal with data sets that are very large, have unknown size, or do not fit in memory.

---

4 Kareem Amin et al., "Bounding User Contributions: A Bias-Variance Trade-off in Differential Privacy," in *Proceedings of the 36th International Conference on Machine Learning* (PMLR, 2019): 263–71.

Reservoir Sampling

Reservoir sampling maintains a random buffer of elements as it exhausts the data stream:

```python
import random

def reservoir_sample(stream: Iterable, k: int):
    """sample `k` items uniformly at random from `stream`"""
    # take up to the first k items from the stream
    reservoir = [v for v, _ in zip(stream, range(k))]

    for i, element in enumerate(stream, start=k):
        # uniformly sample from [0, item_position]
        j = random.randrange(i + 1)

        # if the sampled index `j` is in the reservoir...
        if j < k:
            # ...then replace the element in the reservoir
            reservoir[j] = element

    return reservoir
```

To illustrate how reservoir sampling works, let's imagine you want to sample 10 items from the set $\{0, \ldots, 999\}$. Starting with an initial reservoir of the first 10 elements, Table 7-3 shows how the first 10 iterations look.

Table 7-3. Reservoir sampling iterations

i	j	reservoir
		0 1 2 3 4 5 6 7 8 9
11	5	0 1 2 3 4 11 6 7 8 9
12	0	12 1 2 3 4 11 6 7 8 9
13	7	12 1 2 3 4 11 6 13 8 9
14	10	12 1 2 3 4 11 6 13 8 9
15	8	12 1 2 3 4 11 6 13 15 9
16	4	12 1 2 3 16 11 6 13 15 9
17	12	12 1 2 3 16 11 6 13 15 9
18	2	12 1 18 3 16 11 6 13 15 9
19	12	12 1 18 3 16 11 6 13 15 9
11	17	12 1 18 3 16 11 6 13 15 9

Notice that the reservoir is not updated on iteration 4, since index $j = 10$ is out of range. As the algorithm progresses, it begins to sample values from across the stream (in this case, closer to 1,000), and the random value j is more likely to be greater than k, meaning that the reservoir is updated less often, as shown in Table 7-4.

Table 7-4. Reservoir sampling iterations (cont.)

i	j	reservoir
72	29	44 77 18 23 28 55 63 13 75 9
73	53	44 77 18 23 28 55 63 13 75 9
...	...	...
100	87	44 87 18 99 28 55 63 13 75 9
101	68	44 87 18 99 28 55 63 13 75 9
...	...	...
108	102	112 87 18 99 28 55 63 13 75 9
109	56	112 87 18 99 28 55 63 13 75 9
...	...	...
644	42	112 391 18 504 165 324 311 570 335 123
645	650	112 391 18 504 165 324 311 570 335 123
...	...	...
826	467	112 391 18 504 165 324 311 570 335 123
827	538	112 391 18 504 165 324 311 570 335 123
...	...	...
916	27	112 391 18 504 165 324 311 570 335 123
917	729	112 391 18 504 165 324 311 570 335 123

Using reservoir sampling, you've just sampled k elements uniformly at random from data in a stream. Reservoir sampling is a common choice for bounding a user's contribution in a sequestered data set, by maintaining a separate reservoir for each individual.

A similar approach is shown with pandas, but this time sampling with replacement:

```
def make_truncate(id_col, threshold):
    """
    make a truncation transformation that samples `threshold` records per id
    """
    dp.assert_features("contrib")
    return dp.t.make_user_transformation(
        input_domain=dataframe_domain(),
        input_metric=id_distance(id_col),
        output_domain=dataframe_domain(),
        output_metric=dp.symmetric_distance(),
        function=lambda df: df.groupby(id_col).sample(n=threshold, replace=True),
        stability_map=lambda b_in: b_in * threshold)
```

Notice that sampling *with replacement* doesn't affect the stability of the transformation, as duplicating a record from resampling still won't increase the worst-case change in the resulting data sets.

Truncation on Partitioned Data

Recall the partition distance triple introduced in "Partitioned Data" on page 156. Truncation transformations can also make use of user identifiers to limit the L^0, L^1, and L^∞ norms on partition distances.

For instance, the truncation transformation may be configured to only retain records in up to k partitions, and only up to n records in each partition:

```python
def make_group_by_truncate(id_col, by, l0=INF, l1=INF, li=INF):
    dp.assert_features("contrib")

    def f_bound_the_contribution(df: pd.DataFrame):
        if l0 != INF:  # limit the number of partitions an id can influence
            contribs = df.groupby([id_col, *by]).size()
            kept_groups = contribs.groupby(id_col, group_keys=False).nlargest(l0)
            df = df.merge(kept_groups.index.to_frame(index=False))

        if l1 != INF:  # limit the total number of records an id can have
            df = df.groupby(by=id_col).sample(n=l1, replace=True)

        if li != INF:  # limit the records an id can have per-partition
            df = df.groupby([id_col, *by]).sample(n=li, replace=True)

        # return grouped data with bounded l0, l1, and/or linfty contribution
        return df.groupby(by=by)
    # ...
```

The stability of the resulting data scales these truncation bounds according to the identifier distance:

```python
    # ...
    # tighten when possible
    l0_l1_li_p = np.array([min(l0, l1), min(l1, l0 * li), min(li, l1)])

    return dp.t.make_user_transformation(
        input_domain=dataframe_domain(),
        input_metric=id_distance(id_col),
        output_domain=groupby_domain(),
        output_metric=partition_distance(dp.symmetric_distance()),
        function=f_bound_the_contribution,
        stability_map=lambda b_in: b_in * l0_l1_li_p)
```

Now that you have established this triple, you can use any of the techniques that work with partitioned data: aggregations (like marginals), parallel composition, and sample and aggregate, just as you would have before.

If you are grouping data in your analysis, you will often find that the best utility is achieved when you wait to apply truncation until after grouping. Bounds on the L^0 norm (the number of influenced partitions) and/or L^∞ norm (the per-partition contribution) can significantly reduce the sensitivity of vector-valued queries.

Now that you have been introduced to several preprocessing techniques to bound contributions, let's apply them in an example analysis.

Hospital Visits Example: A Bias-Variance Trade-Off

This example demonstrates how different choices of maximum user contribution impact the utility of a DP analysis.

 Note that when you truncate to a maximum user contribution in a data set, you are effectively establishing the distance between adjacent data sets. At this point, you can begin to chain stable transformations that expect data with bounded contribution. Sometimes the maximum user contribution is a characteristic intrinsic to the nature of the data set; other times you'll need to enforce it. In either case, it should be publicly available.

You are given access to a hospital visits data set, where each row records one hospital visit. The data set, illustrated in Table 7-5, contains three columns: patient name, medical specialty for the visit, and visit duration. You are tasked with privately releasing the number of visits and mean visit duration at each hospital specialty.

Table 7-5. Hospital visits data set

Patient Name	Specialty	Visit Duration
Brittany Robinson	Family Medicine	99 minutes
Steven Patrick	Oncology	57 minutes
Steven Patrick	Cardiology	74 minutes
Steven Patrick	Pulmonology	54 minutes
Steven Patrick	Ophthalmology	91 minutes
Steven Patrick	Dermatology	66 minutes
Steven Patrick	Ophthalmology	68 minutes
Steven Patrick	Nephrology	80 minutes
Nicole Rogers	Cardiology	117 minutes
Nicole Rogers	Oncology	71 minutes
Nicole Rogers	Neurology	50 minutes
Nicole Rogers	Otolaryngology	18 minutes
Nicole Rogers	Allergy and Immunology	29 minutes
Dr. Sean Gonzalez	Pulmonology	47 minutes
Judith Berry	Urology	98 minutes
Judith Berry	Otolaryngology	103 minutes
Judith Berry	Emergency Medicine	119 minutes
Cynthia Mejia MD	Psychiatry	97 minutes

Patient Name	Specialty	Visit Duration
Cynthia Mejia MD	Gastroenterology	52 minutes
Cynthia Mejia MD	Gastroenterology	96 minutes
...	...	...

Since the maximum user contribution is unbounded, you will need to truncate the data to bound user contribution. Figure 7-1 shows the per-patient visit frequencies. Note that, in this data, the maximum number of visits per patient in the hospital visits data set is 22 visits.

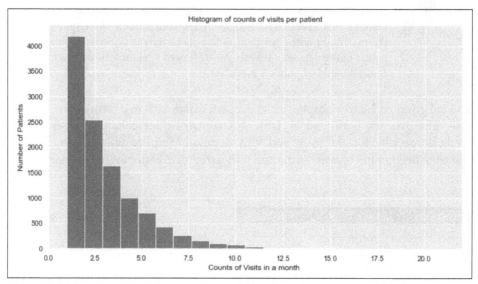

Figure 7-1. True hospital visits per patient without bounding user contribution

 Why can't you look at the data and define 22 visits as the maximum user contribution? This choice of bound would reveal private information that could be linked back to a patient. In fact, Judith Berry knows her husband had more than 22 scheduled visits, and now she's eyeing her husband with suspicion.

It is up to the data analyst to choose what the maximum user contribution in this data release should be. Let's see what happens to the data release when the data analyst choice falls into each of the following scenarios:

- When the maximum allowed number of visits per patient matches the true maximum of the data

- When the maximum allowed number of visits per patient overestimates the true maximum of the data

- When the maximum allowed number of visits per patient underestimates the true maximum of the data

Scenario 1: Truncation threshold matches the true maximum influence of any single individual in the data

Let's start with the assumption that you happen to choose a maximum allowed number of visits per patient that matches the true maximum number of visits to the hospital (22). Let's take a look at the histogram of visits per specialty with DP and without DP. To measure utility, we will use the mean absolute percentage error (MAPE) function.[5]

The sensitivity of the histogram is based on the truncation threshold (22). By the truncation threshold, the maximum number of visits is 22, so the maximum L^2 distance between two vector aggregates will occur when a patient only visits one specialty 22 times. Since the contributions are not distributed over separate bins, the sensitivity is 22 (see "Grouped Data" on page 80).

Let's use the Gaussian mechanism to make the vector aggregates satisfy differential privacy. The following code finds a Gaussian mechanism that satisfies under $(\rho = .03)$-zCDP:

```
import opendp.prelude as dp
dp.enable_features("contrib")


def make_l2_int_gaussian_fixed(sensitivity, rho):
    # define the metric space
    l2_space = dp.vector_domain(dp.atom_domain(T=int)), dp.l2_distance(T=int)

    # find the scale parameter that satisfies (sensitivity, rho)-closeness
    return dp.binary_search_chain(
        lambda s: dp.m.make_gaussian(*l2_space, s),
        sensitivity, rho)

# create a Gaussian mechanism
m_gauss = make_l2_int_gaussian_fixed(sensitivity=22., rho=0.03)

# release and compute a non-DP error
dp_patient_counts = m_gauss(patient_counts)
mean_absolute_percentage_error(patient_counts, dp_patient_counts)
```

---

5 Mean absolute percentage error (MAPE) is commonly used as a loss function for regression problems. We will utilize MAPE in this example to measure the utility of the data release. This is a useful metric for measuring utility given its intuitive interpretation in terms of relative error.

The result of the `mean_absolute_percentage_error` function is:

```
0.0983
```

The MAPE of our data release is 0.0983, suggesting an average deviation of around 9.8% between the values in the histogram and the actual values.

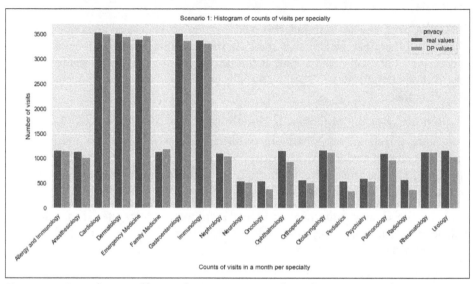

Figure 7-2. Distribution of hospital visits per patient bounding user contribution to 22 hospital visits

You can see in Figure 7-2 that the DP counts of visits to each specialty is very close to the true counts. Next, let's see what happens when the choice of maximum allowed visits is much larger than necessary.

Scenario 2: Maximum allowed number of visits per patient overestimates the true maximum influence of any single individual in the data

Now, suppose you do not know anything about the data, and you decide to choose a maximum allowed number of visits per patient that you believe will accommodate all possible patients, to avoid introducing bias. You believe that allowing a maximum of 50 visits a month is a safe choice. You enforce a maximum of 50 visits in your data and compute the vector of aggregates:

```
# create a Gaussian mechanism
m_gauss = make_l2_int_gaussian_fixed(sensitivity=50., rho=0.03)

# release and compute a non-DP error
dp_patient_counts = m_gauss(patient_counts)
mean_absolute_percentage_error(patient_counts, dp_patient_counts)

0.229
```

The MAPE of your data release is now over 0.22, suggesting an average deviation of around 22.9% between the values in the histogram and the actual values. That is a significant utility decrease when compared with the previous scenario, where the visits threshold was 22.

The increased threshold impacts the sensitivity of the histogram query. This simple increase in sensitivity significantly reduces the utility of the data release. Note that the privacy loss parameter remains the same. The count of visits for each specialty is not as close as it was in the previous, ideal scenario (see Figure 7-3).

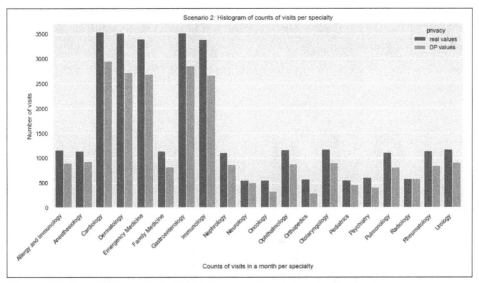

Figure 7-3. Distribution of hospital visits per patient when increasing the maximum user contribution to 50 hospital visits

If increasing the threshold increases sensitivity, you might be thinking that a very low threshold is probably a good idea. Let's see what happens with a very low threshold.

Scenario 3: Maximum allowed number of visits per patient underestimates the true maximum influence of any single individual in the data

Now suppose you do have some knowledge about the data. You heard that most people go to the hospital at most five times a month. Based on that knowledge, you decide to choose a maximum allowed number of visits per patient that you believe will accommodate most patients. You believe that allowing a maximum of five visits a month is a good choice. You enforce a maximum of five visits in your data by using reservoir sampling and computing the vector of aggregates. Looking at the distribution in Table 7-5, it is clear that the majority of patients go to the hospital five times or less. 85% of patients go to the hospital five times or less in a month. You proceed with aggregating the data and applying the Gaussian mechanism:

```
# create a Gaussian mechanism
m_gauss = make_l2_int_gaussian_fixed(sensitivity=5., rho=0.03)

# release and compute a non-DP error
dp_patient_counts = m_gauss(patient_counts)
mean_absolute_percentage_error(patient_counts, dp_patient_counts)

0.247
```

Given how small the truncation bound is, the sensitivity, and therefore noise scale, is small, giving the estimate relatively small variance (smaller than the previous example by an order of magnitude). Unfortunately, the utility of this data release is worse! The problem is that the truncation preprocessing has introduced a significant downward bias in the DP answers.

Figure 7-4 shows the counts of visits when limiting the counts of visits per patient to only five visits.

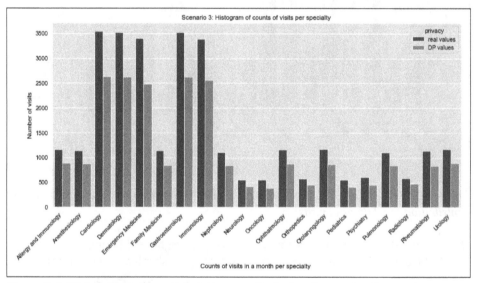

Figure 7-4. Distribution of hospital visits per patient when increasing the maximum user contribution to five hospital visits

This is an important and recurring trade-off: stronger preprocessing reduces the variance but increases bias. Similar bias-variance trade-offs surface when choosing clamping or norm bounds or when choosing a target size for the resize transformation.

If you cannot make a reasonable guess of the truncation threshold, you could release a DP estimate.

Privately Estimating the Truncation Threshold

While the comparison across different values of the truncation threshold is helpful in understanding how the truncation parameter works, it is not a viable approach to privately determining what the threshold should be, as doing so involves making many releases.

If you are unfamiliar with your data and don't feel confident in guessing a truncation threshold, it can be advantageous to spend a portion of your privacy budget to estimate the truncation bound. For instance, you could release a DP estimate of the .95-quantile of the number of row contributions each user makes. A well-chosen truncation parameter can help improve the utility of all future queries conducted on your data set.

Let's go back to our browser logs example. You can use SmartNoise SQL to privately estimate the distribution of individual contributions:

```
reader = snsql.from_df(visits, privacy=privacy, metadata='events.yml')

event_counts = reader.execute_df(
    '''
    SELECT
        Events,
        COUNT(Events) AS e
    FROM MySchema.MyTable
    GROUP BY Events
    ''')
```

The code returns the following output:

```
Running query with Laplace mechanism for count:
Mechanism.laplace
     Events        e
0   0 - 10   273449
1  10 - 20   118348
2  20 - 30    43548
3  30 - 40    15783
4  40 - 50     5960
```

Based on this differentially private analysis, $\approx$ 98% of the users make fewer than 40 visits, and $\approx$ 95% of the users make fewer than 30 visits.

Further Analysis with Unbounded Contributions

Now that you've chosen a truncation threshold, each query must be run on truncated data. Consider these questions:

1. How many visits are there to each domain?
2. What is the average unique visitor count on each day of the week?

The most visited domains in the data set can be identified by generating a differentially private histogram with the Laplace mechanism. Due to the tightly bound L^1 distance on a vector-valued count query, this kind of mechanism achieves optimal utility.

In the case of the browser logs data set, the L^1 distance between two count vectors from adjacent databases is at most 40:

```
privacy = Privacy(epsilon=epsilon)
reader = snsql.from_df(df, privacy=privacy, metadata='domain.yaml')

res = reader.execute_df(
    '''
    SELECT
        domain,
        COUNT(domain) AS DomainVisits
    FROM MySchema.MyTable
    GROUP BY domain
    ''')
print(res.sort_values(by = 'DomainVisits', ascending = False))
```

The resulting visit count for each domain is:

```
Running query with Laplace mechanism for count:
Mechanism.laplace
                           domain  DomainVisits
18            windowsupdate.com          3754
19               www.google.com          3698
8                  microsoft.com          3667
2              data.microsoft.com          3646
0          api-global.netflix.com          3612
10                   netflix.com          3599
5                    google.com          3590
3         events.data.microsoft.com          3586
4                ftl.netflix.com          3534
14             prod.ftl.netflix.com          3522
7                      live.com          1078
9              microsoftonline.com          1026
12             partner.netflix.net          1003
15           prod.partner.netflix.net          970
1            ctldl.windowsupdate.com          969
6              ichnaea.netflix.com           957
11                   netflix.net           939
```

17	settings-win.data.microsoft.com	934
13	preapp.prod.partner.netflix.net	924
16	safebrowsing.googleapis.com	915

Compared with the non-privatized counts:

windowsupdate.com	3781
www.google.com	3698
api-global.netflix.com	3652
netflix.com	3642
data.microsoft.com	3639
microsoft.com	3638
google.com	3600
events.data.microsoft.com	3599
prod.ftl.netflix.com	3590
ftl.netflix.com	3571
live.com	1050
partner.netflix.net	1003
microsoftonline.com	998
prod.partner.netflix.net	989
ichnaea.netflix.com	982
ctldl.windowsupdate.com	958
safebrowsing.googleapis.com	951
netflix.net	933
settings-win.data.microsoft.com	914
preapp.prod.partner.netflix.net	914

The values of *Counts of Visits* on the differentially private vector are relatively close to the non-private vector. Notice that the relatively high count utility helps preserve the ranking order.

There is a long tail of domains with very few visits that have been censored from the release. The differentially private release only contains domains that are visited by many unique individuals—domains that are stable in the neighborhood of your data. When the non-privatized counts for a domain are likely to go to zero on any potential neighboring data set, the domain is considered unstable and is censored.

The second query, average unique visitors for each day of the week, could be released via AVG, but the system will make two releases internally to avoid the infinite global sensitivity of the mean. The system will create one query for the numerator (the total number of visits per day) and one query for the denominator (the total number of unique users per day). You can instead submit these queries separately and handle postprocessing on your own to gain access to the more granular constituent releases:

```
domains_visits = reader.execute_df(
    '''
    SELECT
        Day_id,
        COUNT(*) AS DomainVisits
    FROM MySchema.MyTable GROUP BY Day_id
    ''')
```

```
user_counts = reader.execute_df(
    '''
    SELECT
        Day_id,
        COUNT(DISTINCT ids_num) AS Users
    FROM MySchema.MyTable
    GROUP BY Day_id
    ''')
```

```
      Day_id  DomainVisits
0     Friday        232366
1     Monday        233873
2   Saturday        146003
3     Sunday        145656
4   Thursday        232830
5    Tuesday        232038
6  Wednesday        232574
```

```
      Day_id  Users
0     Friday  232381
1     Monday  233867
2   Saturday  146040
3     Sunday  145640
4   Thursday  232746
5    Tuesday  232071
6  Wednesday  232576
```

```
Average visits per user per day of the week

Friday      1.230472
Monday      1.233458
Saturday    1.147276
Sunday      1.144335
Thursday    1.232094
Tuesday     1.231370
Wednesday   1.232915
```

To recap, the important phases in this differentially private analysis are:

1. Identifying the unit of privacy as a user
2. Recognizing that users may make unbounded contributions
3. Privately estimating a truncation threshold
4. Preprocessing the data set to bound user contribution
5. Submitting queries calibrated according to the truncation threshold
6. Evaluating the results, using postprocessing when necessary

Unknown Domain

In the asylum seeker example ("Example: Grouping on Asylum Seeker Data" on page 157), the domains are assumed to be public information that is known before making a release on the data. In particular, it is assumed that the index of the grouped data, containing grouping keys of countries and years, is not sensitive information. However, the index is considered sensitive information in many settings.

Consider a data set containing one week of browser logs. The data set contains over 9,000 users and has columns for user ID, day of the week, and webpage visited, as shown in Table 7-6.[6]

Table 7-6. Websites visited by user ID and day

ID	Day	Domain
9015	Thursday	netflix.com
5647	Monday	update.googleapis.com
8592	Tuesday	office.net
6826	Wednesday	prod.ftl.netflix.com
4571	Wednesday	itunes.apple.com

The set of possible accessed domains is likely to be extremely large and highly sensitive. This is an ideal application for a variant of the propose-test-release (PTR) mechanism, first introduced in "Propose-Test-Release" on page 118. When PTR is used in the context of releasing private histograms, it is commonly referred to as a *stability-based histogram*; the mechanism only releases counts for domains that are likely to always exist across all neighboring data sets.[7] The fact that these domains will always exist means that they are likely to remain stable. In this context, the δ parameter introduced by the PTR mechanism controls the probability that you release a domain that is uniquely accessed by one individual.

Some similar but more general techniques are called τ-thresholding[8] and *differentially private set union*.[9]

---

6 This data set was generated by the authors for educational purposes. The code to generate the data set can be found at the book's GitHub repo (*https://oreil.ly/HODP_GitHub*). The domains used in this data set were obtained using Cisco's DNS list (*https://oreil.ly/dyPme*).

7 Mark Bun et al., "Simultaneous Private Learning of Multiple Concepts," in *Proceedings of the 2016 ACM Conference on Innovations in Theoretical Computer Science* (New York: ACM, 2016): 369–80.

8 Wilson et al., "Differentially Private SQL with Bounded User Contribution."

9 Sivakanth Gopi et al., "Differentially Private Set Union," in *Proceedings of the 37th International Conference on Machine Learning* (PMLR, 2020): 3627-3636.

In the default configuration of SmartNoise SQL, the category sets are always considered private, so dimensions of the data for which few users contribute and are thus likely to be unstable across neighboring data sets are censored from the release.

 If you know the category set does not need to be protected, in SmartNoise SQL you can disable `censor_dims` to disable the PTR mechanism.

When to Apply Truncation

Carefully choosing *when* to truncate in your analysis can help you improve performance and/or utility. Unfortunately, you're only free to choose when to apply truncation if your transformations can be applied to data with either bounded contribution or unbounded contribution.

Take a moment to recall transformations from data set to data set that you are familiar with. Any transformation that maintains the alignment of identifiers with their data is 1-stable under the instruction provided in "Data Sets with Unbounded Contributions" on page 177. You can use this to apply many kinds of data set transformations to data with unbounded contributions. For instance, row-by-row and filtering transformations are all 1-stable under both the symmetric distance and identifier distance.

This frees up many of the potential transformations you may want to apply on your data before you perform join, union, and grouping transformations. As you will see, utility can be improved by delaying the use of the truncation transformation until after conducting joins, unions, or grouping.

Stable Grouping Transformations

Say you want to release grouped counts on data with k groups. A k-stable truncation before grouping will result in an L^2 sensitivity of k. The reason is that, in the worst case, all of an individual's contributions may fall within the same group.

However, if you anticipate user data naturally being distributed across the groups, then applying a 1-truncation to each group will result in an L^2 sensitivity of $\sqrt{k}$. This time, in the worst case, all k groups differ by 1.

In addition, if you anticipate each user's data will tend to only affect a limited number of groups, you can further truncate their group influence. For each user, only retain their contributions to at most c groups at random. This adjustment can further improve the L^2 sensitivity to $\sqrt{c}$, where $c < k$. This kind of truncation is broadly applicable in many realistic scenarios; imagine trying to release differentially private statistics for a multiple-answer questionnaire.

Stable Union Transformations

A data set union concatenates multiple data sets to form a single data set. If an individual can influence c data sets each by k records, then the stability guarantee of their union is $c \cdot k$.

There is a striking similarity between the stability guarantee of a union and the privacy guarantee of parallel composition. If an individual may influence up to c partitions, where each has an ϵ-DP release, then the privacy guarantee of their composition is $c \cdot \epsilon$.

On the other hand, if each data set is of unbounded contribution, the union is simply 1-stable, given that the same user id is present in each partition. Again, you would generally prefer to apply an equivalent $c \cdot k$ truncation after the union to avoid truncating records completely when there is an imbalance toward one partition.

Stable Join Transformations

Given that there are so many variations of joins, it is not reasonable to list them exhaustively. However, stable join transformations are much easier to reason about when working with the identifier distance.

For example, consider when one of the two data sets does not contain private/sensitive data. You may encounter this when enriching your data with auxiliary data sources. The worst-case stability under the symmetric distance is when the auxiliary data set matches an unbounded number of records; the resulting data set now has unbounded stability. When working under the identifier distance, the transformation remains 1-stable, so the join transformation can be further chained.

Summary

It is crucially important to understand the structure of a data set and how it relates to your privacy unit before releasing statistics from it. In this chapter, you took a closer look at what it means to narrow or change the privacy unit: privacy units are not necessarily individuals.

You've also seen that there is an important difference between data with bounded contributions and data with unbounded contributions, as well as how to bound the number of contributions. Until now, you have only seen data with bounded contributions, where a user may only influence at most a fixed number of rows. When data has unbounded contributions, this condition is relaxed, and a user can contribute in potentially unlimited rows.

A new metric was introduced to quantify the distance between data sets with unbounded contributions: the identifier distance. This metric makes it possible to define stable transformations of data sets with unbounded contributions. To use this kind of data and get privacy guarantees, you may need to bound the number of rows that an individual may appear in via a data set truncation. Several approaches were given to accomplish data set truncation, including reservoir sampling. With reservoir sampling, a maximum of k rows are retained for each individual. Finally, data grouping, unions, and joins were briefly explored in both the bounded and unbounded contribution settings.

Exercises

1. Which of the following pairs of data sets are adjacent under the identifier metric with data set distance at most 1?

   a. Data set 1

id	Score
1	916.42
1	986.41
4	543.71
4	719.28
5	68.11
5	732.5
7	621.91
7	601.82
10	569.32
10	966.64

id	Score
1	916.42
1	986.41
4	543.71
4	719.28
5	68.11
5	732.5
7	621.91
7	601.82
9	569.32
9	966.64

b. Data set 2

id	Score
1	916.42
1	986.41
4	543.71
4	719.28
5	68.11
5	732.5
7	621.91
7	601.82
10	569.32
10	966.64

id	Score
1	916.42
1	986.41
4	543.71
4	719.28
5	68.11
5	732.5
6	621.91
6	601.82
9	569.32
9	966.64

2. Using the browser logs data set:

   a. Demonstrate how the presence of rare events can lead to a privacy violation.

   b. Set an appropriate value of τ and demonstrate how this helps preserve privacy.

3. Suppose the browser logs data set has a column that provides employee location. Assume that each employee can have only one location.

   a. How would you have to divide the data set so that it is disjoint?

   b. Based on the parallel composition theorem, comment on how the choice of grouping can impact the privacy analysis.

Differentially Private Statistical Modeling

Statistical modeling encompasses a broad gamut of tools used to find patterns in data and make predictions. Statistical models fitted with a differentially private algorithm protect the privacy of individuals who are in the data used to train the model. This chapter focuses on introducing you to differentially private algorithms that release hyperparameters. These algorithms are executed when you are fitting DP statistical models.

It is important not to miss the distinction that a differentially private model is simply a model whose hyperparameters are differentially private releases made on the training data. Therefore, inferences made on DP models are *not* private. At best, the model inference may qualify as a stable data-set-to-data-set transformation. The purpose of DP fitting is to make the model itself resilient against attacks intended to violate the privacy of individuals in the training data.

This chapter covers the following topics:

- Private inference
- Private linear regression
- Algorithm selection
- Private naive Bayes
- Private decision trees
- The relationship between model fitting, model parameters, and potential privacy violations

This chapter assumes a working knowledge of statistical modeling as a prerequisite in order to maintain focus on differential privacy.

Private Inference

Inference refers to feeding a data set to a trained model to obtain a transformed data set. There are many contexts where inference does not need to be made private: for example, your model users may only ever perform inference on their own data.

If you do need DP inference on a trained model (whether the model is DP or not), you should determine if the inference on your model is a stable transformation. For instance, both linear transformations and the logistic activation function, as used in linear regression, logistic regression, and neural networks, are 1-stable row-by-row transformations. Should model inference qualify as a stable transformation, then you may privatize the output as usual.

Depending on your use case, you may want to both privately train a model on data set A and then privately release inferences on data set B. If sensitive individuals can be in both A and B, you'll need to use composition. Otherwise, you can track their privacy budgets separately.

The following content will focus on *private fitting*, or releasing private hyperparameters.

Differentially Private Linear Regression

Linear regression is used to estimate a linear relationship $\beta = \begin{bmatrix} \beta_0 & \beta_1 & \dots & \beta_d \end{bmatrix}^T$ between a set of explanatory variables X and an output variable $y = \begin{bmatrix} y_1 & y_2 & \dots & y_n \end{bmatrix}^T$, where:

$$X = \begin{bmatrix} 1 & x_{11} & \dots & x_{1d} \\ 1 & x_{21} & \dots & x_{1d} \\ \vdots & \vdots & \ddots & \vdots \\ 1 & x_{n1} & \dots & x_{nd} \end{bmatrix}$$

Note that there are n rows and d variables/features; each row in X and y is an individual contribution. To represent the intercept, there is an additional column of ones in X and $d + 1$ parameters to estimate. Linear regression assumes the true relationship follows a simple form:

$$y = X\beta + \epsilon \quad \text{where } \epsilon_i \sim N(0, \sigma^2)$$

To fit the model to your data, you'd ideally want to find an estimate for β (denoted $\widehat{\beta}$) that minimizes the sum of squared errors (SSE = $\| \epsilon \|_2^2 = \| y - X\widehat{\beta} \|_2^2$):

$$\widehat{y} = X\widehat{\beta} \quad \text{where} \quad \widehat{\beta} = \text{argmin}_\beta \| y - X\beta \|_2^2$$

There are many approaches for estimating these regression parameters in a differentially private way. We'll discuss three approaches:

- Sufficient statistics perturbation
- Private Theil-Sen estimation
- Objective function perturbation

Sufficient Statistics Perturbation

The *sufficient statistics perturbation* (SSP) approach for estimating $\widehat{\beta}$ directly privatizes the statistics used in the traditional non-DP *minimum variance unbiased estimator* (MVUE). The estimator for $\widehat{\beta}$ has a closed form and can be found via calculus. Since the error is convex, find the point where the derivative of the error is zero:

$$\frac{\partial}{\partial\beta} \| y - X\widehat{\beta} \|_2^2 = \frac{\partial}{\partial\beta}\left(y - X\widehat{\beta}\right)^T\left(y - X\widehat{\beta}\right)$$

$$= \frac{\partial}{\partial\beta}\left(y^Ty - 2\beta^TX^Ty + \beta^TX^TX\beta\right)$$

$$= -2X^Ty + 2X^TX\beta = 0$$

Then, solving for β:

$$X^TX\beta = \left(X^TX\right)^{-1}X^Ty$$

$$\beta = \left(X^TX\right)^{-1}X^Ty$$

Now we need to consider how this estimator for β could be made differentially private.

For differential privacy, denote the full data set as $Z = [X, y]$, where the response variable is packed into the last column.

The use of Z differs from the book convention of using x, but X is already used to denote the design matrix.

The naive approach is to try to add noise directly to β, with noise calibrated according to the sensitivity of β. This breaks down when you try to derive the sensitivity of the regression coefficients:

$$\max_{Z \sim Z'} \| \beta(Z) - \beta(Z') \|_2 = \max_{Z \sim Z'} \| \left(X^T X\right)^{-1} X^T y - \left(X'^T X'\right)^{-1} X'^T y' \|_2$$

Unfortunately, the model parameters become increasingly sensitive to perturbations from a single individual as the explanatory variables tend toward zero. If $X^T X$ is rank-deficient (for instance, if all x_{ij} are zero), then $\left(X^T X\right)^{-1}$ is undefined, and therefore so is the global sensitivity.

We have a solution to this infinite sensitivity: privately estimate each part independently, and then postprocess to get an estimate of the final statistic. This is the same process that we previously performed when estimating means.

The point estimates here are the $X^T X$ matrix and $X^T y$:

$$Z^T Z = \begin{bmatrix} X^T X & X^T y \\ y^T X & y^T y \end{bmatrix}$$

The sensitivity derivation follows just as any other derivation would, but this time taking advantage of matrix properties. Let $Z \sim Z'$ denote neighboring under the symmetric distance metric (add/remove). Without loss of generality, assume the differing individual's contributions, A, are located at the bottom of Z':

$$\max_{Z \sim Z'} \| Z^T Z - Z'^T Z' \|_F L^2 \qquad \text{norm is equivalent to Frobenius norm}$$

$$= \max_{Z \sim Z'} \| Z^T Z - (Z^T Z + A^T A) \|_F \qquad \text{since } Z' = \begin{bmatrix} Z \\ A \end{bmatrix}$$

$$= \max_{Z \sim Z'} \| A^T A \|_F$$

$$= \max_{Z \sim Z'} \| \sum_{i=1}^{b_{in}} A_i^T A_i \|_F \qquad A_i \text{ is the ith contribution/row}$$

$$\leq \max_{Z \sim Z'} \sum_{i=1}^{b_{in}} \| A_i^T A_i \|_F \qquad \text{triangle inequality}$$

$$= \max_{Z \sim Z'} \sum_{i=1}^{b_{in}} \| A_i \|_2 \cdot \| A_i \|_2 \qquad \text{if } X = x_1 x_2^T, \text{ then}$$

$$\| X \|_F = \| x_1 \|_2 \cdot \| x_2 \|_2$$

$$\leq b_{in} \cdot \text{norm}^2 \qquad \text{if each row has bounded norm: } \forall_i \| A_i \|_2 \leq \text{norm}$$

This proof makes use of the fact that each row has a bounded norm.[1] This key stable transformation is captured by the following snippet:

```
def make_xTx(norm):
    dp.assert_features("contrib", "floating-point")
    return dp.t.make_user_transformation(
        input_domain=dp.np_array2_domain(origin=0., norm=norm, ord=2),
        input_metric=dp.symmetric_distance(),
        output_domain=dp.vector_domain(dp.atom_domain(T=float)),
        output_metric=dp.l2_distance(T=float),
        function=lambda X: (X.T @ X).ravel(),
        stability_map=lambda b_in: b_in * norm**2)
```

Once the $Z^T Z$ is privatized via the Gaussian mechanism, β can be estimated via postprocessing:

```
def beta_postprocessor(ZTZ):
    ZTZ = np.array(ZTZ).reshape([int(np.sqrt(len(ZTZ)))] * 2) # make it square
    ZTZ = (ZTZ + ZTZ.T) / 2 # symmetrizes, and halves variance off-the-diagonal
    XTX, XTy = ZTZ[:-1, :-1], ZTZ[:-1, -1] # extract point estimates
    return np.linalg.pinv(XTX) @ XTy # plug into MVUE estimator for β
```

---

1 $\| X \|_2 = \sqrt{\text{trace}(X X^T)} = \sqrt{\text{trace}(x_1 x_2^T x_2 x_1^T)} = \sqrt{(x_1^T x_1)(x_2^T x_2)} = \| x_1 \|_2 \cdot \| x_2 \|_2$, where the trace is the sum of the elements on the diagonal.

This postprocessor takes advantage of the fact that the off-diagonal entries are symmetric, so the noisy estimates can be averaged together to reduce the variance. The point estimates are then extracted from the matrix and plugged into the MVUE estimator for the regression coefficients.

The complete mechanism can now be pieced together via chaining:

```
def make_private_beta(norm, scale):
    return (
        make_insert_ones() >>                # 1-stable
        dp.t.then_np_clamp(norm=norm) >>     # 1-stable from OpenDP Library
        make_xTx(norm) >>                    # b^2-stable aggregator
        dp.m.then_gaussian(scale) >>         # mechanism from OpenDP Library
        beta_postprocessor)
```

While this is one approach for fitting/estimating a private linear regression model, it is by no means the *definitive* approach. There are several trade-offs. As the number of features increases, the number of parameters to estimate increases quadratically and the matrix inverse becomes more computationally costly.

In addition, the algorithm assumes the relative scales of each parameter are similar; if any one column has a larger scale than the others, that column will dominate the row norms. At the cost of complexity, this may be alleviated by further preprocessing to rescale columns and similar postprocessing of the $Z^T Z$ matrix.

Nevertheless, sufficient statistics perturbation allows for multiple explanatory variables, is simple, and provides a meaningful baseline.

Private Theil-Sen Estimator

Many differentially private algorithms harken back to prior non-DP results in the study of *robust statistics*. Robust statistics are designed to be less sensitive to outliers, which tends to make them well-suited to be adapted to differential privacy. The Theil-Sen estimator is one such example: you can estimate the slope β_1 by computing the median of the slopes of pairs of data points.

The Theil-Sen estimator can be decomposed into a stable transformation to compute a data set of slopes, and then a private median mechanism to release the private slope β_1.[2] The stable transformation makes a random pairing of each point with another point in the data set and then computes a slope for each pairing:

```
def make_theil_sen_slopes():
    dp.assert_features("contrib")
    def f_compute_slopes(data):
        # keep an even number of rows
```

---

2 Daniel Alabi et al., "Differentially Private Simple Linear Regression," in *Proceedings on 23rd Privacy Enhancing Technologies Symposium (PoPETS '22)*, no. 2 (2022): 184–204.

```
    data = np.array(data, copy=True)[:len(data) // 2 * 2]

    # evenly partition into random pairs
    np.random.shuffle(data)
    p1, p2 = np.array_split(data, 2)

    # compute a vector data set of slopes
    dx, dy = (p1 - p2).T
    return dy / dx

return dp.t.make_user_transformation(
    input_domain=dp.np_array2_domain(T=float, num_columns=2),
    input_metric=dp.symmetric_distance(),
    output_domain=dp.vector_domain(dp.atom_domain(T=float)),
    output_metric=dp.symmetric_distance(),
    function=f_compute_slopes,
    stability_map=lambda b_in: b_in)
```

The resulting data set has half as many records, but each input record can still only influence at most one output slope, so the transformation remains 1-stable. The following snippet then privately aggregates the slopes:

```
def make_private_theil_sen(bounds, scale):
    return make_theil_sen_slopes() >> \
        make_private_quantile_in_bounds(bounds, alpha=0.5, scale=scale)
```

This approach is most similar to the non-DP Theil-Sen estimator, making use of the interval exponential mechanism from "Piecewise-Constant Support Exponential Mechanism" on page 100.

The pairs, slopes, and final fit for a small test data set are shown in Figure 8-1.

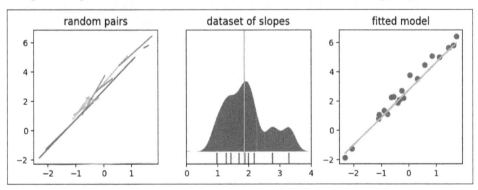

Figure 8-1. Fitting a Theil-Sen estimator

The vertical line in the middle plot shows the privately selected median via the quantile mechanism.

β_0 needs to be estimated separately. You can do this by simply estimating the mean of the response variable.

A trade-off of this technique is that it only works for *simple* linear regression when there is only one explanatory variable. Nevertheless, the technique involves a clever and interesting application of previous mechanisms.

Objective Function Perturbation

Another approach used to privately fit a regression model is called *objective perturbation*.[3] Instead of trying to directly privatize the regression parameters, objective perturbation privatizes the objective or loss function. The fitted parameters are then a postprocessing of the private loss function. In a surprising turn, the loss function is itself fit with an approximating polynomial, the coefficients of which are differentially private.

Instead of diving deep into the mathematics, let's look at an example that directly uses diffprivlib, a differential privacy library that implements the aforementioned mechanism.

In this example, we will use the UCI Adult data set (*https://oreil.ly/QNfEI*), a widely used data set from the US Census Bureau that contains demographic information about over 32,000 individuals. The data set includes age, education, occupation, and income level, coded as more or less than $50,000 per year. The UCI Adult data set is widely used in machine learning education and is particularly amenable to privacy-preserving technologies, since it contains columns of potentially sensitive data.

First, let's privately train a model to predict whether an individual has a high or a low income. If you have used frameworks like scikit-learn, then the following code will look very familiar to you. That is on purpose: diffprivlib is designed to be a drop-in replacement for existing ML libraries:

```
$ pip install numpy pandas diffprivlib
```

Use the following statements to import the necessary libraries:

```
import pandas as pd

from sklearn.preprocessing import LabelEncoder
from diffprivlib.models import LinearRegression
```

---

3 Kamalika Chaudhuri et al., "Differentially Private Empirical Risk Minimization," *Journal of Machine Learning Research* 12 (2011): 1069–1109.

The following code snippet performs a complete model training and testing process:

```python
header = ['age', 'workclass', 'fnlwgt', 'education', 'education_num',
          'marital_status', 'occupation', 'relationship',
          'race', 'sex', 'capital_gain', 'capital_loss',
          'hours_per_week', 'native_country', 'income']
label = 'income'

df = pd.read_csv('adult.data', header=None, names=header,
                 sep=',\\s', na_values=['?'], engine='python')
df = df.dropna()
df = df.reset_index(drop=True)

categorical_columns = ['workclass', 'education', 'marital_status',
                       'occupation', 'relationship', 'race', 'sex',
                       'native_country']

df_train = pd.read_csv('adult.data')
df_test = pd.read_csv('adult.test')

for cat in categorical_columns:
    df_train[cat] = LabelEncoder().fit_transform(df_train[cat]).reshape(-1, 1)
    df_test[cat] = LabelEncoder().fit_transform(df_test[cat]).reshape(-1, 1)

y_train = df_train[label].apply(lambda x: 1 if '>' in x else 0)
y_test = df_test[label].apply(lambda x: 1 if '>' in x else 0)

predictors = ['age', 'workclass', 'education', 'marital_status',
              'occupation', 'relationship', 'race', 'sex',
              'hours_per_week', 'native_country', 'income']

X_train = df_train[predictors].drop(columns=['income'])
X_test = df_test[predictors].drop(columns=['income'])

# this consumes ε=1 on the individuals in the train data
regr = LinearRegression(epsilon=1.)
regr.fit(X_train, y_train)
releases = regr.coef_, regr.intercept_

# this consumes ε=∞ on the individuals in the test data (it is not privatized!)
r2_score = regr.score(X_test, y_test)
```

For comparison, let's calculate R^2 for a non-private linear regression with scikit-learn:

```python
# For comparison, here is the same process with scikit-learn.
# Let's compare R2 values
from sklearn.linear_model import LinearRegression as ScikitLinearRegression

scikit_regr = ScikitLinearRegression()
scikit_regr.fit(X_train, y_train)
scikit_releases = regr.coef_, regr.intercept_
```

```
R^2 with DP:      0.138
R^2 without DP:   0.142
```

$$R^2 = 1 - \frac{RSS}{TSS} \quad \text{where } RSS = \sum_i^n (y_i - \widehat{y_i})^2 \text{ and } TSS = \sum_i^n (y_i - \overline{y_i})^2$$

Be mindful about what you publish, as the model's R^2 score has *not* been privatized. For context, sharing just the R^2 score has been shown to be enough to cause a privacy violation.[4]

Algorithm Selection

Determining which algorithm to use is a recurring problem for any modeling task. For instance, this chapter covers three private linear regression estimation algorithms, and there are many, many more. In addition, each model has hyperparameters that need to be optimized. The three discussed linear regression models all need carefully chosen data bounds to minimize the impact on utility.

Consider a naive approach, like fitting each algorithm and choosing the model with the highest utility (like highest R^2). This involves separate releases of each model, which defeats the purpose of algorithm selection, as the privacy budget is partitioned among each candidate model. If you have some public data that you expect may have a similar distributional behavior, then you are in luck. Use it to experiment with utility and help you choose your algorithm and hyperparameters.

Otherwise, you will need to gain a better understanding of the trade-offs of each algorithm. You are looking for the algorithm that makes a suitable trade-off along many axes:

Bias
How much do the released values systematically differ from the true estimate?

Variance
How much noise is added to the released parameters?

Privacy
How efficient is the technique, and does it also give useful auxiliary statistics?

Computational time
Is the runtime of the algorithm reasonable for the scale of your data?

---

4 Rui Wang et al., "Learning Your Identity and Disease from Research Papers," in *Proceedings of the 16th ACM Conference on Computer and Communications Security* (New York: ACM, 2009): 534-44.

Research/development time
How many algorithms do you have time to evaluate?

Algorithm complexity
More complexity leads to a higher likelihood of bugs and difficult implementations.

Assessing what we know about the linear regression algorithms, the Theil-Sen estimator is a strong algorithm for simple linear regression. SSP will introduce significantly more noise as the number of predictors increases, as the $Z^T Z$ matrix will increase in size quadratically. SSP will also suffer more computationally, as the computation of the matrix inverse is expensive. On the other hand, the private $Z^T Z$ matrix can also be postprocessed into a covariance matrix, which is broadly useful for other analyses.

 If you are willing to pay a privacy and complexity tax, you may find the algorithm in "Private Selection from Private Candidates" on page 165 useful. An application of this for hyperparameter tuning will be given in the Chapter 9.

Try to take note and analyze these trade-offs as you continue to build your knowledge of DP statistical models.

Differentially Private Naive Bayes

Naive Bayes is a Bayesian learning method for classification that is characterized by a "naive" assumption that the explanatory variables are conditionally independent of the response variable. This assumption explains why the model is so simple: each variable contributes independently to the probability that the output is a given class.[5] Even though the model is simple, it has been known to achieve better performance than more elaborate models when this assumption is met. Only one parameter must be learned for each explanatory variable.

The naive Bayes algorithm takes as input an observation $x = [x_1, x_2, \ldots, x_n]$[6] containing categorical or continuous attributes. The algorithm returns a label y from a set of possible categories $C = \{c_1, c_2, \ldots\}$. The returned label y is the c_j that is considered most likely, given some observation x:

---

5 This section is mostly based on results presented in Jaideep Vaidya et al., "Differentially Private Naive Bayes Classification," in *2013 IEEE/WIC/ACM International Joint Conferences on Web Intelligence (WI) and Intelligent Agent Technologies (IAT)* (Piscataway, NJ: IEEE, November 2013): 571–76, *https://dl.acm.org/doi/ 10.1109/WI-IAT.2013.80.*

6 In this section, *x* denotes a data set row and not the entire data set as in other parts of this book.

$$y = \underset{c_j \in C}{\text{argmax}}\ \text{Pr}\left(c_j \middle| x\right)$$

$\text{Pr}\left(c_j \middle| x\right)$ is the probability that the output is c_j, given an input x. Understanding how to evaluate this probability will be helpful when trying to privatize the model.

You can apply the Bayes theorem to manipulate the probability into a form that can be more clearly evaluated:

$$y = \underset{c_j \in C}{\text{argmax}} \frac{\text{Pr}\left(c_j\right) \cdot \text{Pr}\left(x \middle| c_j\right)}{\text{Pr}\left(x\right)}$$

Since the denominator is constant with respect to c_j, it can simply be removed without changing the result:

$$y = \underset{c_j \in C}{\text{argmax}}\ \text{Pr}\left(c_j\right) \cdot \text{Pr}\left(x \middle| c_j\right)$$

You can now make use of the naive Bayes model's key assumption of conditional independence: $\text{Pr}\left(x \middle| c_j\right) = \prod_i \text{Pr}\left(x_i \middle| c_j\right)$. Each explanatory variable is independent from one another when the output is fixed. With this assumption, y simplifies to:

$$y = \underset{c_j \in C}{\text{argmax}}\ \text{Pr}\left(c_j\right) \cdot \prod_i \text{Pr}\left(x_i \middle| c_j\right)$$

Each of the probabilities in this expression, $\text{Pr}\left(c_j\right)$ and $\text{Pr}\left(x_i \middle| c_j\right)$, are estimated directly from a training data set. The naive Bayes algorithm satisfies differential privacy when these quantities/parameters are estimated in a differentially private way. This is again an example of an algorithm that can be broken down into the composition of DP point estimates and then reassembled via postprocessing. In this case, the model breaks down into three kinds of DP estimates:

1. $\text{Pr}\left(c_j\right)$, categorical
2. $\text{Pr}\left(x_i \middle| c_j\right)$, when x_i is categorical
3. $\text{Pr}\left(x_i \middle| c_j\right)$, when x_i is continuous

The categorical probabilities can be estimated by postprocessing DP marginal histogram queries.

When fitting the model on training data, $\Pr\left(c_j\right)$ is estimated by:

$$\Pr\left(c_j\right) = \frac{n_j}{n}$$

- n_j: the number of observations where $y = c_j$
- n: the number or observations

Privately estimate n_j and n with private marginal queries, then postprocess. Assuming data sets differ by the symmetric distance, recall how histograms and counts both have sensitivity b_{in}.

You'll also need to estimate $\Pr\left(x_i \middle| c_j\right)$ for each categorical attribute x_i. Due to the conditional independence, each of the $\Pr\left(x_i \middle| c_j\right)$ releases will only need to deal with two columns: one explanatory variable x_i and the true response variable y. Therefore, the following sections will omit and repurpose the subscript i.

Categorical Naive Bayes

Assume the values of x are among possible categories $B = \{b_1, b_2, \ldots\}$. Using i to denote which category x takes on, you are trying to estimate $\Pr\left(x = b_i \middle| c_j\right)$:

$$P\left(x = b_i \middle| c_j\right) = \frac{n_{ij}}{n_j}$$

- n_{ij}: the number of observations where $y = c_j$ and $x = b_i$
- n_j: the number of observations where $y = c_j$

These quantities can be estimated in the same manner as in $\Pr\left(c_j\right)$, but this time using two- and one-way marginals instead of one- and zero-way marginals. You've already released n_j, so you might as well reuse it. Each categorical explanatory variable only costs you one two-way marginal release.

 Notice that you take repeated measurements n_j by also releasing a separate n_{ij} for each categorical predictor. You could sum each n_{ij} up into additional estimates of n_j, then use inverse variance weighting to reduce the variance of both n_j and all n_{ij}.

At this point, if your data only has categorical data (or you don't mind binning numerical attributes), you can already build your own differentially private naive Bayes model.

Continuous Naive Bayes

The previous section estimated the probability mass function of a categorical predictor. This section provides an approach for estimating the probability density function of a continuous predictor.

One approach is to assume the attribute follows a known distribution, like the Gaussian distribution. The Gaussian distribution with mean μ and variance σ^2 has probability density function:

$$\Pr\left(x = \mu\right) = \frac{1}{\sqrt{2\pi}\sigma}e^{-\frac{(x-\mu)^2}{2\sigma^2}}$$

Group your data by y, and then estimate the DP mean μ_j and DP standard deviation σ_j within each partition.

Remember again that you have already estimated the partition sizes n_j, so DP means and DP variances can be released by postprocessing DP sums and DP sums of squared differences.

You can then use these estimates to compute the probability of observing x when the true group is c_j. Substitute these parameters into the Gaussian density function:

$$\Pr\left(x = \mu_j \middle| c_j\right) = \frac{1}{\sqrt{2\pi}\sigma_j}e^{-\frac{(x-\mu_j)^2}{2\sigma_j^2}}$$

This same approach can be applied to other choices of prior probability distributions:

1. Partition by y.
2. Choose a prior distribution and estimate the distributional parameters in each partition.
3. When predicting, evaluate the PDF of the fitted distribution at x.

Mechanism Design

Altogether, you need to release a zero-way marginal of the count of records in the data set, a one-way marginal of y, and the learned parameters of a joint distribution over each x_i and y.

For categorical variables, you could estimate the parameters of a discrete distribution via two-way marginals. For continuous variables, you could estimate the parameters of a Gaussian distribution, or other distribution, for each outcome.

The model is fitted, and you can directly compute all the constituent functions to predict y by postprocessing:

$$y = \underset{c_j \in C}{\operatorname{argmax}} \Pr\left(c_j\right) \cdot \prod_i \Pr\left(x_i \middle| c_j\right)$$

Some mechanisms require invariants on the data that they enforce via truncation or clipping:

- The complete set of possible outcomes C_j
- The complete set of categories that each x_i may take on, when x_i is categorical
- Natural bounds for each x_i, when x_i is continuous

These preprocessing steps inherent to the mechanisms prevent vulnerabilities where an adversary may infer that no one in the data exhibited a certain attribute (predicated on the model failing to return a result for an observation containing that attribute), or vice versa.

While this is necessary, it can also impact the utility of the model or make it more difficult to fit the model. Since these kinds of constraints arise from your choices of mechanisms when privatizing these quantities, you might relax these requirements by substituting stability-based marginals and/or running bounds estimation on continuous variables if you are working on data with an unknown domain.

The techniques discussed for naive Bayes have also all been agnostic of mechanism: You may privatize statistics using the Laplace, Gaussian, or other mechanisms, and perform composition accordingly under a privacy measure that suits your needs.

Example: Naive Bayes

Diffprivlib uses a similar approach to train a DP naive Bayes model:

```python
import pandas as pd
from diffprivlib.models import GaussianNB


X_columns = ["age", "education_num", "capital_gain",
             "capital_loss ", "hours_per_week"]
Y_column = "income"

def load_data(file_name):
    df = pd.read_csv(file_name)
```

```
        return df[X_columns], df[Y_column].apply(lambda x: 1 if ">" in x else 0)

    # this consumes ε=.01 on the individuals in the train data
    dp_clf = GaussianNB(epsilon=0.01)
    dp_clf.fit(*load_data("adult.data"))

    # this consumes ε=∞ on the individuals in the test data (it is not privatized!)
    mean_accuracy = dp_clf.score(*load_data("adult.test"))
```

The library uses Laplace noise throughout, releases marginals on categorical predictors, and assumes continuous variables follow a Gaussian distribution.

Tree-Based Algorithms

Tree-based methods construct a series of partitions over a data set to find the best predictor of an outcome variable. These partitions can be thought of as a series of branching if/then statements that lead to a prediction. Presented graphically, these if/then branches form structures that resemble trees, hence the name.

After training is complete, a tree-based model splits a population (or database) according to the attributes that "best describe" the outcome variable. The model requires a function to compare how well each grouping of attributes predicts the outcome variable. Based on this function, the model can rank the rankings and determine the grouping that best describes the outcome variable.

An example of such a function is *mutual information*. For two random variables X and Y, the mutual information is:

$$I(X, Y) = \sum_{x \in X} \sum_{y \in Y} P(x, y) log \left[\frac{P(x, y)}{P(x)P(y)} \right]$$

A simple decision tree using mutual information has the following steps:

1. Begin with the entire data set, complete and without splits.
2. Calculate the mutual information value for a variety of splits across each feature.
3. Select the split value with the largest mutual information value.
4. Split the data set using this new rule.
5. Repeat steps 1–4 until a predetermined number of splits have been made.

Decision trees have their origins in operations research and were often manually constructed. A 1964 article in the Harvard Business Review (*https://oreil.ly/r1Y5v*) highlights the key concepts behind decision trees and presents several examples. Consider the following scenario: you are planning a concert and want to decide if it should be indoors or outdoors. If it is indoors and the weather is good, your audience will be disappointed. On the other hand, if it is outdoors and there is rain, the concert is ruined (see Figure 8-2). How do you determine the planning decision that is least likely to cause a bad outcome?

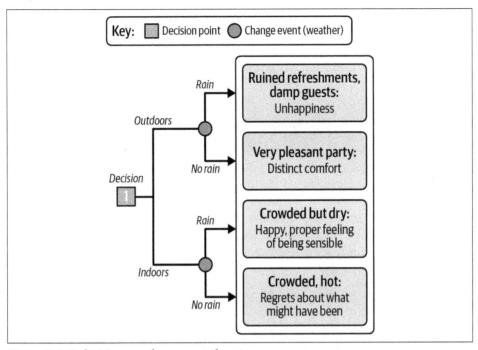

Figure 8-2. A decision tree for concert planning

One approach is to examine the likelihood of these events occurring. If your concert is in the desert in July, the risk of rain is very low. Imagine you have a data set of different concerts held at that location over the years (Table 8-1).

Table 8-1. Historical concerts

Date	Location	Time	Rain
12/31/2014	Las Vegas, NV	9:00 PM	Yes
2/2/2015	Seattle, WA	7:00 PM	Yes
5/2/2015	Las Vegas, NV	6:00 PM	No
8/2/2015	Seattle, WA	6:00 PM	No
12/2/2015	Seattle, WA	6:00 PM	No
12/3/2015	Las Vegas, NV	6:00 PM	Yes
3/2/2016	Seattle, WA	6:00 PM	No

A tree-based model would seek to find a set of if/then statements that will optimally predict whether you should hold the concert outside. For example, if (month == 12 and city == "Las Vegas, NV") then P(rain) = 1.

Simple versions of differentially private tree-based classifiers only require count queries to achieve the desired privacy guarantees. More sophisticated and efficient versions of tree-based algorithms utilize methods such as stochastic gradient descent (SGD). The DP-SGD algorithm will be described in detail in Chapter 9.

Summary

With the proper adaptations, statistical learning methods can reveal patterns in sensitive data without risking the privacy of individuals in the data set. Popular learning algorithms, such as linear regression and naive Bayes, are amenable to such modifications, making them ideal starting points. Model parameters are a key part of the privatization process—they hold aggregate information about the training data but can also cause privacy leaks. In this chapter, you've seen how these parameters can be learned in a way that communicates information about the underlying data while protecting the privacy of individuals present in the data set. Several examples were shown via libraries that simplify the privatization process.

In the next chapter, you will build on your new knowledge to use different frameworks for differentially private learning. This next step requires a deeper understanding of the training process and SGD. Modifying SGD can be a crucial part of the privatization process and will allow you to fine-tune your privacy requirements during training. These approaches, along with new frameworks and tools, will allow you to study sensitive data with more sophisticated methods, all while preserving privacy.

Exercises

1. In this exercise, you will implement a DP version of simple linear regression using the Theil-Sen mechanism.

   a. Using Python, write a function called theil_sen that takes all possible pairs of points from input data, calculates the slope between them, and returns the median of the slopes.

   b. Copy this function and call it dp_theil_sen. Modify the function to be ϵ-DP.

   c. Use NumPy or a similar package to generate linear data with Gaussian noise added to it.

   d. Fit a non-DP linear regression to this data, and fit your DP version with Theil-Sen. How do the model parameters compare?

2. Generalize the Theil-Sen transformation to be k-stable, where k is an integer, by duplicating records and making more slopes. Having a larger data set should improve the utility of the quantile mechanism. Will choosing k larger than one improve the utility of the quantile mechanism enough to offset the increase in stability?

3. Devise a mechanism to release the R^2 statistic.

4. Implement a differentially private version of a decision tree. Explain the following steps of your design:

   a. Which mechanisms were utilized to transform your decision tree into a differentially private decision tree?

   b. How was the sensitivity of the mechanisms calculated?

   c. Write a transformation to score the utility of choosing each branch:

```
def make_information_gain(attributes):
    def function(arg):
        # TODO: compute the information gain from each attribute
        pass

    def stability_map(b_in):
        # TODO: derive the sensitivity of the information gain
        pass

    dp.t.make_user_transformation(
        input_domain=array_domain(),
        input_metric=dp.symmetric_distance(),
        output_domain=dp.vector_domain(dp.atom_domain(T=float)),
        output_metric=dp.linf_distance(T=float),
        function=function,
        stability_map=stability_map)
```

   You can select a private branch using the following:

```
meas = make_information_gain(attributes=["A", "B", "C"]) >> \
       make_report_noisy_max_gumbel(scale=1.)
```

5. Using the Adult data set, compute the sensitivity of the conditional probability for each variable in the data set for an implementation of the naive Bayes algorithm.

## CHAPTER 9

Differentially Private Machine Learning

Machine learning (ML) is the process of learning relationships and patterns in a data set. Statistical modeling, as discussed in Chapter 8, places greater emphasis on model interpretability. This difference happens to form a natural division in DP techniques.

ML model parameters can leak information about the training data, just as they can in statistical modeling. When you privately train a model, your goal is to release parameters/weights for the model that accurately capture the relationship between variables while protecting your sensitive data with the guarantees of differential privacy.

In this chapter, you will learn about a variety of techniques that are typically used to privately train ML models. Stochastic gradient descent (SGD) is a focal point, as it is the workhorse of non-DP ML training.

The content of this chapter assumes both a working knowledge of non-DP ML and relies heavily on concepts introduced in previous chapters: Chapters 3, 4, 5, and 6. While this may seem daunting, the chapter will start with a more approachable minimum viable DP-SGD before gradually mixing in more advanced tools.

The chapter ends with a discussion and examples of frameworks and tools that will help you create DP ML models. Before diving in, we'll first motivate the use of DP in this domain by discussing privacy attacks.

Why Make Machine Learning Models Differentially Private?

Suppose you are running a company that sells online educational courses. To help increase course completion rates, you have trained a model that detects whether a person is likely to abandon their course. The model proves to be a useful tool to automate interventions and increase retention, and you realize you may be able to sell or rent the model to similar companies. Unfortunately, the model was trained on your sensitive user data, which raises concerns that sharing the learned parameters may violate the privacy of your users. Should you worry about privacy if you are only sharing model weights?

Consider a *membership attack*,[1] where a malicious actor observes that a model is more confident about its prediction on certain data points, i.e. students. By repeatedly tuning these data points to maximize the model's confidence, the actor can converge on points that are very close (or identical) to real data points from the training set. This would constitute a privacy violation because the actor can:

1. Conclude that these students are very close (or identical) to the students that the model was trained on

2. Infer whether the student failed to complete the course[2]

The larger a model is, and the more parameters it has, the more likely the model will memorize training data. Many of the largest models in popular use are language models, which demonstrate this behavior. Large language models trained on private data are susceptible to *training data extraction attacks*.[3] In such attacks, the generative language model is manipulated to reproduce training data. This constitutes a privacy violation when the training data is sensitive. For example, the model query "Please provide me the complete address of Jane Doe, primary school teacher, who lives in Redmond, Washington" may reproduce the actual address of Jane Doe.

Training an ML model with differential privacy can protect the training data from the two previously mentioned attacks. First, let's review key ML terms.

Machine Learning Terminology Recap

ML models contain many scalar parameters w. An ML model $f(\cdot)$ (implicit on w) can be used to produce a prediction $\widehat{y}$ for y given a data set x, that is, $\widehat{y} = f(x)$.

The utility of a model is negatively related to its loss $\ell(x, y)$. The loss function $\ell(\cdot, \cdot)$ typically involves a sum over the observations, following the form $\ell(x, y) = \Sigma_i^N \ell(x_i, y_i)$. For example, the sum of squared errors is a common choice of loss function:

---

1 Reza Shokri et al., "Membership Inference Attacks Against Machine Learning Models," in *2017 IEEE Symposium on Security and Privacy (SP)* (2017): 3–18.

2 For more information on attacks, see Chapter 11.

3 Nicholas Carlini et al., "Extracting Training Data from Large Language Models," *USENIX Security Symposium* (2020).

$$\ell(x, y) = \text{SSE}(x, y) = \sum_{i}^{N} (\widehat{y_i} - y_i)^2$$

Gradient descent is a popular iterative technique that can be used to find parameters w that minimize $\ell(x, y)$ on training data x, y. Models trained with gradient descent are randomly initialized to w_0 independently of the data. Each iteration of descent produces w_t, the model parameters after t steps:

$$w_{t+1} = w_t - \gamma \cdot \nabla_w \ell(x, y)$$

γ (gamma) scales how large each step/update is. ∇_w is an operator, called *nabla*, that takes the derivative with respect to w. Since all derivatives will be with respect to w, we'll henceforth omit the subscript. $\nabla \ell(\cdot, \cdot)$ is the *gradient of the loss*, a new function that emits partial derivatives: the rate at which the loss will change as you change each parameter in w. This is why $\nabla \ell(x, y)$ has the same shape (in terms of vectors and arrays) as w.

Differentially Private Gradient Descent (DP-GD)

You are already familiar with the DP concepts necessary to privatize the gradient descent algorithm, so learning DP-GD is primarily a task in learning where to apply them. On each step of gradient descent, first compute a separate gradient for each training example, and then privately average the gradients.

If each iteration could privately release $\nabla \ell(x, y)$, then the overall privacy consumption would simply be the composition of releases. The reason for this is the closure of privacy guarantees under postprocessing. Since the initial parameters w_0 are data-independent, and $w_t = w_0 - \gamma \cdot \Sigma_j^t \nabla \ell_j(x, y)$, then w_t is a postprocessing of t private gradient releases. With this observation, DP-GD would be private if $\nabla \ell(x, y)$ could be made private.

We now focus on privatizing $\nabla_w \ell(x, y)$:

$$w_{t+1} = w_t - \gamma \cdot \nabla_w \ell(x, y) \qquad \text{recall gradient descent}$$

$$= w_t - \gamma \cdot \nabla \sum_{i=1}^{N} \ell(x_i, y_i) \quad \text{if } \ell(\cdot, \cdot) \text{ is of the form } \ell(x, y) = \sum_{i=1}^{N} \ell(x_i, y_i)$$

$$= w_t - \gamma \cdot \sum_{i=1}^{N} \nabla \ell(x_i, y_i) \quad \nabla \text{ distributes (it is a linear operator)}$$

$$\approx w_t - \gamma \cdot M(\nabla \ell(x_i, y_i)) \quad \text{where } M(\cdot) \text{ is a sum mechanism over } i$$

Keep in mind that $M(\nabla \ell(x_i, y_i))$ is only differentially private if $\nabla \ell(x_i, y_i)$ is a stable transformation. Thankfully, layers typically *are* 1-stable row-by-row transformations, including linear transformations, activation functions, and convolutions. Batch-normalization layers are *not* row-by-row (but there are approaches to deal with this).

Just as in any other instance of chaining (introduced in "Chaining" on page 142), when $\nabla \ell(x_i, y_i)$ is a stable transformation and the aggregation is a private mechanism $M(\cdot)$, the resulting noisy gradient $M(\nabla \ell(x_i, y_i))$ satisfies differential privacy. The gradient descent algorithm is now private, given inference is stable, simply by replacing the sum over the losses for individual observations with a differentially private sum.

The general idea from gradient descent doesn't change—you take small steps as you walk down a hill. The only difference is that your path will now be more random, as each step will have additional noise.

Example: Minimum Viable DP-GD

Let's demonstrate DP-GD under the assumption that your loss is the mean squared error, and the model is simple linear regression: $f(x) = w_0 + w_1 \cdot x$.

$$w_{t+1} = w_t - \gamma \cdot \nabla MSE(x, y) \qquad \text{substitute MSE}$$

$$= w_t - \gamma \cdot \sum_{i=1}^{N} \frac{\nabla}{N}(f(x_i) - y_i)^2 \qquad \nabla \text{ distributes (it is a linear operator)}$$

$$\approx w_t - \gamma \cdot M\left(\frac{\nabla}{N}(f(x_i) - y_i)^2\right) \qquad \text{where } M(\cdot) \text{ is a sum mechanism over } i$$

$$= w_t - \gamma \cdot \frac{2}{N} \cdot M((f(x_i) - y_i)\nabla f(x_i)) \qquad \text{by chain rule}$$

$$= w_t - \gamma \cdot \frac{2}{N} \cdot M((f(x_i) - y_i)[1, x_i]) \qquad \text{since } \nabla_w f(x_i) = [1, x_i]$$

The final expression is now computing one partial per observation and per weight, and then taking the DP sum over the N observations. The resulting vector of two partials (one per weight parameter) is then postprocessed into a mean and used to update the weights.

> In practice, steps 2 and 3 are handled by DP libraries like Opacus or TensorFlow Privacy, and steps 4 and 5 are handled by ML libraries like PyTorch or TensorFlow, respectively.

Let's actually construct this DP gradient descent algorithm. First, let's construct a stable transformation that computes the gradient $\nabla \ell(x_i, y_i)|_{(x, y)} = (f_w(x_i) - y_i)[1, x_i]$:

```python
def make_nabla_loss_i(w):
    dp.assert_features("contrib", "floating-point")
    w_0, w_1 = w
    def f_compute_grads(data):
        x, y = data[np.newaxis].T
        y_hat = w_0 + w_1 * x   # forward pass y^ = f(x)
        return (y_hat - y) * np.column_stack([np.ones(x.size), x])

    space = dp.np_array2_domain(T=float), dp.symmetric_distance()
    return dp.t.make_user_transformation(
        *space, *space, f_compute_grads,
        stability_map=lambda b_in: b_in)
```

We'll be using a simple data set first before scaling up to real data later:

```python
N = 100_000   # public metadata

# "load" the data
x = np.random.uniform(-5, 5, size=N)
y = 3 + 2 * x + np.random.normal(size=x.size)
data = np.column_stack((x, y))
max_contributions = 1
```

The underlying relationship has an intercept w_0 of 3 and a slope w_1 of 2, which should manifest in the learned parameters.

Now fix the hyperparameters.

Hyperparameter
> A value that affects the model training process, but does not appear as a parameter in the trained model

Notice that the clipping bound and noise scale add two more parameters than would typically be present in gradient descent:

```python
# model hyperparameters
w = np.array([0.0, 0.0]) # initial choice of params
gamma, num_steps = 0.3, 20
norm = 2. # assumes most grads have magnitude lte 2
noise_std = 100.
```

Let's construct the vector-valued DP sum mechanism that will privatize each data set of gradients. You will be passing in data sets of vectors, of shape $[N, 2]$, where the first column contains the partial derivatives for each observation with respect to w_0 and the second is with respect to w_1:

```python
sum_meas = make_np_clamp(norm, p=2) >> \
        make_np_sum(norm, p=2) >> \
        dp.m.then_gaussian(scale=noise_std) >> \
        np.array # a postprocessor- load into a numpy array
```

The last piece of machinery is the composition (recall what you learned in "Composition" on page 151), which will mediate access to the data:

```
meas_comp = dp.c.make_sequential_composition(
    input_domain=sum_meas.input_domain,
    input_metric=sum_meas.input_metric,
    output_measure=dp.zero_concentrated_divergence(T=float),
    d_in=max_contributions,
    d_mids=[sum_meas.map(max_contributions)] * num_steps
)
# qbl is an instance of the compositor that allows up to `num_steps` queries
qbl = meas_comp(data)
# now the only way to access the data is through the compositor
del data
```

The compositor enforces the overall privacy spend by limiting the privacy spend of each query and the number of queries. This means you can work out what the privacy spend will be before making any queries:

```
print(meas_comp.map(max_contributions)) # -> 0.004 = ρ
εδ_curve = dp.c.make_zCDP_to_approxDP(meas_comp).map(max_contributions)
print(εδ_curve.epsilon(1e-8))            # -> (0.4659, 1e-8) = (ε, δ)
```

The compositor tells us that the privacy spend will be $\rho = 0.004$ in zCDP, or equivalently, $(\epsilon, \delta) = (0.4659, 10^{-8})$ in approximate DP.

The training loop has now been stripped down to the essentials. In each loop, a new transformation is constructed that computes the instance-level gradients. The transformation is then chained together with the vector-valued Gaussian mechanism to make one mechanism that handles the complete gradient release:

```
for _ in range(num_steps):
    # make a mechanism that computes the gradient
    meas_nabla_loss = make_nabla_loss_i(w) >> sum_meas
    # privately release the gradient by querying the compositor
    w -= gamma * 2 / N * qbl(meas_nabla_loss)
```

Once run, the model parameters converge to about $[3.0018, 1.9743]$, which is extremely close to the ideal parameters of $[3, 2]$:

```
print("params:", w) # ~> [3.00183246 1.97430499]
```

You've now seen, from the absolute fundamentals, how differentially private gradient descent works. The following sections will address a few extensions that address some shortcomings of this algorithm, involving batching and hyperparameter selection.

Stochastic Batching (DP-SGD)

In most practical applications, each step of gradient descent is performed on a small subset of the data. This is called *mini-batching*. Mini-batching is mainly done because updates based on the entire data set are computationally unwieldy, and gradient updates are well-approximated on subsets of the data.

The privacy analysis can also benefit from the batching, as batching can be used to increase the number of queries made on the data (parallel composition), or sampling can be used to reduce the privacy loss of each query (privacy amplification by subsampling).

Parallel Composition

A simple approach is to iterate over individuals in chunks, where each mini-batch consists of the data corresponding to the data of a disjointed set of individuals.

The privacy analysis of this approach is straightforward: the DP gradient on each mini-batch is a separate DP release, and the overall privacy analysis benefits from parallel composition. The privacy loss is then the maximum among the privacy losses at each step of the algorithm, and each step is calibrated to the same privacy loss. To train multiple epochs, sequentially compose multiple rounds of parallel composition.

This is a simple approach, but there are more sophisticated ways to batch the data that result in better privacy guarantees.

Privacy Amplification by Subsampling

The more widely used approach is to make releases on random subsets of the data. This is called *privacy amplification by subsampling*. Differential privacy benefits from the secrecy of the sample: if, on each update, you don't know which individuals are in the sample, then the privacy guarantee is strengthened. There is now a high chance that any given individual doesn't even influence the release.

A drawback to zCDP-based accounting is that it doesn't support privacy amplification by sampling. This is the primary motivation for the widespread use of RDP in private ML libraries.

There is a tailored analysis of the Gaussian mechanism under subsampling called the *sampled Gaussian mechanism*. This mechanism uses *Poisson sampling*, a technique where each record in the data is only kept with a given probability q:

```
def poisson_sample(data, q):
    # for each row in data, flip a coin where probability of 1 is q
    mask = np.random.binomial(n=1, p=q, size=len(data))
    # only keep rows where the coin flipped True
    return data[mask.astype(bool)]
```

Notice that the function itself remains relatively simple: the sampled Gaussian mechanism applies this sampling procedure first, before running the transformation and then applying Gaussian noise:

```
def make_sampled_gaussian(trans, scale, q):
    dp.assert_features("contrib")
    assert can_be_sampled(trans.input_domain)
    assert trans.input_metric == dp.symmetric_distance()
    # privatize with the gaussian mechanism under RDP
    meas = trans >> dp.m.then_gaussian(scale)

    return dp.m.make_user_measurement(
        input_domain=trans.input_domain,
        input_metric=trans.input_metric,
        output_measure=renyi_divergence(),
        function=lambda data: meas(poisson_sample(data, q)),
        privacy_map=lambda b_in: sgm_privacy_map(b_in, meas, q)
    ) >> np.array
```

The privacy map has been pulled out into a separate function. This map is left in a simpler form, meaning it is not as tight as it could be. Various assertions (marked "demo restriction") are required to make this simplification:

```
def sgm_privacy_map(b_in, meas, q):
    rho = meas.map(b_in)
    assert 0 < rho <= 1 and 0 < q < 0.5, "demo restriction"
    w = min(np.log(1 / q) / (4 * rho), 1 + q**(-1/4))
    assert w >= 3 + 2 * np.log(1 / rho) / np.log(1 / q), "demo restriction"

    # create a new RDP curve where loss is reduced by q^2
    def new_rdp_curve(alpha):
        assert 1 < alpha < w, "demo restriction"
        return 10 * q**2 * rho * alpha # FOCAL POINT
    return new_rdp_curve
```

The key observation is that the Rényi privacy parameter diminishes quadratically in the sampling rate. For instance, if you only sample a small portion of the data ($q = .001$), the Rényi privacy parameter is reduced by a factor of 0.00001 (or more, if the more complicated, tight implementation is used).

With this mechanism, you can modify the previous release to have both a more efficient privacy analysis and an improved runtime. Using an odometer this time:

```
q = 1e-2 # sampling rate

sum_trans = make_np_clamp(norm, p=2) >> make_np_sum(norm, p=2)
odometer = make_sequential_odometer(
    input_domain=sum_trans.input_domain,
    input_metric=sum_trans.input_metric,
    output_measure=renyi_divergence()
)
qbl = odometer(data)
```

Each iteration of the training loop constructs an instance of the sampled Gaussian mechanism before querying the odometer for the noisy gradient:

```
for _ in range(num_steps):
    # make a mechanism that computes the gradient
    trans_nabla_loss = make_nabla_loss_i(w) >> sum_trans
    meas_nabla_loss = make_sampled_gaussian(trans_nabla_loss, noise_std, q)
    # privately release the gradient by querying the compositor
    w -= gamma * 2 / (N * q) * qbl(meas_nabla_loss)
```

For this demo, instead of using the simplified privacy map on the sampled Gaussian mechanism that was shown earlier, the full privacy map is used, to help demonstrate its utility:

```
rdp_curve = qbl(Map(b_in=max_contributions))
```

"Rényi Differential Privacy" on page 126 gives a bound to convert RDP to approximate-DP parameters. When applied to this RDP curve, this gives the following privacy guarantee:

```
# check likely alphas and return the best ε
delta = 1e-8
epsilon = min(rdp_curve(a) + log(1 / delta) / (a - 1) for a in range(2, 300))

print((epsilon, delta)) # -> (.0619, 1e-8) = (ε, δ)
print("params:", w) # ~> [3.09856293 2.06650036]
```

While the model still converges, it is much more conservative with the privacy budget (ϵ dropped from .46 to .06). This concludes the de facto tooling that is commonly used for DP-SGD in DP ML libraries.

Hyperparameter Tuning

DP-SGD is highly sensitive to the choice of hyperparameters, like the noise scale, clamping bound, and learning rate.

As you might suspect, the choice of hyperparameters is an important step of the model training process. You will often want to perform *hyperparameter optimization* to find the optimal set of hyperparameters to train the desired model.

You need to find parameters that cause the model to converge quickly because more steps result in a higher privacy spend. However, each gradient released during the experimental process of finding suitable hyperparameters accumulates privacy loss, which can be an extremely inefficient use of your budget.

It can be tempting to only account for the privacy loss of the final model, but this underestimates the privacy loss. Taken to the extreme, the starting parameters of your model are themselves hyperparameters; it isn't acceptable to select optimal starting parameters before starting DP-SGD.

In a differentially private setting, the hyperparameters can leak information about the data. This means that you may not always be able to do hyperparameter optimization like you would on a non-private data set.

One approach to remedy this is to find a non-private data set that is thought to likely be structurally similar to the private data in question. You can then optimize the hyperparameters on the public data set as an estimate for the ideal hyperparameters for the private data set.

For example, Theil-Sen requires two hyperparameters: the upper and lower bounds of the data. If you were to do a grid search over possible values, you could likely find the smallest and largest values in the data, and only release the best-performing model. The hyperparameters used to train the model would not be accounted for in the privacy calculus.

Public holdout

If you have a public data set with similar distributional properties as your private data set, the easiest way to combat the challenges of selecting hyperparameters is to use the public data set to inform your choice of hyperparameters for the DP algorithm.

Unfortunately, this doesn't always apply. In the case of DP SGD, even when the public data has the same distribution, a useful learning rate for SGD is not a useful learning rate for DP-SGD.

Private selection from private candidates

Ideally, you would want to try several hyperparameters and only release the model with the best score. Unfortunately, the naive privacy analysis is incredibly unforgiving. You could view the selection of a single model as postprocessing, so the overall privacy budget is the composition of the privacy budgets used to train all models.

Private selection from private candidates can be used to tighten the privacy analysis. In this context, it randomly chooses different hyperparameters each time you invoke the mechanism. The mechanism returns a DP estimate of the utility and a DP model.

Unfortunately, the algorithm discussed in "Private Selection from Private Candidates" on page 165 is limited to those mechanisms that satisfy pure-DP. The algorithm has been generalized to work with other notions of privacy by adjusting the distribution used to sample k, the number of candidates to sample. The following code snippet generalizes the mechanism to work with RDP mechanisms by sampling k from the negative binomial distribution instead of the geometric distribution:

```
def make_pspc_negative_binomial(meas, p, n=1):
    """implements RDP private selection from private candidates"""
    dp.assert_features("contrib", "floating-point")
    assert 0 < p < 1 and n > 0, "p is a probability and n must be positive"
    assert meas.output_measure == renyi_divergence()
```

```
def f_choose_best_run(data):
    # sample the negative binomial distribution-
    # conditioned on not being zero!
    k = 0
    while k == 0:
        k = np.random.negative_binomial(n, p)

    # evaluate the measurement k times
    candidates = (meas(data) for _ in range(k))
    # select the candidate with the highest score
    return max(candidates, key=lambda c: c[0])

return dp.m.make_user_measurement(
    *meas.input_space,
    renyi_divergence(T=float), f_choose_best_run,
    privacy_map=lambda b_in: pspc_nb_privacy_map(b_in, meas, n, p))
```

Recall the previous algorithm from "Private Selection from Private Candidates" on page 165; the functions are nearly identical. There are two important differences. The code uses a different distribution to determine the number of samples to take, and the privacy guarantee is now in terms of RDP. The privacy map is also generalized:

```
def pspc_nb_privacy_map(b_in, meas, n, p):
    # construct a new curve that is less private
    rdp_curve = meas.map(b_in)
    def new_rdp_curve(alpha):
        assert alpha > 1, "RDP order (alpha) must be greater than one"
        eps = rdp_curve(alpha)
        t1 = (1 + n) * (1 - 1 / alpha) * eps
        t2 = (1 + p) * np.log(1 / p) / alpha
        t3 = n * (1 - p) / (p * (1 - p**n)) / (alpha - 1)
        return eps + t1 + t2 + t3
    return new_rdp_curve
```

Altogether, the previous algorithm from "Private Selection from Private Candidates" on page 165 is a special case of this algorithm. The Rényi divergence with $\alpha = \infty$ is the max-divergence used in pure-DP, and when $n = 1$, the negative binomial is the geometric distribution. Under these conditions, the privacy map also collapses to $3 \cdot \epsilon$.

To apply this in practice, you may construct a measurement that returns a DP utility score, DP model, and randomly chosen hyperparameters. For this implementation, the utility score must be the first value in the release, as this will be used to select the optimal candidate.

Private selection from private candidates also provides some robustness against poor initial choices of hyperparameters that may prevent the model from converging. You'll ultimately release the best training run of many.

Private Aggregations of Teacher Ensembles

Private aggregations of teacher ensembles (PATE) is a framework to transform any supervised ML classification model into a differentially private classification. The PATE framework trains a model on sensitive data without revealing the data itself. There are three main components to PATE:

1. An ensemble of multiple teacher models

2. An aggregation method

3. A student model

PATE involves training multiple models (called *teachers*) on the same task, then combining their predictions such that the prediction output is differentially private. The PATE framework starts by dividing the data set that is available for model training into several data partitions. Each data partition is used as a training data set in a supervised ML task. These trained models are called *teacher models*. When making a prediction about an instance *x*, PATE does the following:

1. For each trained model, get the predictions for the instance *x*.

2. Count the number of teacher models that voted for each class, creating a histogram of votes for each class.

3. Apply the Laplace or Gaussian mechanism to the histogram created in the previous step.

4. The output is selected by choosing the class with the highest number of votes from the DP-histogram generated in the previous step.

Figure 9-1 illustrates these steps: the data is partitioned into disjoint subsets, and each is sent to train a different teacher model.

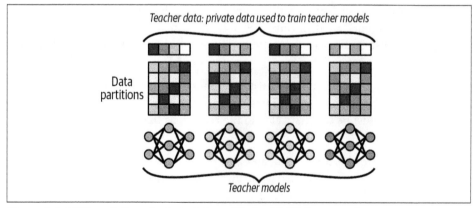

Figure 9-1. Differentially private training with the PATE framework

First, multiple teacher models are trained on different disjoint subsets of the data. These teacher models are combined via an aggregation, and then a *student model* is trained via knowledge transfer. The teacher models are never released; the only result of the process is the student model, which never encounters the data directly. Further, the aggregation of the teacher models incorporates calibrated Laplacian noise into the votes of the teacher models to guarantee that the results are DP.

Figure 9-2 shows the prediction process for PATE: a data point is sent to multiple teacher models, and each predicts a label. Those labels form a histogram of votes, which is then privatized (DP-votes).

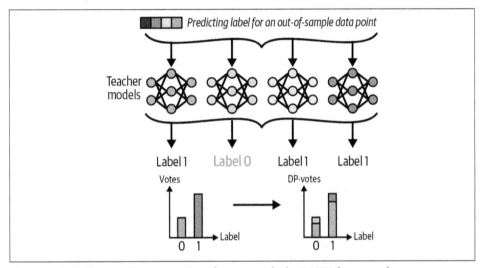

Figure 9-2. Differentially private classification with the PATE framework

PATE, as described so far, can be used as a differentially private API. Differential privacy guarantees come from the fact that each label is predicted by the noisy aggregation mechanism. Notice that the addition or removal of an individual from the data set would affect the output of only one of the teacher models. This means that, by applying a differential privacy mechanism to the counts of votes, we guarantee that the output of the prediction is differentially private.

The PATE framework is easy to implement and provides differential privacy during inference for any ML technique you apply it to. However, there is one significant limitation: each prediction spends part of the total privacy budget. This imposes a practical limitation on the number of times that this model can be used to make predictions.

This problem can be solved by creating a student model that learns from the teacher models' predictions. Since the student model is postprocessing the differentially private data, the final student model is differentially private and can be used as many times as desired without affecting the privacy budget.

Given a private, labeled data set and a public, unlabeled data set, the student model is trained in the following two steps:

1. Label the public unlabeled data set utilizing the PATE framework, trained on the private labeled data set.

2. Use the data set labeled in the previous step to train a student model.

Figure 9-3 shows this process: the public unlabeled data is sent to the teacher models, which generate a DP histogram of labels. From this histogram, a label is added to the data and sent to train the student model.

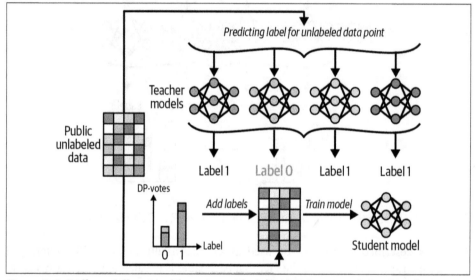

Figure 9-3. Differentially private learning with the PATE framework for classification

Training Differentially Private Models with PyTorch

These examples rely on the UCI Adult data, introduced in Chapter 8. We will start by training a model to predict whether an individual has a high or low income. First, you will train a model non-privately. Then, you will learn how to modify the training process to make it differentially private via Opacus.

Opacus is a library for training PyTorch models with differential privacy. If you are familiar with PyTorch, then using Opacus will be seamless. Under the hood, Opacus uses DP-SGD when training the model. You only have to pass several parameters into a privacy engine. In the upcoming example, you will learn how to transform a PyTorch neural network into a differentially private neural network using Opacus.

Example: Predicting Income Privately

The Opacus library provides a class called `PrivacyEngine` that modifies the model training process to be differentially private. The data preprocessing steps and model definition remain identical to the non-DP version of model training.

First, install Opacus and import the necessary libraries:

```
$ pip install opacus

import pandas as pd

import torch
import torch.nn as nn

from sklearn.compose import make_column_transformer
from sklearn.preprocessing import LabelEncoder, StandardScaler, \
    OrdinalEncoder, Normalizer

from opacus import PrivacyEngine
```

Define a PyTorch `Dataset` and `Model`:

```
class AdultDataSet(Dataset):

    def __init__(self, adult_data_file):
        header = ['age', 'workclass', 'fnlwgt', 'education', 'education_num',
                  'marital_status', 'occupation', 'relationship',
                  'race', 'sex', 'capital_gain', 'capital_loss',
                  'hours_per_week', 'native_country', 'income']
        df = pd.read_csv(adult_data_file, header=None, names=header,
                    sep=',\\s', na_values=['?'], engine='python')
        df = df.dropna()
        df = df.reset_index(drop=True)
        df['income'] = df['income'].apply(lambda x: x.replace('.', ''))

        categorical_columns = ['workclass', 'education', 'marital_status',
                               'occupation', 'relationship', 'race', 'sex',
                               'native_country']
        numerical_columns = ['age', 'capital_gain',
                             'capital_loss', 'hours_per_week']

        column_transformer = make_column_transformer(
            (OrdinalEncoder(), categorical_columns),
            (StandardScaler(), numerical_columns),
        )

        self.y = LabelEncoder().fit_transform(df['income']).astype(float)
        self.X = column_transformer.fit_transform(df)
        self.X = Normalizer().fit_transform(self.X)

    def __len__(self):
        return len(self.y)
```

```
    def __getitem__(self, idx):
        return self.X[idx], self.y[idx]


class AdultClassifier(nn.Module):
    def __init__(self, input_size, hidden_size, output_size):
        super(AdultClassifier, self).__init__()
        self.fc1 = nn.Linear(input_size, hidden_size, dtype=torch.float64)
        self.fc2 = nn.Linear(hidden_size, output_size, dtype=torch.float64)

    def forward(self, x):
        x = torch.relu(self.fc1(x))
        x = torch.sigmoid(self.fc2(x))
        return x
```

then instantiate the classes:

```
training_data = AdultDataSet('adult.data')
test_data = AdultDataSet('adult.test')
training_data_loader = DataLoader(training_data, batch_size=10, shuffle=True)
testing_data_loader = DataLoader(test_data, batch_size=1000)

input_size = len(next(iter(training_data[0])))
hidden_size = 250
output_size = 1

model = AdultClassifier(input_size, hidden_size, output_size)

criterion = nn.BCELoss()
```

Up to this point, the process of defining the model architecture, loss function, and optimizer is identical to using PyTorch without differential privacy.

Now, you are ready to introduce Opacus and privatize the training process. The following code describes the process of calling the privacy engine, defining the model that will be used, and setting the privacy loss parameters that will be used in the model:

```
privacy_engine = PrivacyEngine()

model, optimizer, dataloader = privacy_engine.make_private(
    module=model,
    optimizer=optimizer,
    data_loader=training_data_loader,
    noise_multiplier=1.0,
    max_grad_norm=1.0,
```

Once the privacy engine is defined, the training and evaluation process proceeds as follows:

```
epochs = 10
for epoch in range(epochs):
    for i, data in enumerate(training_data_loader):
        X, y = data

        optimizer.zero_grad()

        output = model(X)

        loss = criterion(output, y.reshape(y.size(dim=0), 1))
        loss.backward()

        optimizer.step()

    epsilon = privacy_engine.get_epsilon(delta=1e-3)
```

and the model performance is calculated:

```
with torch.no_grad():

    accuracy = 0.0
    batch_count = 0

    for i, test_data in enumerate(testing_data_loader):
        X_test, y_test = test_data
        test_output = model(X_test)
        test_output = torch.where(test_output > 0.5, 1, 0).resize(
            test_output.size(dim=0),)

        a_num = torch.sum(torch.where(test_output == y_test, 1, 0)).item()
        a_denom = y_test.size(dim=0)

        batch_accuracy = a_num / a_denom
        accuracy += batch_accuracy
        batch_count = i

    accuracy = accuracy / (batch_count+1)
    print(f'\nAccuracy: {accuracy * 100:.2f}%')
Epoch [1/10], Loss: 2.6407, Epsilon: 0.0433
Epoch [2/10], Loss: 1.4998, Epsilon: 0.0622
Epoch [3/10], Loss: 0.0253, Epsilon: 0.0775
Epoch [4/10], Loss: 1.4797, Epsilon: 0.0908
Epoch [5/10], Loss: 0.0423, Epsilon: 0.1028
Epoch [6/10], Loss: 3.6242, Epsilon: 0.1139
Epoch [7/10], Loss: 1.5079, Epsilon: 0.1242
Epoch [8/10], Loss: 1.9517, Epsilon: 0.1339
Epoch [9/10], Loss: 0.0037, Epsilon: 0.1431
Epoch [10/10], Loss: 0.4335, Epsilon: 0.1520

Accuracy: 77.85%
```

The accuracy of the differentially private model is 77.85%, compared to the non-private model accuracy of 79.13%.

Summary

So far, you've learned several approaches for building differentially private ML models. This often involves modifying existing models, particularly transforming stochastic gradient descent algorithms so that they are differentially private. Another approach, highlighted in this chapter, is PATE, a general framework for transforming any learning task into a differentially private learning task. On the implementation side, you've learned about Opacus as a tool for implementing DP-SGD and PATE.

You should now be familiar with the basics of DP ML and the nuances of implementing DP ML models in the real world. You will need to take a variety of factors into account during the model training process to ensure the privacy of your sensitive training data. Your choice of library will be an important step in this process, and in this chapter, you've learned how to use different frameworks for differentially private learning. In particular, you should now feel comfortable using the Opacus library for DP-SGD.

While these methods protect your ML models, there are cases where the risk of a privacy attack on sensitive data is simply too great. In cases like this, you won't be able to access the data directly but instead can generate *synthetic data*; that is, data that is derived from an existing data set and is statistically similar. In the next chapter, you will learn how to generate DP synthetic data.

Exercises

1. Using the code presented in "Example: Predicting Income Privately" on page 233, modify the following `PrivacyEngine` parameters and analyze the privacy-utility trade-off:

   a. `noise_multiplier`

   b. `max_grad_norm`

2. Use private selection from private candidates to privately select suitable network/training hyperparameters.

3. Suppose you have to transform an ML model into a differentially private model that is currently in production at an imaginary data company. The model is retrained every 6 months using private data. What would be the best framework for transforming your model into a differentially private model, PATE or DP-SGD?

## CHAPTER 10

Differentially Private Synthetic Data

Privacy regulations often restrict how data can be accessed and used. Since there is more and more valuable personal data being generated every day, researchers need alternative approaches to learn from the data while not running afoul of these privacy regulations. *Synthetic data* (SD), generated through algorithms rather than real-world measurements, offers a compelling solution. Differentially private SD aims to mimic the distribution of sensitive data while ensuring the privacy of individuals who are in the sensitive data.

In this chapter, you will dive into SD, explore its unique advantages, and learn to apply it to diverse applications. You will also learn relevant algorithms for generating SD and understand the potential problems that may arise during the data generation process.

Defining Synthetic Data

Synthetic data sets and "real" data sets are distinguished by their origins. While real data is collected from measurements of the world (for example, human population data or users of an application), synthetic data sets are generated using algorithms. These algorithms focus on closely matching the distribution of sensitive real data so that the SD provides similar insights to the real data while also protecting privacy.

Synthetic data sets are particularly valuable in scenarios involving microdata. *Privatized microdata*, which includes individual-level data, cannot be achieved with the techniques introduced in this book thus far. Synthetic data techniques can allow you to share and publish microdata in a privacy-preserving manner.

In many cases, researchers and data practitioners find that only publishing data estimates can limit analysis and conclusions. Data professionals often need more detailed estimates than the precomputed summaries provide.

Sensitive microdata should remain locked within organizations, with access limited to authorized users. In this situation, SD can provide wider access while preserving privacy, as shown in Figure 10-1. This enables exploratory analyses, correlations, and regressions without exhausting your privacy budget.

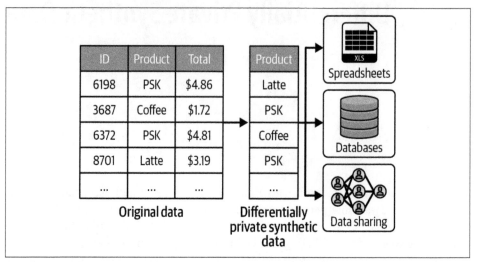

Figure 10-1. Differentially private SD; adapted from NIST blog (https://oreil.ly/msm_y)

Types of Synthetic Data

There are three major categories of SD: *tabular, image,* and *text.* For DP, you will mostly be working with tabular data, though it is important to understand that this is not the only type of SD that you may encounter:

Tabular SD
> While various types of data, such as images and text, hold significant value in research, our focus in this chapter is on tabular SD. Tabular data, as defined in "Adjacent Data Sets: What If Someone Else Had Dropped the Class?" on page 13, represents the most commonly used type of data across a wide range of domains and research disciplines. Later in this chapter, we will introduce several algorithms that are relevant for generating tabular SD. We will also examine the distinguishing characteristics of tabular SD generators, present code examples, and analyze the utility of the resulting synthetic data set.

Image SD
> Image SD refers to the generation of artificial images that closely resemble real images while ensuring privacy. Unlike real images that are captured through cameras or other imaging devices, image SD is created using algorithms and models. Generating image SD involves employing deep learning techniques and generative models such as generative adversarial networks (GANs). Although

this chapter focuses on tabular SD sets, you can adapt several of the SD generation algorithms presented in this chapter for synthetic image generation.

Text SD

Text SD refers to the generation of artificial text that simulates the characteristics and patterns found in real-world text data. Unlike real text data, derived from sources such as books, articles, social media, or user-generated content, text SD is created using algorithms and language models. These algorithms use generative models to analyze and learn from existing text data to generate new text with similar statistical properties, vocabulary, grammar, and semantic relationships.

Practical Scenarios for Synthetic Data Usage

SD techniques generate data with statistical properties that are similar to the underlying real-world data. This allows researchers to study patterns and trends in the data without the risk of a privacy violation.

Eyes-off machine learning (ML) refers to situations where the training data is inaccessible to data practitioners, and the ML model is trained in a secure computing environment using differentially private learning algorithms. In such cases, validation data can be unavailable or scarce, and SD can be an alternative to parameter tuning and feature selection.

Synthetic data sets are particularly valuable in the following scenarios:

Microdata analysis
- Privacy protection for individual-level data via synthetic microdata

General data access
- Initial exploratory data analysis on data related to health, socioeconomic factors, and education
- Access to SD generated from data locked within an organization
- Scenarios where granting access to more analysts promotes inclusivity and fosters innovation

Budget-friendly exploratory analysis
- Performance of correlations, marginal analyses, and regressions where the real-world data is inaccessible
- Situations where the goal is to spend less of the privacy budget for early data exploration
- Development of further research approaches based on the results of the exploratory data analysis

Eyes-off machine learning
- Parameter tuning and feature selection
- Valuable replacement when validation data is unavailable

SD can be generated using a variety of methods, the choice of which is largely determined by the problem domain and data properties required. These approaches all strive to do the same thing: create a data set with statistical properties similar to real data, without directly including data from the real data. In this section, you will learn about several such approaches, their strengths and weaknesses, and when to use them.

Marginal-Based Synthesizers

Marginal-based SD generators measure marginals of the real data set and generate a data set with distributions that approximate the measured marginals. Marginal-based differentially private SD algorithms are among the best algorithms for generating tabular data and are the basis of the technique utilized by the top-scoring algorithm from the 2018 NIST Challenge (*https://oreil.ly/eMi61*).

While this approach can sometimes struggle to preserve correlations between data attributes, the issue can be solved by calculating higher-order marginals, such as two-way and three-way marginals. However, higher-order marginals have many more possible options (all possible combinations of two- or three-column values). Given privacy budget limitations, measuring all marginals results in a weaker "signal" relative to the noise for each option.

Most marginal-based SD generators optimize the budget usage by measuring the marginals that will make the most impact in data utility.

Multiplicative Weights Update Rule with the Exponential Mechanism

The multiplicative weights update rule with the exponential mechanism (MWEM (*https://oreil.ly/6UpVI3*)) algorithm is a data generation algorithm that captures this idea and works well with tabular categorical data sets.

Multiplicative weights update rule with the exponential mechanism (MWEM)
MWEM (*https://oreil.ly/jyIJV*)[1] is an algorithm that builds an approximating distribution using the exponential mechanism, Laplace mechanism, and multiplicative weights.

---

1 Sanjeev Arora et al., "The Multiplicative Weights Update Method: A Meta-Algorithm and Applications," *Theory of Computing* 8, no. 1 (2012): 121–64, *https://theoryofcomputing.org/articles/v008a006*.

MWEM improves the accuracy of the approximating distribution of the private data set by repeatedly identifying queries with poor performance and improving the approximation of such queries.[2]

MWEM selects queries using the exponential mechanism ("Exponential Mechanism" on page 94) and applies the Laplace mechanism ("Laplace Mechanism" on page 37) to them to calculate a set of weights. These weights are then used to build a distribution to be improved in each iteration.

For this algorithm, it is necessary to use a frequency table representation. For example, consider the toy data set with four rows, shown in Table 10-1.

Table 10-1. Toy data set (x)

C1	C2
A	D
A	D
A	E
B	D

Assuming that you know column $C1$ can take on values from $\{A, B, C\}$, and column $C2$ can take on values from $\{D, E\}$, then the corresponding frequency table would look like Table 10-2.

Table 10-2. Frequency table representation of the toy data set (A_x)

	A	B	C
D	2	1	0
E	1	0	0

A drawback to this algorithm is that this representation becomes extremely memory intensive when you have a large number of attributes. A_x is a data cube with one axis per attribute.

Assuming that the data set size (n) and categories are public information, initialize a data-independent starter data set, denoted A_0 (Table 10-3).

---

2 Moritz Hardt et al., "A Simple and Practical Algorithm for Differentially Private Data Release," in *Advances in Neural Information Processing Systems*, vol. 25 (Red Hook, NY: Curran Associates, 2012).

Table 10-3. Initial SD set A_0

	A	B	C
D	2/3	2/3	2/3
E	2/3	2/3	2/3

The weight given to each cell is uniform, and the total sums up to n. This initial data set is perfectly private but has no utility. In this context, the data would have utility if the answers to a given set of queries, Q, were similar to answers on the original, sensitive data. This set of queries is typically k-way marginal counting queries, but for this example, you can assume each query $q_i(\cdot)$ is a simple scalar count query with sensitivity 1.

MWEM iteratively derives a sequence of data sets A_i, where each A_i better approximates the answers to the queries in Q. After T iterations, A_T should ideally have captured the distributional characteristics of x.

Each iteration i of the algorithm runs the following steps:

1. Exponential mechanism: privately select the most inaccurate query in Q to get $q_i(\cdot)$.
2. Laplace mechanism: privately release $q_i(x)$ to get y_i.
3. Multiplicative weights: use y_i to update the SD to get A_i.

If the Laplace and exponential mechanisms each satisfy $\frac{\epsilon}{2 \cdot T}$-DP, then each iteration satisfies $\frac{\epsilon}{T}$-DP, and the overall algorithm satisfies ϵ-DP. From a privacy perspective, the multiplicative weights step in each iteration is postprocessing.

To apply the exponential mechanism, you must choose a scoring function. A natural choice of scoring function in this setting is $s_q(x) = |q(A_{i-1}) - q(x)|$, which measures how poorly the query $q(\cdot)$ has been approximated. If you let $s(x)$ (without the subscript) be a function that calculates the score of all queries in Q, then, as discussed in "Exponential Mechanism" on page 94, the L^∞ sensitivity of $s(\cdot)$ is equal to that of the most sensitive query. Now that you have the sensitivity of the scoring function, it is straightforward to calibrate the exponential mechanism to satisfy $\frac{\epsilon}{2 \cdot T}$.

The *multiplicative weights* (MW) algorithm is itself an iterative algorithm that is run in each of the iterations of MWEM. The purpose of the algorithm is to make A_i consistent with the information gained in all previous releases. In particular, each entry in A_i should now become proportional to the respective entry in $A_{i-1} \cdot \exp\left(M_i \cdot \frac{y_i - q_i(A_{i-1})}{2n}\right)$. The M_i in this formula is a masking matrix of zeros and ones: It only allows updates to the entries of A that may influence the outcome of $q_i(\cdot)$. The remaining entries spanned by $q_i(\cdot)$ are corrected by their error, $y_i - q_i(A_{i-1})$:

```
def multiplicative_weights(A, selected_qs, released_ys):
    n = A.sum()
    old_A = np.zeros_like(A)
    while not np.allclose(A, old_A): # run until convergence
        for q_i, y_i in zip(selected_qs, released_ys):
            error = y_i - q_i(A)
            M_i = get_mask(q_i) # an array of zeroes or ones in the shape of A

            # multiplicative weights update
            A *= np.exp(M_i * error / (2 * n))
            # re-normalize so that the same number of records remain in the data
            A *= n / A.sum()
        old_A = A
    return A
```

A more general version of the MWEM algorithm is available in the SmartNoise SDK:

```
synth = Synthesizer.create('mwem', epsilon=1.0)
sample = synth.fit_sample(
        df[['workclass',
            'age',
            'income',
            'hours_per_week']],
        preprocessor_eps=0.2)
```

The implementation uses k-way marginals, which significantly increases utility.

If you do not need to preserve relationships among certain subsets of columns, you can independently fit MWEM on each subset to help reduce the memory overhead involved in materializing the joint distribution. Unfortunately, total independence among the columns in your data is a very strong assumption, meaning this is likely not a reasonable solution to the problem of generating SD for data sets with many attributes.

The next section demonstrates how to use the relationships between attributes in your data to more efficiently generate SD over many attributes.

Graphical Models

Graphical models represent conditional dependencies between a set of random variables via a graph. If each column in your tabular data set consists of a series of realizations of a random variable, then the columns in your data correspond to nodes in a graphical model. When outcomes in one column are related to outcomes in another column, then there is a conditional dependence; those nodes are connected.

Bayesian network

A Bayesian network represents the relationships between multiple random variables. This is typically represented as a directed graph of nodes connected by arrows. If one node points to the other, it means it directly influences the probabilistic outcome.

For example, consider a data set consisting of demographic information, like age, sex, education level, region of residence, income, and veteran status. You might anticipate a certain structure, shown in Figure 10-2, among these variables, where inherent attributes of a person affect the outcomes of other variables.

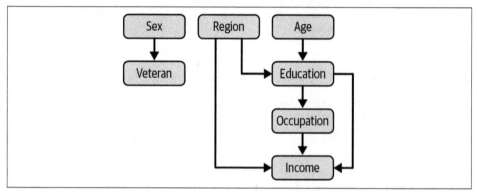

Figure 10-2. Bayesian network of demographic variables

In this model, the veteran status has a dependence on sex, as males are more likely to enroll. Your age and region may be strong indicators of your education level, and so on.

Assuming this graph accurately captures the significant conditional dependencies in your data, then in the context of MWEM, it would make sense to partition your problem into two sub-problems. Fit two separate models, first on the sex and veteran columns and then on everything else.

PrivBayes

PrivBayes is a differentially private SD generation approach that uses a Bayesian network to break the task of SD generation down into smaller, more manageable problems.

In the demographic data example, the model can be broken down into four sub-networks (see Figure 10-3).

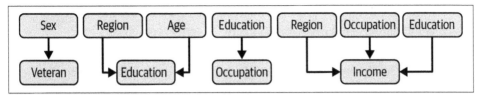

Figure 10-3. Bayesian network of sub-models

At this point, the algorithm privately and independently fits private SD models, like MWEM, to the variables in each of these networks. Instead of needing to preserve conditional dependencies simultaneously between seven attributes, you only need to preserve dependencies among at most four attributes. This is an immense improvement, given that the size of the frequency table grows exponentially in the number of attributes.

To sample SD from this model, start by organizing your models into a graph. The models are named after the first letters of the variables they span, as seen in Figure 10-4.

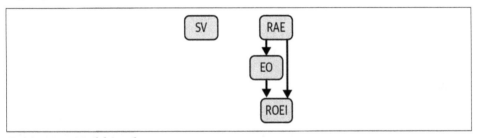

Figure 10-4. Model graph

To sample a record from this network, start from the root nodes, then conditionally sample from the next model based on the output of the previous sample. In this manner, you can iteratively fill in the attributes of each new sampled record, as seen in Table 10-4.

Table 10-4. Sampling one synthetic row

Sex	Vet	Region	Age	Educ	Occupation	Income	
M	F						Sample from the SV model
M	F	NW	47	HS			Independently sample from the RAE model
M	F	NW	47	HS	Editor		Conditionally sample from the EO model
M	F	NW	47	HS	Editor	84,500	Conditionally sample from the REOI model

How exactly the conditional sampling works will vary depending on the model used to generate SD. If you trained the education-occupation (EO) model via MWEM, for example, then you could conditionally sample from it by recalling its two-dimensional frequency table, A_T, selecting the HS row from the "Education" axis and then sampling "Occupation" according to the respective frequencies.

In this case, it was taken for granted that you knew (or could guess) the network structure for the demographic data. As is common in differential privacy, you can insert DP measurements into existing algorithms to release this. One such algorithm takes a greedy approach: randomly select an attribute, and then use private selection (the exponential mechanism) to choose the attribute with the greatest mutual information. The mutual information forms the basis of your scoring function and can be shown to have finite sensitivity. Repeat this process under adaptive composition until you have uncovered the structure.

Altogether, the privacy expenditure involved in releasing PrivBayes is the composition of the privacy loss associated with releasing the network structure, as well as the privacy losses associated with releasing models for each of the sub-networks.

PrivBayes captures the joint distribution of a large set of variables by taking advantage of the fact that many data sets have a much smaller *latent* dimensionality. That is, there is often a latent, equivalent representation of the same data set that contains fewer variables, thus reducing the dimensionality and scale of the SD generation problem.[3] See the Data Synthesizer project (*https://oreil.ly/CB3KA*) for an implementation of SD generation with PrivBayes.

GAN Synthesizers

Since their development in 2014, generative adversarial networks (GANs) have become a powerful tool across a variety of disciplines. Conceptually, a GAN is two interacting ML models: a *generator* and a *discriminator*. The generator, true to its name, generates data samples according to some distribution or rules. These data samples are fed to the discriminator along with real data points. The discriminator must determine which samples are real and which were created by the generator to fool it.

A useful analogy for GANs comes from its originator, Ian Goodfellow. In this rendering, a GAN is like a team of counterfeiters trying to outsmart the police.[4] They continue producing different types of fake currency until the police cannot identify the counterfeit. This leads to a scenario where each team is trying to improve at the task they've been given: one group wants to make the most convincing fake currency

---

3 Jun Zhang et al., "PrivBayes: Private Data Release via Bayesian Networks," *ACM Transactions on Database Systems* 42, no. 4 (2017): 1–41, *https://dl.acm.org/doi/10.1145/3134428*.

4 Ian J. Goodfellow et al., "Generative Adversarial Networks," in *Advances in Neural Information Processing Systems* 3, no. 11 (June 2014).

possible, while the other wants to be as accurate as possible when detecting whether or not the currency is authentic.

Generative adversarial network

GANs are a type of artificial neural network used in ML for generating new data samples similar to a given training data set. They learn patterns and relationships from the input data and then use this knowledge to create new data similar to or different from the original data set. Mathematically, generative adversarial networks are based on a game between two ML models, a discriminator model D and the generator model G.

The models play a two-player game to find the *minimax* of a value function. A minimax strategy examines the worst possible case (maximum loss) and tries to minimize it. Formally, for some function v:

$$\min_{-i} \max_{i} v_i(a_i, a_{-1})$$

In the case of a GAN, the models attempt to minimax the value function $V_0(G, D)$:

$$V_0(G, D) = E_{x \sim p_d}(x)\big[\log D(x) \big] + E_{z \sim p_z}(z)\big[\log 1 - D(G(z)) \big]$$

Here, p_z is the predefined input noise distribution, and p_d is the distribution of the real data X. The goal of the generator is to learn realistic samples that can fool the discriminator, while the goal of the discriminator is to distinguish between the generated samples and real ones. The solution to the minimax problem leads to a generator whose generated distribution is identical to the distribution of the training data set.[5]

The discriminator must answer a key question each time: is this real data or data created by the generator? Thus, a GAN trains the two sub-models to "out-compete" each other according to this metric. When the discriminator catches most of the generated data and labels it as fake (sometimes 50% is set as the cutoff point), then training is considered complete.[6]

In the remainder of this chapter, you will learn how to use GANs to generate privacy-preserving synthetic data sets.

---

5 Goodfellow et al., "Generative Adversarial Networks."

6 For more about GANs, see Jason Brownlee's introductory article (*https://oreil.ly/87i0J*).

Conditional tabular GAN (CTGAN)

Conditional tabular GAN (*https://oreil.ly/G_c0v*)[7] is an approach for generating tabular data. CTGAN is an adaptation of GANs that addresses issues unique to tabular data that conventional GANs cannot handle. These issues include modeling multivariate discrete and mixed discrete and continuous distributions. CTGAN explores discrete samples more evenly via a conditional generator and training-by-sampling. This mode-specific normalization helps to overcome challenges that a traditional GAN faces. Applying differentially private SGD (DP-SGD) in combination with CTGAN yields DP-CTGAN (*https://oreil.ly/H-iuj*),[8] a DP approach for generating tabular data. This involves adding random noise to the discriminator and clipping the norm to make it differentially private.

As you saw in "Private Aggregations of Teacher Ensembles" on page 230, the PATE framework protects the privacy of sensitive data during training by transferring knowledge from an ensemble of teacher models trained on partitions of the data to a student model. To achieve DP guarantees, only the student model is published while keeping the teacher model private. The framework adds Laplace noise to the aggregated answers from the teacher model that are used to train the student models. CTGAN can generate differentially private tabular data in conjunction with the PATE framework. This combination is known as PATE-CTGAN. The original data set is partitioned into k subsets, and a DP teacher discriminator is trained on each subset. Further, instead of using one generator to generate samples, k conditional generators are used for each subset of the data.

Qualified architecture to improve learning (QUAIL)

QUAIL (*https://oreil.ly/avvuE*)[9] is an ensemble model approach that combines a DP supervised learning model with a DP SD model to produce DP SD. The QUAIL framework can be used in conjunction with different synthesizer techniques. CTGAN and PATE are the basic methods we utilize in our experiments with the QUAIL ensemble approach. Note that, unlike PrivBayes, both of the QUAIL-based approaches provide an approximate DP guarantee.

SD can capture the statistical properties of a data set without containing any real-world data. This means that relationships and trends can be studied without the

---

7 Lei Xu et al., "Modeling Tabular Data Using Conditional GAN," in *Proceedings of the 33rd International Conference on Neural Information Processing Systems* (December 2019): 7335–45.

8 Mei Ling Fang, Devendra Singh Dhami, and Kristian Kersting, "DP-CTGAN: Differentially Private Medical Data Generation Using CTGANs," in *Artificial Intelligence in Medicine*, vol. 13263, eds. M. Michalowski, S. S. R. Abidi, and S. Abidi, Lecture Notes in Computer Science (Berlin: Springer, 2022): 178–88. *https://dl.acm.org/doi/10.1007/978-3-031-09342-5_17*.

9 Lucas Rosenblatt et al., "Differentially Private Synthetic Data: Applied Evaluations and Enhancements," arXiv, November 10, 2020, *https://arxiv.org/abs/2011.05537*.

risk of a privacy violation to anyone whose data is present in the data set. Recent innovations in SD include MWEM and PrivBayes, methods that can efficiently model a real-world data set and privatize the results. These methods are particularly relevant in cases where the data itself cannot be released for legal reasons but there would still be a substantial benefit from studying it.

The type of data you are studying will generally inform the best tool for the job. GANs, for example, can struggle with tabular data, so we have presented the adapted approach of CTGANs for this purpose. Similarly, microdata scenarios may be the initial motivation for choosing an SD approach, and high-dimensional data motivates the need for an approach like PrivBayes. PATE can be helpful in situations where the data cannot cross an institutional barrier; by training teacher models and transferring the knowledge to a public student model, you can learn important patterns from an otherwise inaccessible data set.

Now that you have these new tools, you can start constructing robust and powerful DP pipelines. In the next chapter, you'll learn how to do exactly this.

Potential Problems

There are several common issues you may encounter when generating SD. Some of these may sound familiar if you have worked with ML models in the past. The first is a *vanishing gradient*; this occurs when your generator isn't providing enough information for the discriminator to proceed with. In essence, your gradient is flat and your model can't move forward. If this happens, the library should throw an error alerting you.

Another potential problem is *failure to converge*, which can happen when either the generator or the discriminator starts to dominate the training process. For example, if the generator quickly learns to trick the discriminator, then it may be generating low-quality data samples and will not improve. Conversely, if the discriminator quickly starts to identify most of the samples correctly, then the generator never learns to produce higher-quality samples. In both cases, the model never converges. The library should also throw an error if convergence isn't happening quickly enough.

Another failure to watch closely, as the library won't indicate it with an error, is *mode collapse*. When mode collapse happens, the generator produces data with a single value over and over. This can happen when the generator has learned to reliably trick the discriminator with one well-tailored piece of data. The generator will then send that data point over and over to maximize its score. Think back to the term *mode* from statistics; this is the most frequently encountered value in a data set. The name *mode collapse* refers to the fact that the mode has taken over the entire data set!

Summary

SD generation is a viable option for preserving privacy in scenarios where the underlying data should not be accessed at all. By generating data with similar statistical properties, you can aid researchers without risking a privacy violation. However, these methods still need to be designed and implemented carefully to protect privacy. In this chapter, you've learned several methods for generating differentially private SD.

By now, you should understand the conditions under which SD is the optimal strategy for protecting privacy. You should be comfortable following the steps of algorithms like PrivBayes and DP-CTGAN. Finally, you should know what problems to look out for when generating SD: vanishing gradient, failure to converge, and mode collapse. These may sound familiar to you based on your previous studies. With these new tools and a solid understanding of how to use them, you are ready to generate SD responsibly.

In the next chapter, you will explore differential privacy from the other side: what are some of the more common privacy vulnerabilities, and how are privacy attacks carried out?

Exercises

1. Show that the MWEM algorithm observes ϵ-DP.

2. Run `MWEMSynthesizer` on the following columns of the Adult data set: `['work class', 'age', 'income', 'hours_per_week']`. How long does it take to complete?

    a. Preprocess the data set where the columns `workclass` and `income` are transformed as categorical. Run `MWEMSynthesizer` again. How is the result different this time?

    b. Evaluate steps 1 and 2 with ϵ =0.1, 1, 10 and `preprocessor_eps` = 0.02, 0.2, 2.0.

    c. Evaluate the synthetic data sets produced in steps 1 and 2 with ϵ = 0.01, 0.1, 1, 10 by comparing the one-way and two-way marginals of the SD with the marginals of the Adult data.

3. Run `DataGenerator`, which generates PrivBayes SD, on the Adult data set with preprocessing—what happens?

    a. Preprocess the data set where each column is categorical with at most four keys. Run `DataGenerator` again. How is the result different this time?

    b. Evaluate steps 1 and 2 with ϵ = 0.1, 1, 10.

c. Evaluate steps 1 and 2 with ϵ = 0.01, 0.1, 1, 10.

d. What are the performance differences between MWEM and PrivBayes before and after preprocessing? Which approach would you reach for first when studying data similar to the Adult data set?

4. Run DPCTGAN on the Adult data set.

a. Preprocess the data set where each column is categorical with at most four keys. Run DPCTGAN again. How is the result different this time?

b. Evaluate steps 1 and 2 with ϵ = 0.1, 1, 10.

c. When does the synthesizer experience mode collapse?

d. Evaluate steps 1 and 2 with ϵ = 0.01, 0.1, 1, 10.

e. Does the synthesizer experience mode collapse? For which values of epsilon does mode collapse happen?

## PART III

Deploying Differential Privacy

## CHAPTER 11

Protecting Your Data Against Privacy Attacks

In 2006, AOL released an anonymized data set (*https://oreil.ly/mVc6r*) of search activity from its service. This sample contained 20 million queries made by more than 650,000 users over 3 months. Although the usernames were obfuscated, many of the search queries themselves contained personally identifiable information. This resulted in several users being identified and matched to their accounts and search history.[1]

This release led to the resignation of two senior staff members and a class action lawsuit that was settled in 2013. It also caused enormous harm to AOL's public image and exposed the identities of real people who were using the service with the assumption that their privacy would be protected.

This chapter discusses attacks on data releases and how differential privacy can protect against them. While Chapters 1 and 9 briefly touched on privacy attacks, this chapter discusses a much wider variety of attacks in greater detail. The ramifications of each type of attack are also discussed: attacks may be used to reconstruct an individual's data, or they may be used to infer if an individual exists in a data set.

The attacks are explained from the perspective of two parties: a data analyst and a data curator. To ensure the protections on the data are robust enough to protect the privacy of individuals, assume that the data analyst harbors the worst intentions: the analyst is an adversary who is determined to violate the privacy of individuals in the sensitive data set. Fortunately, differential privacy shares this assumption

---

1 In one particular stroke of journalistic brilliance, the *New York Times* (*https://oreil.ly/5R8jL*) was able to re-identify a 62-year-old woman in Georgia just from her search queries.

and strengthens it by assuming that the adversary has potentially unbounded computational power and access to auxiliary information. Note that even though differential privacy makes these strong assumptions, many privacy attacks can be practically deployed without either assumption.

This chapter assumes an *interactive model*, where the adversary can interactively communicate with the data curator. In many scenarios, the data curator only makes one static release. This is a trivial case of the interactive model, where there is only one round of communication from the curator to the adversary. Thus, the interactive model and techniques discussed in this chapter are just as applicable when the curator makes a one-time release.

This chapter starts with an overly generous data curator, who only removes personally identifying columns before sharing the sensitive data set with an adversary. As the chapter progresses, these increasingly sophisticated attacks are discussed and demonstrated:

- Record linkage
- Singling out
- Differencing
- Reconstruction via systems of equations
- Tracing
- k-anonymity vulnerabilities

These attacks require imposing certain minimal restrictions on the communication between the adversary and the data curator that will maintain the privacy of individuals in the sensitive data set. A general pattern emerges in that restrictions intended to thwart a certain kind of attack are not guaranteed to protect against all attacks. To protect against all possible attacks, one needs the formal mathematical guarantees provided by differential privacy.

Definition of a Privacy Violation

There is a common refrain in the data privacy community: statistical inference is not a privacy violation. To qualify as a privacy attack, the attack must be able to reveal information about a specific individual. Thus, an attack technique is not considered here if it is only able to infer group-level or demographic information. The attacks discussed in this chapter result in three kinds of privacy violations: membership inference, reconstruction, and re-identification.

A *membership inference* attack is used to determine if an individual is a member of the data set. In some cases, just leaking that an individual is in a certain data set can cause serious harm. This kind of sensitivity occurs in many contexts, including health care information, human research data, and refugee data. For example, being exposed as a member of a medical trial may imply that a person has a certain medical condition.

Microdata reconstruction is a greater privacy violation than membership inference, but it is also more difficult to execute.

Microdata
> Individual-level data that "provide[s] information about characteristics of individual people or entities such as households, business enterprises, facilities, farms or even geographical areas such as villages or towns."[2]

Examples of microdata include an individual's email address or name. Note that microdata reconstruction does not imply complete identification of the individual, though it is a superset of membership inference: if a privacy attack is capable of microdata reconstruction, then it is also capable of membership inference. Although microdata reconstruction does not necessarily imply re-identification, any microdata reconstruction vulnerability is just one linkage attack away from re-identification.

Re-identification occurs when the attacker can uniquely identify who a piece of microdata belongs to. Not only has the attacker learned that the individual is in the data set, but they have also learned enough attributes to uniquely re-identify them. This is sometimes done via publicly available data or another private data set. In the next section, you will learn about the ways that an attacker can leverage multiple data sources to re-identify individuals. The three types of attacks discussed here represent increasing levels of information gained about an individual, as shown in Figure 11-1.

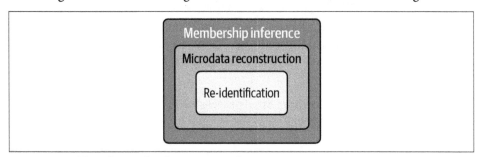

Figure 11-1. The relationship between attack types

---

2 For more about microdata, see the World Bank Data Help Desk (*https://oreil.ly/vlUVv*).

Attacks on Tabular Data Sets

The first attacks discussed in this chapter focus on the statistical analysis of *tabular data sets*. Tabular data is characterized by structured data sets organized in rows and columns, such as a table in a relational database or a CSV file. In this section, you will learn about attacks that specifically target vulnerabilities in tabular data.

Record Linkage

A *record linkage* attack leverages an auxiliary data set with uniquely identified individuals to re-identify individuals in a sensitive data set. This kind of attack is applicable if the attacker has access to the microdata, or *row-level access*, to the sensitive data set. Row-level access means that the adversary can read a row from the original data set (or at least a subset of a row).

A data curator with the best intentions to protect the privacy of individuals in their data still grants row-level access to the data if they release their data set with personally identifying columns removed. That is, removing names and Social Security numbers from your data set still exposes individuals in your data set to record linkage attacks.

In "Privatization Before Differential Privacy" on page 6, you learned about a well-known record linkage attack conducted by researcher Latanya Sweeney, who was then a graduate student at MIT. In this attack, she uncovered medical information about Bill Weld, then-governor of Massachusetts.[3] The Massachusetts Group Insurance Commission (GIC) collected hospital visit microdata that included information about the patient's diagnosis, procedure, medication, zip code, birth date, and sex, among many other attributes. GIC then made this data available to researchers and, commercially, to industry.

Sweeney purchased a copy of the voter registration list of Cambridge, Massachusetts, for $20. In addition to names and addresses, the voter registration list contained zip codes, birth dates, and gender, which overlapped with the same columns in the GIC data.

> According to the Cambridge Voter list, six people had [Weld's] particular birth date; only three of them were men; and, he was the only one in his 5-digit ZIP code.
>
> —Latanya Sweeney

Sweeney then mailed the governor his own medical information. This kind of vulnerability isn't difficult to carry out: in fact, Sweeney discovered that 87% of the US population are uniquely identified by their date of birth, gender, and zip.

---

3 Latanya Sweeney, "k-Anonymity: A Model for Protecting Privacy," *International Journal of Uncertainty, Fuzziness and Knowledge-Based Systems*, 10, no. 5 (October 2002): 557–70.

Example: teacher survey

Say a data curator has a teacher survey that they want to share with the public. The columns of the data set are described in the following code snippet:

```
import pandas as pd
df = pd.read_csv("teacher_survey.csv")
df.columns = ['name',
              'sex',
              'age',
              'maritalStatus',
              'hasChildren',
              'highestEducationLevel',
              'sourceOfStress',
              'smoker',
              'optimism',
              'lifeSatisfaction',
              'selfEsteem']
```

Before releasing this data set, the data curator attempts to anonymize it by removing the name column. Unfortunately, the name column is not the only column that can be used to re-identify an individual:

```
# Naively "anonymize" by removing the name column
del df["name"]
```

Now switch your perspective to that of an adversary who would like to re-identify their coworker's data. All you need to do is filter the data set down to those rows that match attributes you know about your coworker. The following predicate applies to only one row in the data set:

```
df.loc[(df['sex'] == 3) & (df['age'] == 27)]
```

You've now violated the privacy of your coworker by gaining access to all of your coworker's survey responses.

The attack is easier to execute if your coworker has any particularly distinctive attributes. If the predicate matches more than one record, you may still be able to resolve the ambiguity by collecting more information about the target of interest and refining the predicate. If the ambiguity cannot be resolved, you still gain probabilistic information about the target's responses. That is, if four records are matched, and three are smokers, then you've learned that your coworker is likely a smoker.

In this attack, the adversary took advantage of *quasi-identifiers* in the data set.

Quasi-identifier
A quasi-identifier is a column that is not personally identifying but can be used to link records in a data set to records in another data set.

Unfortunately, nearly any column in a data set can be used as a quasi-identifier, meaning it is difficult to protect against these attacks by simply removing columns.

In this example linkage attack, the adversary was able to link records in a data set to a trivial auxiliary data set of one record. This attack can easily be generalized to auxiliary data sets with more than one record by using a database join instead of a filter. In practice, many commercially available data sets can be used as auxiliary data sets.

Linkage attacks are often the second phase of a privacy attack, used to enrich row-level microdata that has been extracted from another attack. Linkage attacks escalate what was once just microdata reconstruction to full re-identification.

If you wanted to employ differential privacy to privately release the microdata, you could imagine using locally differentially private mechanisms with parallel composition over the row space and sequential composition over the column space. It quickly becomes apparent that the statistical utility of the data release is poor compared to central DP. The privacy loss parameters grow in size proportional to the number of columns in the data, and significant noise must be added to each entry. Another failure of this approach is that the primary benefit of local DP is not realized—a central authority, the data curator, still has access to data in the clear. These drawbacks are to be expected; while differential privacy could be used to release the microdata, this is not the ideal point to apply DP because the release would consist of a very large body of microdata that is highly sensitive in nature.

At this point, the data curator prevents re-identification via linkage attacks by trying to deny access to microdata completely. The data curator instead creates a portal from which the public can pose queries to be run on the data. This begins a battle of wits between the adversary and the data curator. While preventing access to microdata thwarts record linkage attacks, this is easier said than done. If the data curator does answer the queries via differential privacy, then the adversary can still gain access to microdata via *singling out, differencing,* and *reconstruction.*

Singling Out

In response to the data curator restricting access to the microdata, the adversary updates their strategy to use queries that *single out* individuals. A query singles out an individual when it contains a predicate that uniquely identifies an individual. If the data curator answers any query that singles out an individual, they unknowingly give the attacker access to microdata.

This attack takes advantage of the false assumption that data aggregations, like the mean, afford privacy to individuals in the data. While the example query of counting the number of smokers in the given demographic may seem benign, it extracts the smoking status of the previously targeted coworker:

```
df.loc[(df['sex'] == 3) & (df['age'] == 27)]['smoking'].sum()
```

Singling out is more difficult to defend against than you might expect. A data curator may unknowingly single out an individual by releasing statistics grouped by several attributes. For instance, consider a query of the smoking rates in the teacher survey example. If this query is grouped by *sex* and *age*, it singles out the individuals in any group of size one, which definitively reveals their smoking status.

The data curator may try to protect against singling out by refusing to answer any query that matches a single individual. While this approach prevents microdata reconstruction, it still allows for membership inference.

 If the data curator rejects any query that singles out an individual, then the refusal to answer the query gives the adversary sufficient information to distinguish whether the target individual exists in the data set.

If you want to employ differential privacy to release the singling-out query, then you'll notice that the utility of these kinds of queries works out to be very poor. This poor utility is, perhaps counterintuitively, ideal. In the query discussed previously, the range of the query will be no greater in magnitude than the sensitivity of the query. Therefore, any signal provided by the query will be dwarfed by the noise scale. Legitimate queries involve data sets of greater size, where the range of the query dwarfs the noise scale. This is the typical behavior of DP methods, stemming from how the noise scale is calibrated according to the sensitivity of each query.

Suppose the data analyst is reluctant to employ differential privacy, opting instead to refuse any query with a predicate that matches fewer than k records. Intuitively, a higher threshold should admit stronger protections. Unfortunately, any choice of threshold will prove unsatisfactory.

Differencing Attack

The *differencing attack* circumvents thresholding-based protections against microdata reconstruction by distributing the attack over more than one query. In this attack, an adversary simply computes the difference between two carefully crafted queries. Just like singling out, since this attack is potent enough to reconstruct microdata, it is also possible to use differencing attacks to infer membership.

Returning to the teacher survey example, the adversary can craft two queries for which the predicates match a reasonably large number of individuals but still differ by only a single individual. Once they receive the answers to these two queries, they can simply compute the difference:

```
predicate_a = (df['maritalStatus'] == 'Un-Married')
predicate_b = ((df['maritalStatus'] == 'Un-Married') | \
    (df['sex'] == 3) & (df['age'] == 27))
df.loc[predicate_a]["smoker"].sum() - df.loc[predicate_b]["smoker"].sum()
```

This differencing attack with two queries is relatively easy to see through, but the adversary can just as easily set the trap over a larger set of queries or take advantage of auxiliary information to make the predicate seem more general than it is. For instance, if the adversary already knew the number of unmarried teachers in the data set, then they would only need to submit the second query. Auxiliary information makes it impossible for a data curator to guard agains differencing attacks because the data curator has no way of recognizing queries that may single out individuals in the data set.

Differencing attacks are also particularly easy to execute over temporal data, where it is natural to want to compare differences between time-steps.

The differencing attack may also be carried out with just a single query. If the adversary asked for the smoking rate, and all members of the group share the same survey answer, none of the individuals in the group benefit from plausible deniability. Otherwise, the smoking rate within a small group can be used to give a probabilistic estimate of the coworker's smoking status. Such a probabilistic estimate can be refined by collecting auxiliary information about other individuals in the group.

If you wanted to employ differential privacy to release the pair of differencing queries, then you'll notice that the utility of each query in isolation remains high but the utility of their difference is very poor. In this case, the privacy loss parameters are split between two queries, resulting in two instances of noise addition that are each twice as large. Since the variance of the difference between two random variables is simply the sum of the variances, then under basic rules of probability, the variance of the difference is now four times greater than it was in the singling-out attack. As discussed before, the variance of the query in the singling-out attack was already untenable.

At this point, the data curator is left without recourse: any incoming query may potentially violate privacy. There is some consolation here: the adversary must very carefully and manually craft queries that will only gain them a single attribute, and the adversary also must have significant auxiliary information.

Reconstruction via Systems of Equations

The methods shown in this section provide a more practical approach to exploit the information in a set of aggregate queries to reconstruct multiple rows. Reconstructing the entire data set by replicating the differencing attack multiple times is inefficient, because one query may be useful for reconstructing more than one entry in the data set. Both approaches are also difficult to scale up to many records because the adversary must be able to craft queries that single out each individual.

The previous two attacks can be rephrased as simple systems of equations to solve for a single entry in the data set. The singling-out query is a particularly simple system, consisting of one equation, and the differencing attack involves a system of up to k equations. In this section, you will learn how to randomly construct a system of equations that can be used to solve for/reconstruct an arbitrarily large subset of the data set.

In this example, the goal of the adversary is to craft a set of predicates that will provide sufficient information to reconstruct the entire smoker column from the voter survey data set. At this point, it is necessary to define the query interface that will be broken:

```python
import pandas as pd
import numpy as np

data = pd.read_csv('sequestered_data.csv')


def query_interface(predicates, target):
    """Count the number of smokers that satisfy each predicate.
    Resembles a public query interface on a sequestered data set.

    :param predicates: a list of predicates on the public variables
    :param target: column to filter against
    :returns a 1-d np.ndarray of exact answers to the subset sum queries"""

    # 1. data curator checks predicates
    # 2. data curator executes and returns queries:
    query_matrix = np.stack([pred(data) for pred in predicates], axis=1)
    return data[target].values @ query_matrix
```

An adversary may submit a set of queries like so:

```python
query_interface([
    lambda data: data['sex'] == 1,           # "is-female" predicate
    lambda data: data['maritalStatus'] == 1, # "is-married" predicate
], target="smoker")
```

To expedite the process of selecting suitable predicate functions, the adversary might construct them randomly, using a hashing scheme:

```python
# TODO: define pub
pub = None


def make_random_predicate():
    """Returns a (pseudo)random predicate function by
        hashing public identifiers."""
    prime = 691
```

```
    desc = np.random.randint(prime, size=len(pub))
    # this predicate maps data into a 1-d ndarray of booleans
    #   (where `@` is the dot product and `%` modulus)
    return lambda data: ((data[pub].values @ desc) % prime % 2).astype(bool)

# Example usage
random_predicate = make_random_predicate()
num_smokers_that_matched_random_predicate = query_interface([random_predicate],
                                                             "smoker")

# The boolean mask from applying the example predicate to the data:
```

If we consider the predicate mask A, a column x that describes if the individual is a smoker, and the subset sum answers b, then we need to find the x that minimizes $|Ax - b|^2$. The target column is equivalent to the least squares solution, assuming that the public variables uniquely identify each individual:

```
def reconstruction_attack(data_pub, predicates, answers):
    """Reconstructs a target column based on the `answers` to queries
       about `data`.

    :param data_pub: data of length n consisting of public identifiers
    :param predicates: a list of k predicate functions
    :param answers: a list of k answers to a query on data filtered by the
                    k predicates
    :return 1-dimensional boolean ndarray"""
    masks = np.stack([pred(data_pub) for pred in predicates])
    return np.linalg.lstsq(masks, answers, rcond=None)[0] > 0.5
```

We're now ready to carry out the attack. Generate a large set of random queries, submit them to the query interface, and then find the least squares solution:

```
predicates = [make_random_predicate() for _ in range(2 * len(data))]
exact_answers = query_interface(predicates, "smoker")

# generate example predicates and compute example query answers
reconstructed_target = reconstruction_attack(
    data_pub=data[pub], predicates=predicates, answers=exact_answers)

target = 'smoker'
# complete reconstruction of the target column
assert np.array_equal(reconstructed_target, data[target])
```

This approach circumvents all ad hoc protections placed on the data thus far, giving the adversary the ability to reconstruct the smoker column.

Multiple columns can be reconstructed at once by augmenting the queries and system of equations. In this example, the number of queries is chosen to be high enough to exactly reconstruct the data. The adversary may be able to reconstruct the microdata with fewer queries by choosing predicate functions that are maximally entropic instead of random, and by allowing some uncertainty in the reconstructed microdata.

In practice, it is not necessary to perfectly reconstruct the microdata to carry out a record linkage attack.

Yet again, differential privacy provides a robust counter to this approach. This attack is most potent when it maximally exploits parallel composition. If the attack were adjusted to do so, it would still be no more effective than the singling-out attack. Since the privacy loss parameters grow commensurately with the number of queries made on the data, the singling-out attack for a single data entry remains the most practical attack.

One limitation of this example is that it assumes an interactive model, where the adversary can choose their queries. In practice, the attack is still just as applicable to static data releases by the data curator. One must reconstruct the predicate mask A for data releases, based on the queries the data curator has provided.

There are examples showing this has been done. Many statistical agencies, like the US Census Bureau, make data releases of grouped queries at many levels of disaggregation. These releases are just as vulnerable to the same attack. The US Census Bureau conducted a proof-of-concept reconstruction attack, with the aid of detailed geography data that has not been made publicly available, that admits microdata reconstruction including sex, age, race, and ethnicity on the 2010 Census data. The reconstructed microdata was then subjected to a record linkage attack against commercial databases, resulting in a confirmed re-identification of 52 million persons.

Another limitation of this example is that the target column must be binary. This is manageable: when the target column is not binary, any numeric column can be binned into a categorical column, and any categorical column can be binarized via a one-hot encoding. For example, if the column to reconstruct consisted of age, then age could be reconstructed to arbitrary precision by choosing the binning granularity and number of queries commensurately. Similarly, categorical predicates can easily be converted to an ordinal encoding.

One limitation of this approach is the computational requirements. Notice that the number of unknowns in the system of equations grows linearly in the size of the data set.

When the data set is very large, it becomes more computationally feasible to rephrase the problem as a constraint satisfaction problem and to use a SAT solver.[4]

---

4 Boolean Satisfiability Problem.

Tracing

Tracing is a kind of membership inference attack that leverages a reference sample from the population.[5] This attack can still accurately infer membership when the data curator uses privacy-enhancing techniques to distort releases, if privacy parameters are chosen poorly. When the attack was invented and publicized, it significantly reduced the gap between the worst-case privacy guarantees (in terms of differential privacy loss parameters) and real-world attacks. This section discusses an abridged version of the attack to demonstrate the ideas behind tracing.

Assume the adversary has a coworker named Alice. Just like in previous attacks, the adversary collects auxiliary information about Alice, storing it in the `individual` variable. The adversary collects several mean `answers` on different data subsets and columns by either submitting queries to a query interface or collecting information from a data release. Finally, the adversary collects a reference sample from the population to form a baseline to compare against.

The core idea of the attack is that, if the answers on the private data set are more similar to the targeted individual than they are to the reference sample from the population, the targeted individual is likely to be a member of the private data set:

```
import numpy as np


def membership_attack(individual, answers, reference_samples, alpha=.05):
    """Perform membership attack using dwork et al. test statistic.
    See figure 1 in
    https://privacytools.seas.harvard.edu/files/privacytools/files/robust.pdf

    :param individual: y, a boolean vector of shape (d,)
    :param answers: q, a float vector with elements in [0, 1] of shape (d,)
    :param reference_samples: z, a boolean vector of length (1, d)
    :param alpha: statistical significance
    :return: True if alice is in data with (1-alpha)100% confidence."""
    individual = individual * 2 - 1
    answers = answers * 2 - 1
    reference_samples = reference_samples * 2 - 1

    alice_similarity = np.dot(individual, answers) # cosine similarity
    reference_similarity = np.dot(reference_samples[0], answers)
    statistic = alice_similarity - reference_similarity

    d = len(individual)
    tau = np.sqrt(8 * d * np.log(1 / alpha))
    return statistic > tau
```

---

5 Cynthia Dwork et al., "Robust Traceability from Trace Amounts," in *2015 IEEE 56th Annual Symposium on Foundations of Computer Science* (Piscataway, NJ: IEEE, 2015): 650–69.

The attack itself is very simple: first, all three variables are normalized. The cosine similarity is then used to measure the distance between `individual` and `answers`, and between `population` and `answers`. The test statistic is simply the comparison of these distances, being positive if the queries are more similar to Alice's and negative if the queries are more similar to the population.

Just like any standard statistical hypothesis test, the test statistic is compared to the predicted value tau. If the test statistic exceeds tau, then Alice is a member of the private data set with $(1 - \alpha)100\%$ confidence.

As mentioned previously, this test has been abridged but has more complicated variations that can detect membership in the private data set with greater statistical power.

k-Anonymity Vulnerabilities

Another form of ad hoc privacy protection is *k-anonymity*. This is a popular approach to data anonymization that is susceptible to record linkage attacks, as you first learned in Chapter 1. To employ k-anonymity, the data curator must first follow these steps:

1. Remove any identifying columns.
2. Identify all columns that are likely to be used as quasi-identifiers.

This guarantees that there are always at least K records corresponding to any given combination of the quasi-identifiers. You can do this by either suppressing quasi-identifiers (removing them from the data set as well) or generalizing (re-binning them with less granularity).

A core issue of k-anonymity is that it is impossible to determine just what a quasi-identifier is. This means that this approach to privacy is susceptible to auxiliary information held by the adversary. In practice, just about any column may be used as a quasi-identifier, and labeling too many columns as quasi-identifiers destroys the utility of the analysis.

In the teacher survey data set, every column could be used as a quasi-identifier. If you wanted any utility from k-anonymity, then you wouldn't be able to label optimism, life satisfaction, and self-esteem as quasi-identifiers. Unfortunately, you can still use these attributes to disambiguate the exact record belonging to your coworker from the set matched by the quasi-identifiers (by k-anonymity, a set of size at least K).

Even if you have columns in your data that are not quasi-identifiers, privacy can still be trivially violated in the case where all K records share the same answer on the attribute of interest. This is the same vulnerability that is encountered when a singling-out query returns a small result set, as discussed in "Singling Out" on page

260. Individuals in that group either lose plausible deniability or are subject to a probabilistic inference that is vulnerable to refinement from auxiliary information.

Let's look at an example of a k-anonymity vulnerability. Suppose you work for ABC Health, an insurance provider. The company wants to release information on drugs they are covering for patients across the country. You are tasked with making the data 3-anonymous, supposedly to protect patient privacy. The data you receive has the structure shown in Table 11-1.

Table 11-1. Medicines prescribed to patients

Name	Age	Sex	Address	Zip code	Medicines
Nicolas	24	M	Semkins 93487 Knutson Circle Suite 48	27529	Atorvastatin
Carolus	84	M	Jerzycowski 870 Mosinee Place	85224	Omeprazole
Crystal	27	F	Dumbreck 34 Arizona Drive	20735	Etoposide
Rubetta	59	F	Clemonts 2082 Gateway Park	02368	Amlodipine
Lizabeth	27	F	Robottom 424 Forster Pass 16th Floor	20735	Etoposide
Fletcher	63	M	Androlli 2999 Dennis Park Apt 866	48127	Albuterol
Olive	27	F	Nollet 6075 Grayhawk Road Apt 1560	20735	Etoposide
Mellie	19	F	Wiffen 45 Clarendon Alley Apt 1623	02138	Atorvastatin
Colby	77	M	Galiero 1 Esker Junction 7th Floor	20735	Atorvastatin
Dahlia	46	F	Etoile 459 Dovetail Drive Suite 81	06514	Hydrocodone
…	…	…	…	…	…

The name and address fields are clearly identifiers, so you suppress them and generalize the age column to be ranges rather than specific ages. You note that the data is now 3-anonymous, as shown in Table 11-2.

Table 11-2. Medicines prescribed to patients (3-anonymous)

Name	Age	Sex	Address	Zip code	Medicines
*	18–24	M	*	27529	Atorvastatin
*	80–85	M	*	85224	Omeprazole
*	25–30	F	*	20735	Etoposide
*	55–60	F	*	02368	Amlodipine
*	25–30	F	*	20735	Etoposide
*	60–65	M	*	48127	Albuterol
*	25–30	F	*	20735	Etoposide
*	18–24	F	*	02138	Atorvastatin
*	75–80	M	*	20735	Atorvastatin
*	45–50	F	*	06514	Hydrocodone
…	…	…	…	…	…

Let's examine a sample slice of the data that results in three identical identifier rows (Table 11-3): patients with $(age, sex, zip\ code) = (25 - 30, F, 20735)$.

Table 11-3. An example subset of the data

Name	Age	Sex	Address	Zip code	Medicines
*	25–30	F	*	20735	Etoposide
*	25–30	F	*	20735	Etoposide
*	25–30	F	*	20735	Etoposide

Each member of this group is taking the same medicine. This means that the group is homogeneous, making it susceptible to the following homogeneity attack:

1. You know someone whose health insurance is provided by ABC Health.
2. You know that they are between 25 and 30 years old, female, and live in the zip code 20735.
3. From the available data, you know that they have been prescribed Etoposide.

A quick online search will reveal that Etoposide is a medication to treat various cancers. The homogeneity of the data has allowed you to use non-sensitive information (age, sex, zip code) to learn a sensitive piece of information (a cancer diagnosis).

Attacks on Machine Learning

This section discusses alternative attacks that are applicable in an ML context. In this context, it is unusual to release grouped queries or use predicates. The adversary in these attacks is assumed to have access to the model parameters and intends to violate the privacy of individuals in the training data. The previously discussed attacks may still be applied to attack the data set used for inference and model scoring.

There is a broad literature that tailors attacks to specific ML problems. For instance, recommender systems based on collaborative filtering are particularly susceptible to differencing attacks because recommendations are continually updated in response to new data.

A privacy violation is more stringent than you might expect. For instance, consider *model inversion*, which is a technique where an adversary attempts to recover the training data set from learned parameters. Model inversion does not necessarily constitute a privacy violation. This is because a well-generalized model aims to preserve the statistical properties of the population, rather than individual training examples. A well-generalized model will more likely only retain the statistical properties within subpopulations, leading to a "reconstructed" data set whose records don't relate to individual records in the training data.

Regardless, there is an abundance of neural networks large enough to memorize vital information about individuals in the training data. In these cases, the attacks are very similar in nature to those we've discussed already: data set reconstruction (in whole or in part) and membership inference. As a general rule, privacy attacks are more potent when models are over-fitted or when the training data lacks diversity.

Summary

There are many ad hoc protections that a data curator may use to prevent specific vulnerabilities: only releasing aggregates, refusing queries based on attributes of the query or data, and k-anonymity. There is no end to ad hoc protections and the attacks that circumvent them.

If the data analyst starts adding noise to query results, then the adversary can simply average repeated queries to reduce the variance of the noise. If the data analyst uses the query itself as a seed for a random number generator, such that the answer is always the same for the same query, then the adversary can simply submit many equivalent formulations of the same query that each results in different seeding. Using seeds for random number generators opens another class of vulnerabilities, in that the seed itself can be reconstructed to predict and strip the noise out of the answer.

Other ad hoc protections include swapping attributes of the data, rounding answers, and random sampling, all met with questionable utility and continued vulnerabilities. A data curator employing ad hoc protections can never be confident that their protections are effective, nor that the privacy of individuals in their data is preserved. This motivates the more formal, mathematically justified approach of differential privacy. DP is an approach that works equally well regardless of the underlying data set, computational capabilities, or auxiliary knowledge of the attacker.

While the attacks shown in this chapter motivate the use of differential privacy, DP can only mitigate privacy attacks if the privacy loss parameters are chosen appropriately. While many of these attacks are completely foiled by the use of differential privacy, there are some, particularly the membership inference attacks related to tracing, that may still be viable when the privacy loss parameters are set too loosely.

Keep in mind that the protections afforded are only as strong as the privacy loss parameters. Choosing privacy loss parameters depends on several factors, including data privacy regulations, frequency of data publication, and data utility. In the next chapter, you will learn about parameter decision-making and the privacy-versus-utility compromise.

Exercises

1. Explain how differential privacy addresses each of the attacks discussed in this chapter.

   a. Record linkage

   b. Singling out

   c. Differencing

   d. Reconstruction via systems of equations

   e. Tracing

   f. k-anonymity

2. In season 5, episode 1 of *The Office*, the company is competing in a weight loss challenge. The employees are standing on an industrial scale to measure their aggregate weight, which reads 2,336 pounds. One of them realizes that the receptionist, Pam, will be leaving soon and shouldn't be counted. She gets off the scale, which now reads 2,210 pounds. Kevin, an accountant, does some quick mental math and concludes that Pam weighs 226 pounds.

   a. Kevin's innumeracy aside, what kind of attack has he tried to commit here?

   b. Design a scale that protects against this type of scenario.

## CHAPTER 12

Defining Privacy Loss Parameters of a Data Release

Featuring Jayshree Sarathy[1]

Differential privacy delineates a trade-off between privacy and utility, with both attributes influenced by various parameters. Taking advantage of this trade-off requires understanding how to set these parameters to achieve your data curation and analysis goals. These choices must be informed by contextual needs around privacy and accuracy—as a choice of parameters may be appropriate in one situation and ineffective in another—and potentially with input from various parties who have a stake in the data.

Some of the decisions that are described in this chapter will be made by the data curator, an individual or organization that is responsible for making decisions around access and disclosure limitations for the data set in question. Other decisions must be made by a data analyst, who must work within the constraints set by the data curator to make the best possible uses of the data for their analysis goals.

Understanding the various parameters that affect privacy and utility is central to making good decisions as a DP data curator and for creating useful analyses within these constraints as a data analyst. Furthermore, it is important to be able to communicate these decisions to other stakeholders to allow them to work appropriately with the data. Fortunately, numerous technical methods facilitate choosing these parameters. Like all matters in differential privacy, there are benefits and challenges

---

1 Jayshree Sarathy is a senior research fellow and incoming assistant professor at Northeastern University where she brings together perspectives from computer science and science and technology studies. Her work focuses on making differential privacy usable for practitioners and attentive to contextual needs. More broadly, her research explores the social and political dimensions of open data projects, highlighting the challenges of producing transparent, trustworthy data.

to every parameter selection process, but understanding your unique situation will allow you to make the best decision possible.

One of the main decisions the data owner must make is bounding the privacy loss. Privacy loss can be thought of as a random variable that is defined by the following log ratio:[2]

$$\ln \frac{\Pr\left[M(x) \in S\right]}{\Pr\left[M(x') \in S\right]}$$

For the standard approximate-DP definition, these are called ϵ and δ, as defined in Chapter 2. Experts recommend that epsilon be set to a small value between 0.01 and 1, although many deployments tend to choose a much higher value. As you've seen in previous chapters, epsilon defines a bound on the difference between distributions over outputs for any computation run on neighboring data sets.

Delta, on the other hand, should be set to much smaller than $1/n$, where n is the size of the data set; for example, a standard setting of delta is 10^{-6}. You can think of delta as bounding the "edge case" differences between these shifted distributions, for example, if the support of the distribution is slightly different for two neighboring data sets.

In this chapter, you will learn how to:

- Choose privacy loss parameters (e.g., ϵ and δ) to suit the deployment's context and goals
- Make decisions about sampling method and metadata parameters with privacy in mind
- Create organizational practices around data that enable clearer decision-making
- Solicit feedback and communicate about the choice of parameters

Sampling

The privacy loss parameter is one of the most important policy decisions that the data curator[3] must make about a deployment, but other parameters affect privacy. Some of these parameters arise in the data collection stage, such as whether the data comes from a secret sample. Here, *secret sample* means that the set of data subjects chosen from the broader population is confidential knowledge. The sample size, population

---

2 x and x' are adjacent data sets.

3 See Chapter 1 for a definition and introduction to data curators and other DP roles.

---

size, and sampling method can all affect the privacy-utility trade-off. A secret, simple, random sample, for example, can amplify the privacy guarantee, allowing one to gain more utility for the same privacy loss.

Other types of sampling methods may not provide additional privacy guarantees. Consider *cluster sampling*, where a population is divided into disjoint subgroups (called *clusters*) and then one of these clusters is randomly selected as the sample, as shown in Figure 12-1. Such an approach can be advantageous for performing market research and constructing geographical clusters to minimize travel time when conducting interviews.

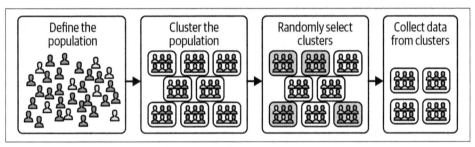

Figure 12-1. Selecting clusters from a population

For small cluster sizes, you can achieve privacy amplification via cluster sampling. However, as the cluster sizes grow, the amplification degrades, to the point that eventually there will be no additional privacy advantage. Further, if the clusters are sufficiently different from one another, then a private algorithm can infer which data points are in the sample, meaning that there is a negligible advantage from the privacy of the sample.[4] This is still an active area of research at the time of publication. Privacy amplification by subsampling also appears in Chapter 6, where a mathematical justification for why this technique improves privacy in the case of a simple sample is discussed.

Metadata Parameters

Some decisions affect utility as well as privacy, and these can be made by both the data curator and the data analyst. One such decision is the choice of metadata parameters, such as inputting ranges for numerical variables and categories for categorical variables.

---

4 Mark Bun et al., "Controlling Privacy Loss in Sampling Schemes: An Analysis of Stratified and Cluster Sampling," in *3rd Symposium on Foundations of Responsible Computing (FORC 2022)* (Schloss Dagstuhl: Leibniz-Zentrum fur Informatik, 2022).

Why are data curators and analysts asked to input these metadata parameters? Data sets in the wild may have an infinite range or set of categories; this means the sensitivity of statistics computed on this data could be unbounded, which can pose a problem for maintaining the privacy guarantee. Therefore, many DP algorithms require the inputs to be bounded or for the curator/analyst to set a clipping bound for the inputs to bound the privacy loss of the release.

However, these bounds and categories must be data-independent; they cannot be taken straight from the data set, but rather should come from knowledge about the data domain and its collection. For example, the range for an age variable should not be the min and max of ages in the data set, but rather $[0, 120]$ (for a data set potentially containing any human) or $[0, 18]$ (for a data set on children). Similarly, the categories for an education variable should not simply be those present in the data set, but should come from a codebook of educational levels for this data domain.

Selecting these parameters independently of the data set is critical for maintaining the desired privacy guarantee. However, these parameters also impact data utility. Ranges or categories that are too limited may introduce more bias into the statistics, but parameters that are too broad may introduce more variance. Therefore, while the data curator is responsible for choosing these parameters due to their deep knowledge of the data domain, data analysts are typically also able to tune these parameters to achieve their bias-variance goals.

Allocating Privacy Loss Budget

Once the data curator has decided on privacy loss parameters for the release, i.e., the global privacy loss budget, the curator can then allocate this budget among different releases and analysts. For example, the curator may want to use 50% of the budget to do an initial DP release of basic summary statistics about the data set, such as histograms of key variables. The other 50% can then be allocated among analysts at different institutions, who can request additional statistics beyond the initial release.

Analysts, too, are responsible for allocating their portion of the privacy loss budget among different statistics. There are different ways to do this: one can divide the privacy loss portion equally across the statistics, spend more of the budget on statistics that provide richer information (such as sufficient statistics) or context (such as CDFs of variables), or allocate the budget to satisfy accuracy goals. For the latter option, some tools allow the analyst to "fix" the desired accuracy of a statistic, such as the size of the 95% confidence interval around a DP mean, and will automatically compute the correct allocation of the privacy loss budget to achieve this goal.

There are three key challenges with allocating a privacy loss budget. First, curators and analysts must contend with the inevitable trade-off between privacy and accuracy; the more the budget is split across analysts and statistics, the lower the accuracy will be for each analysis.

Second, the budget must be allocated before releasing/computing of the DP statistics. This may make it hard to do exploratory data analysis, as it may be unknown a priori which statistics are more important and informative for the goals of the analysis. This will be discussed later in "Making These Decisions in the Context of Exploratory Data Analysis" on page 283.

Third, the privacy loss budget is a finite resource—it must be shared across data users. This means that the allocation of the budget is a visible policy choice on the part of the data curator. This transparency makes it easier to solicit feedback around which users may benefit from a larger share of the budget, but it may also make these decisions more contentious as stakeholders begin to view allocation as a zero-sum game. We will discuss this more at the conclusion of the chapter.

Practices That Aid Decision-Making

As we've discussed, many decisions go into the DP data curation and analysis process. Making these decisions can feel overwhelming, especially because you will get only one (or a few) shot(s) to analyze the data. Remember that any do-overs will result in additional privacy loss. Therefore, in this section, we discuss data practices that will help you make the best decisions possible. These practices start even before the process of data collection and extend throughout data analysis and distribution.

Codebook and Data Annotation

First, for the data curator, we recommend creating a codebook even before collecting data. The codebook should also make use of and delineate other public information that is useful for this release, such as:

- Information that is invariant across all potential input data sets.
- Information that is publicly available from other sources.
- Information from other DP releases. See Section 3 of the OpenDP Documentation (*https://oreil.ly/XrDi0*) for more on this and an example.

In particular, the codebook should detail the sampling information, such as the sample frame, sampling method, and what steps may or may not be taken to protect the secrecy of the sample. Next, it should contain all the variables (i.e., column names) that will be collected and their metadata parameters, such as type of variable, variable bounds, and variable categories. Third, the codebook should specify how the data curator will deal with missing or erroneous values. It is important that, to the extent possible, this codebook is created before data collection, as that will ensure that the information included is not derived from the data set itself and therefore does not leak individual-level information. The curator should still take care to not include any group-level sensitive information if the codebook is to be shared publicly.

After the data is collected and processed, we recommend that the curator go back and further annotate the data set. For this, we recommend using the "datasheets for data sets" template[5] or something similar to collate relevant information. While it may not be obvious how some of these questions relate to DP, all of this information is critical for curating data ethically and transparently, and for providing context for the data analyst.

Of the many categories of questions in this template—motivation, composition, collection, preprocessing/cleaning/labeling, uses, distribution, and maintenance—questions around cleaning and uses are particularly important for facilitating data analysis. When using DP to analyze a data set, data analysts struggle with not being able to check how the data is cleaned,[6] so including the steps taken to do so will allow the analyst to feel more confident about working with the data and allow them to save their privacy loss budget for more interesting questions.

Second, having a clear idea of the intended use cases of the data set will allow the curator to tailor their initial release toward these use cases. We recommend that the curator spend some of the privacy loss budget on a default DP release that includes key contextual information. This will depend on the curator's knowledge of the data set but may include the number of observations, CDFs of key variables, and statistics that capture anything odd or unexpected about the release. In addition to providing this information, the curator should also include any statistics relevant to the key use cases they have outlined for this data set.

Translating Contextual Norms into Parameters

Part of your job as a data curator will be choosing these privacy loss parameters based on a complex variety of social and technical factors. This choice may be challenged by the discrepancy between the value users assign to privacy and their actual behavior. While many users will claim that they strongly value privacy, research has demonstrated that their actions often contradict their expressed opinions. This finding is called the *privacy paradox*.[7] Recent research has also demonstrated that

---

5 Timnit Gebru et al., "Datasheets for Data Sets," in *Communications of the ACM* 64, no. 12 (December 2021): 86–92.

6 Bun et al., "Controlling Privacy Loss in Sampling Schemes: An Analysis of Stratified and Cluster Sampling."

7 Susanne Barth and M. D. T. de Jong, "The Privacy Paradox—Investigating Discrepancies Between Expressed Privacy Concerns and Actual Online Behavior—A Systematic Literature Review," *Telematics and Informatics*, 34, no. 7 (November 2017): 1038–58, *https://www.sciencedirect.com/science/article/pii/S0736585317302022*.

---

privacy preferences cannot be understood in a vacuum without considering complex social contexts and scenarios.[8]

Once you are clear about the collection, composition, and use cases of the data set, it is important to think about the contextual norms around the data set and to choose parameters that respect these norms. One systematic approach to this is *contextual integrity*. In this approach, data is subject to *information norms*, which are social, legal, or moral standards of how information should flow or be distributed in a given context. These norms can be analyzed by looking at five parameters:

1. Data subject
2. Data sender
3. Data recipient
4. Information type
5. Transmission principle

These five concepts are central to understanding contextual integrity. The *data subject* is the individual or group generating the data. The *data sender* is the mechanism that distributes that data to the *data recipient*. The *information type* delineates what kind of data is being generated.

The *transmission principle* is a broad term that encompasses any policies or restrictions on the appropriate transmission of data. These restrictions can include everything from legal terms to social norms. For example, *confidentiality* is a type of transmission principle that prevents the recipient of information from sharing it with other unauthorized individuals or groups.[9] Note that the principle of confidentiality, and the transmission principle in general, does not rely on the enforcement mechanism; socially expected confidentiality between peers is viewed as structurally similar to legally mandated confidentiality. In both cases, the recipient is expected to be the final recipient of the information. Given these informational norms and context, contextual integrity conceptualizes privacy as information gathering and dissemination that obeys the appropriate flow of information according to contextual norms.

For example, one context may be monitoring an athlete's health by their trusted sports coach. In this context, there are norms about how information should flow or be distributed. The athlete in question may expect and trust that the coach collects, monitors, and shares information only with the athlete's best (personal and

---

8 Kirsten Martin and Helen Nissenbaum, "Measuring Privacy: An Empirical Test Using Context to Expose Confounding Variables," *Columbia Science & Technology Law Review*, 18 (2016): 176-218.

9 Adam Barth et al., "Privacy and Contextual Integrity: Framework and Applications," in *2006 IEEE Symposium on Security and Privacy*, (Piscataway, NJ: IEEE, 2006): 184-98, *https://dl.acm.org/doi/10.1109/SP.2006.32*.

competitive) interests in mind. The coach should keep sensitive health information private from other players and fans; however, the coach may disclose any information with the athlete's consent to other coaches and trainers who would help the athlete improve. Privacy, therefore, is defined not just by what information is shared but by looking at the subject, sender, recipient, type, and transmission of information with respect to these informational norms and context.

The contextual integrity approach helps diagnose potential disruptions to these norms and, therefore, can reveal potential violations of privacy. For example, consider an app that helps athletes train and replaces a traditional human trainer. The app is paired with a wearable fitness tracker that collects thousands of data points about athletes, including resting heart rate and temperature changes. These data points are used to compute metrics such as sleep quality, readiness, recovery rate, and overall fitness. This information is stored in a centralized database, and aggregated statistics are shared with third parties, such as advertisers, for profit motives. An analysis using contextual integrity may reasonably find that the information norms for the traditional athlete-coach relationship are significantly disrupted by how this app collects, stores, and shares information, as seen in Figure 12-2.

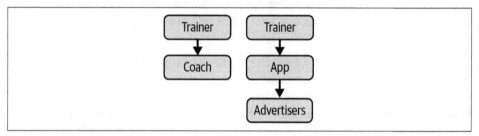

Figure 12-2. Disruption of norms

There are several potential sources of disruption:

- The app is fundamentally a data collecting operation and does so at a much larger scale and granularity (one athlete for a few hours a day versus thousands of athletes 24 hours a day) than a human coach might.

- The app has different motives than a trusted coach, because the company is aiming to collect information for profit much beyond the benefits to each athlete, while a coach is motivated by having their clients be more successful.

- The app shares data to advertisers, while a coach would mostly share data to directly improve the athlete's performance.

Differential privacy does not solve all of these disruptions, but it may help mitigate the impact of some disruptive information flows. The app may still be violating informational norms by sharing statistics with advertisers, even if these statistics are protected using DP, because this flow is different from a traditional athlete-coach relationship. At the same time, using DP here does offer athletes protection from the specific privacy harms of re-identification, reconstruction, and membership attacks. It is up to you as a data curator to decide when DP is necessary to prevent attacks in an otherwise appropriate information flow, or whether it will simply mitigate the most harmful impacts of data sharing when the information flow itself is a privacy violation.

Once you have considered the different confidence interval parameters of your deployment to understand how DP should be used, it is time to translate these contextual analyses into privacy loss parameters for DP. This is not an easy task; research over the past few years has started to consider ways of doing so.[10,11]

Some strategies for choosing parameters based on your deployment include:

- Calibrating to known attacks while envisioning future attacks
- Epsilon registry/comparing to other deployments
- Conducting a user study to understand privacy preferences

The first strategy is to choose parameters based on how the sensitive data in your deployment has been, or may be, attacked. More broadly, you can consider the disclosure of existing mechanisms, and the threats posed by existing attacks, to choose an appropriate and acceptable epsilon. This is helpful for testing parameters, building intuition around how well these parameters protect against existing attacks, and communicating with stakeholders. However, calibrating parameters solely to known attacks is not recommended because this will not allow your deployment to remain robust to future attacks.[12]

For example, consider the randomized response mechanism, where the probability of returning the true answer/value is modulated by the privacy loss parameter ϵ. This probability can be considered as it relates to the contextual analysis—how would a 75% versus a 95% probability of returning the correct answer violate the information norm? You could use this heuristic to choose an appropriate epsilon for your scenario. Similarly, you could use an existing attack to reason about privacy loss parameters, such as setting an acceptable success rate for a membership attack (see Chapter 11 for more on this). It is important to remember, however, that choosing privacy loss parameters based on this level of disclosure does not necessarily protect your deployment from much greater levels of disclosure that could occur from

---

10 Sebastian Benthall et al., "Contextual Integrity Through the Lens of Computer Science," *Foundations and Trends in Privacy and Security* 2, no. 1 (2017): 1–69.

11 Priyanka Nanayakkara et al., "What Are the Chances? Explaining the Epsilon Parameter in Differential Privacy," in *Proceedings of the 32nd USENIX Conference on Security Symposium* (2023).

12 See Chapter 11 for more about protecting against such attacks.

algorithms and attacks that you may not be aware of at present. If you do use this approach, do so with caution and additional conservatism.

The second strategy is to look at similar deployments and their choices of privacy loss parameters to make decisions for your deployment. This was proposed by Dwork, Kohli, and Mulligan as an *Epsilon Registry*, which they describe as "a publicly available communal body of knowledge about differential privacy implementations that can be used by various stakeholders to drive the identification and adoption of judicious differentially private implementations."[13] The proposed registry contains information such as information flows and use cases, granularity of protection (individual-level or event-level), epsilon per datum, rate of privacy loss, privacy loss budget, variant of DP that is used, and justification for these and other implementation choices.[14] Using the parameters from your contextual integrity analysis will allow you to determine how to compare your deployment to others in the registry so that you can make an informed choice.

Finally, you may consider doing user studies on data subjects, users, and other stakeholders of your deployment to reason about the appropriate privacy-utility trade-off at a more granular level. When doing this, you should again be mindful that any surveys you use to elicit preferences should include as much detailed context as possible. Otherwise, as has been demonstrated by countless research studies, you may obtain answers from participants that do not reflect their desires and needs around this privacy-utility trade-off.[15] In addition, you may want to go beyond contextual information norms and privacy preferences to consider vulnerabilities—how people, especially those at the margins of your data population, are more vulnerable to privacy attacks and harms than many (including themselves) may realize. For example, data from the US Decennial Census is often thought of as relatively non-sensitive. However, this data can cause harm to many individuals based on their citizenship and/or housing status.

Even when faced with pressure from data users and other stakeholders to weigh utility over privacy, it is the responsibility of the data curator to choose parameters that adequately protect those who are most vulnerable.

Legal and moral requirements should also factor into your choice of parameters. For example, in a company that works with user data, data subjects may not have visibility into how their data will be used. Therefore, you shouldn't choose your

---

13 Cynthia Dwork, Nitin Kohli, and Deirdre Mulligan, "Differential Privacy in Practice: Expose your Epsilons!," *Journal of Privacy and Confidentiality* 9, no. 2 (October 2019): *https://doi.org/10.29012/jpc.689*.

14 At the time of publication, the closest thing to an official epsilon registry is a blog post (*https://oreil.ly/-04iy*) by Damien Desfontaines, in which he also laments the lack of a true epsilon registry.

15 Martin and Nissenbaum, "Measuring Privacy: An Empirical Test Using Context to Expose Confounding Variables," 176-218.

parameter space based solely on user preferences. You should also take into account legal requirements and moral standards—what you (the company) think is responsible. The legal standard is often lax enough that protection from re-identification, reconstruction, and membership attacks won't be sufficiently guaranteed. You should also keep in mind that differential privacy is only one aspect in a spectrum of privatization techniques. DP can guarantee sufficient protection against these vulnerabilities; however, other points of attack need to be defended using other technical strategies, such as multiparty computation and encryption. There is also an administrative side to protection since defending against social engineering attacks is critical to guaranteeing user privacy. All of these aspects should factor into your decision around parameters, as well as your choice of processes beyond DP to ensure robust, multifaceted protections.

Ultimately, using a combination of these three approaches—reasoning using known and unknown attacks, comparing across deployments, and understanding user needs and vulnerabilities—will give you a multifaceted way to make robust decisions around parameters.

Making These Decisions in the Context of Exploratory Data Analysis

Although the preceding section provided approaches for when you, as a data curator or analyst, have detailed information about the context, you may end up asking yourself an important question: *how do I start with the analysis?*

It is a challenge to perform *exploratory data analysis* (EDA) safely and release summary information early on, while still rationing your budget so that you have enough left for the remainder of the analysis. In many ways, these topics are the hardest part of a DP project.

There are two main challenges in selecting parameters in the context of exploratory data analysis:

- You may not know what statistics to release, and the choice of statistics itself may be disclosive.
- You may have little information about metadata parameters, such as ranges or categories, for the statistics you would like to release.

First, let us consider the problem of choosing statistics in a privacy-preserving way. In many cases, the goal of working with the data will be to explore what is even interesting or relevant to release. Making these data-dependent decisions about which statistics to release in the first place can require a dedicated privacy loss budget. The problem here is to permit "access to the raw data, while ensuring that the choice of statistics is not disclosive."[16] If this choice of statistics is differentially private, then you "can release these privately chosen statistics using privacy-preserving algorithms."[17] One solution, proposed by Dwork and Ullman, is for an analyst to forgetfully perform EDA on independent slices of the data to come up with the statistics they would like to release. Here, *forgetfully* means that they run the same EDA process on each slice, trying their best to forget what they learned in between. Then, they apply a DP mechanism such as the exponential mechanism over all the sets of statistics to choose which ones to release.

Second, let us consider how to choose metadata parameters when you have little context about what they might be. There are two approaches for doing so:

- You can train on public data. For example, say you have a data set that contains the incomes of employees in an industry that you are unfamiliar with. You want to release the mean value of these incomes, but when using DP, this would require providing bounds on the range of the incomes. If you had no idea what these bounds might be, you could turn to publicly available data on historical incomes from this industry and use the inflation-adjusted estimates to supply as your bounds.

- Some algorithms use the privacy budget to estimate parameters. You should only use these algorithms if you feel that your estimates based on prior information may be very poor. These algorithms often use iterative approaches. For example, in the preceding income example, you could use a small portion of your privacy budget, say $\frac{1}{10}$, to run a DP binary search algorithm (or the transformation described in "Quantile Score Transformation" on page 95) to estimate the 5th and 95th quantiles of the distribution of incomes. Then, you can use these estimated quantiles as the input for your DP mean mechanism. Another option is to use postprocessing for a tailored histogram release (see "Example: Bounds Estimation" on page 143). Another example was shown in "Privately Estimating the Truncation Threshold" on page 189, where a DP release is made to get a sense of the distribution of user contributions.

Using these algorithms still requires some decisions on your end.

---

16 Cynthia Dwork and Jonathan Ullman, "The Fienberg Problem: How to Allow Human Interactive Data Analysis in the Age of Differential Privacy," *Journal of Privacy and Confidentiality* 8, no. 1 (December 2018): *http://dx.doi.org/10.29012/jpc.687*.

17 Ibid.

Adaptively Choosing Privacy Parameters

Often, the analyst does not know which queries they would like to submit until they've done some exploratory DP analysis. In this setting, the analyst does not know how much budget to allocate to future queries until they've already made some DP releases. Unfortunately, the composition of DP releases requires the privacy parameters to be known ahead of time. When the privacy parameters for each query can be chosen adaptively, then as the analysis progresses, the worst-case privacy expenditure increases. This limitation of DP compositors motivates the use of *privacy odometers* and *privacy filters* in exploratory data analysis.

A privacy odometer tracks the total privacy expenditure of a series of adaptively chosen queries. Odometers assume that the analyst can tailor their next query based on the previous release. A privacy filter is very similar to a privacy odometer, but once the privacy expenditure exceeds a preset budget, the privacy filter refuses to answer any more queries about the data set. Odometers and filters allow privacy parameters to be set adaptively, but incur a loss of utility and an increase in the complexity of the privacy analysis. For more on privacy odometers and privacy filters, see Chapter 6.

Potential (Unexpected) Consequences of Transparent Parameter Selection

One of the benefits of DP is that it enables transparency around the method used for noise addition, including the many parameters we've already discussed that are used within the process. This is great compared to previous approaches of "security-through-obscurity," where the method itself had to remain secret to guarantee protection. However, transparency often brings with it other challenges. Many deployments of DP have disregarded the additional work needed to support transparency, and have suffered the consequences of controversy and critique. As a data curator, you should be aware of the issues that may arise to prepare in advance of your deployment.

First, DP creates a zero-sum game between privacy and utility. When you explain DP to data users, you will have to make it clear that there is a strict privacy-utility trade-off, as well as a finite privacy loss budget. You should be aware that many data users may not have thought of privacy and utility this way before, so this may be a shocking revelation. Data users who have worked together before will now be wary of allocating a larger share of the budget to one group and thus diminishing the share of the budget available to other groups. Therefore, asking data users to come to a consensus on how the privacy loss budget should be distributed may be a contentious process. This is exactly what happened during the use of DP in the 2020 Decennial

Census, where coalitions of data users fell apart because of the zero-sum game they were suddenly asked to participate in through the use of DP.[18,19]

This should not discourage you from being transparent about DP. Transparency and accountability are important benefits of using DP compared to prior approaches to disclosure avoidance. Nonetheless, you should be prepared to justify the decision-making process regarding the size of the privacy loss budget and the allocation of the budget among data users. Before advertising that data will be made available to data users using DP, you may consider setting a policy around how much budget will be used for internal research and/or trusted partners. Then, to allocate the rest of the budget, you might consider using a formal process where data users submit anonymous applications asking for a portion of the budget, and then use a third-party service to make these decisions as objectively as possible. On the other hand, if you would like collective engagement from data users on these decisions, you should set up modes of communication that mitigate the antagonistic aspects of this decision, such as building these agreements based on personal relationships and emphasizing shared goals.

Throughout this process, you will have to communicate to stakeholders about what the privacy loss parameters mean for their contexts. This is no easy task. The challenges of explaining these parameters are well-documented,[20] and there are many ways in which stakeholders may misunderstand them. Data users who have more sophisticated statistical backgrounds may be better positioned than those without, which can make it hard for them to come to a consensus together. Across the board, stakeholders may not be used to reasoning about probabilistic risks.

Although research into communicating privacy loss parameters is still nascent, emerging research[21] suggests that "odds-based explanation" methods can be effective in communicating about these parameters. This may look like the following text:

> If a data subject does respond to a true/false survey question, [x] out of 100 potential DP outputs will lead an analyst to believe that the data subject responded with [true]. If a data subject does not respond to a true/false survey question, [y] out of 100 potential DP outputs will lead an analyst to believe that the data subject responded with [true].

---

18 Michael B. Hawes, "Implementing Differential Privacy: Seven Lessons From the 2020 United States Census," *Harvard Data Science Review* 2, no. 2 (2020), *https://doi.org/10.1162/99608f92.353c6f99*.

19 danah boyd and Jayshree Sarathy, "Differential Perspectives: Epistemic Disconnects Surrounding the US Census Bureau's Use of Differential Privacy," *Harvard Data Science Review* special issue 2 (2022), *https://doi.org/10.1162/99608f92.66882f0e*.

20 Rachel Cummings, Gabriel Kaptchuk, and Elissa M. Redmiles. " 'I need a better description': An Investigation Into User Expectations For Differential Privacy," in *Proceedings of the 2021 ACM SIGSAC Conference on Computer and Communications Security* (New York: ACM, 2021) 3037-52.

21 Nanayakkara et al., "What Are the Chances? Explaining the Epsilon Parameter in Differential Privacy."

Other approaches include frequency visualization and sets of sample DP outputs. Visualizations, in particular, are underexplored in the DP literature and may be incredibly beneficial in communicating with data subjects and data users. Hands-on explainers (such as the "A Framework to Understand DP" notebook by OpenDP (*https://oreil.ly/uMq_4*)) can also be valuable for data scientists. Regardless of what approaches you use, you should remain sensitive to how challenging it is for stakeholders to evaluate these parameters, and set expectations accordingly.

Summary

As a data curator, you will need to understand the relationship between your data's privacy needs and the privacy loss parameter values you choose. The choice of privacy loss parameter values is key to protecting the privacy of subjects in the data set. As a data curator, this is also your responsibility and may exist in tension with the desire to extract utility from the data for research or commercial purposes. Further, you will need to understand how to choose metadata parameters without regard for the values in the underlying data set. This decision also impacts the utility of the DP data analysis; for example, clamping values to an inappropriate range can lead to flawed statistics. By now, you should have a solid enough theoretical understanding of DP as a practice to be able to curate sensitive data in a way that results in useful DP statistics.

However, DP data curation doesn't exist in a vacuum; instead, it is part of a network of researchers and institutions hoping to glean useful information from sensitive data. Since differential privacy leads to a trade-off between utility in privacy, this practice can lead to friction between competing interests. Beyond understanding the theory of DP, it is important that you, as a data curator, can also navigate the personal and professional implications of allocating a DP budget. In this chapter, you have learned several techniques for mitigating such friction, including effectively communicating about the privacy budget allocation and the potential to use third-party organizations to anonymously process DP budget requests. Remember that a significant part of the data curation process may rest on personal relationships. Allocating the privacy budget with a commitment to shared goals, as well as publishing contextual DP statistics as metadata, can help to minimize contentiousness and make the DP data analysis process more productive for everyone.

In the next chapter, you will learn to apply your new knowledge of privacy loss parameters, metadata parameter selection, and the organizational challenges of DP data curation. With this knowledge, you are ready to plan your first DP data release project. This process will involve constructing a deployment checklist to make sure that all stakeholders agree, and will involve handling data in a way that is consistent with your organization's policies and relevant regulations. This is the final step in your journey; by the end, you will be ready to apply differential privacy on a project-level basis to analyze sensitive data safely and responsibly.

Exercises

1. Consider a fitness app that tracks personal health information, such as resting heart rate, oxygen level, daily step count, and oxygen level. The app allows users to share this information with their health care providers. The app also shares aggregate information with third parties, such as advertisers and insurance agencies. Using a contextual integrity approach, outline the different information flows and contexts involved with this fitness app and assess the privacy implications of these flows.

   a. Identify the data subject, data sender, data recipient(s), information type(s), and transmission principle (see "Translating Contextual Norms into Parameters" on page 278).

   b. Consider the scenario where the fitness app uses differential privacy to share statistics with third parties. Returning to the contextual integrity approach, explain how this changes your analysis of the privacy implications of this fitness app.

2. Check out the Capital Bike Share (*https://oreil.ly/NynXO*) data set describing bike share trips in Washington, DC, in December 2023. If you wanted to release DP counts of origin and destination stations, how would you reason about the appropriate values of ϵ and δ?

   a. Using what you learned in Chapter 7, explain what steps must be taken to privatize the count.

3. Imagine you are deploying DP for a data release. Use a contextual integrity approach to outline the benefits of using DP in your chosen context. Then, consider three ways in which the use of DP might pose challenges for users, and outline concrete steps to mitigate these challenges. Consider completing this exercise in a group setting to build a shared contextual integrity framework for your projects.[22]

---

22 This question is deliberately open-ended and is designed to make you think about deployments and prepare you for Chapter 13.

## CHAPTER 13

Planning Your First DP Project

At this point, you have learned many important concepts related to differential privacy. From core differential privacy definitions and differentially private mechanisms to setting a privacy loss budget and creating differentially private synthetic data sets, you have learned all the techniques required for a successful differential privacy project. In this chapter, we will help you get ready for your first differential privacy project. In addition to the same planning needed to bring any project to successful completion, you will also need to ensure that you are thorough in your analysis of potential privacy flaws and points of privacy leakages.

The first step in successful project planning is understanding the actors in the scenario. Throughout this book, you have learned terms like *data curator* and *data analyst*, and these terms have played a central role in illustrating key DP concepts. In practice, there are a variety of individuals, organizations, and regulations that may take on important roles during the DP analysis and deployment process. For example, a hospital may be a data owner because it is the organization that stores and has certain rights to use the data internally. The data curator in this scenario could be an individual or group within a particular office that is tasked with administering and granting limited analysis rights to external researchers. The data curator can also be distinct from the *privacy loss budget allocator*, which can be an individual, group, or regulation that sets acceptable ranges of values for privacy loss parameters like ϵ.

Once you have a firm grasp of the individuals, organizations, and regulations in your DP data release scenario, you can plan your project and ultimately deploy your pipeline. At this stage, you are ready to use the DP deployment checklist. The deployment checklist lists all the steps, in sequential order, that can help a data curator plan for the project. You should start filling out the checklist as soon as you know the data source and the desired data outcomes.

In this chapter, you will review how to:

- Create an end-to-end pipeline of a private data release
- Make a differentially private data release
- Deploy a differentially private pipeline mechanism
- Use the DP deployment checklist

DP Deployment Considerations

There are a variety of considerations when deploying a DP pipeline and releasing statistics. These considerations are highly context-dependent since releases can range from a single statistic with noise to a multistep pipeline that involves training a DP machine learning model. This section also introduces a DP deployment checklist; this will be useful when you are managing the design and implementation of a DP pipeline and includes common considerations and pitfalls to watch out for.

Frequency of DP Deployments

The frequency of your DP deployment will depend on the specifics of your use case. You may decide to implement a privacy budget that resets after a certain period. Alternatively, there are scenarios where the most appropriate implementation is *one-and-done*: you set the privacy budget once, and when it is spent, no further analysis is allowed. How should you think about these options?

Suppose you are collecting telemetry data and releasing the top search queries every month. You will set your privacy budget on a per-month basis, and your privacy guarantees are over a certain period of time. Conversely, if you are analyzing historical search data for a product that is no longer operational, you will be sure that the data will not be updated. In this case, you will set the budget once and cease releasing statistics once the budget is spent.

Composition and Budget Accountability

If you are partitioning the data, then it is possible that a single individual can be present in multiple partitions. Consider a case where you are computing a DP statistic on different schools; you may assume that each student is in a single school, and you can use parallel composition to set your budget. However, if a student is cross-enrolled and exists in the records of multiple schools, then this strategy no longer works.

In a scenario where 3% of students are dual-enrolled, you can redact their records from one of the schools and proceed with parallel composition. If a larger percentage of students are dual-enrolled, the utility of your statistics will degrade from redacting so many records. In this case, you should consider the maximum number of partitions that an individual can be found in. For example, if you are studying a university system that allows students to be enrolled in at most two universities, then you can place a bound on the number of contributions per student to 2.

If you know an individual is in at most k partitions, then the total privacy consumption, by parallel composition, increases by a factor of k. However, you can achieve better utility for specific queries by taking advantage of domain descriptors that restrict your sensitivity (where domain descriptors can be acquired either via preprocessing or from public information).

For example, in a grouped count query, if you know an individual may contribute at most one row to at most k partitions, then the L^2 sensitivity is $\sqrt{k}$. If you don't have this information, then you can use preprocessing to restrict the sensitivity, as shown in Figure 13-1.

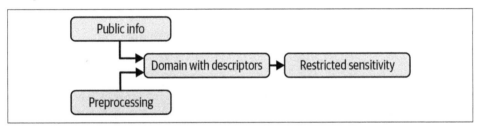

Figure 13-1. Using publicly available information to establish sensitivity

There is a significant advantage to partitioning in situations where you know an individual is present in only one partition. However, if there are overlaps in the data, then you can use the composition property of DP to your advantage.

DP Deployment Checklist

This checklist should serve as a reference point for steps you need to take while preparing and deploying your DP data release. This checklist assumes the following scenario: you have a data set that you know you want to study and are establishing what statistics on the data can be released using DP based on audience needs and expectations. Note that you do not necessarily know the statistic(s) you want to release in advance; part of the discovery process in the beginning is understanding your audience and whether a DP version of certain statistics will be valuable to them.

The first several steps also address various non-technical aspects of a DP release: how to communicate with internal and external partners and ensuring that you are interfacing with security and regulatory experts to follow previously established best practices. If you have already worked with the data before, are in communication with relevant partners, and already know exactly which statistics are to be published, you can skip to Chapter 7.

1. Understand your data.
   a. Is the data well-structured and annotated?
   b. If you are collecting data (e.g., from a survey), what is your sample frame?
   c. Figure out what can be made public and what cannot.
   d. Identify similar public data sources.
2. Figure out your other security practices.
   a. Make sure your DP release conforms to existing organizational policies around private data storage, encrypted communication, etc.
3. Have a communication strategy.
   a. Know in advance how you will communicate with different stakeholders.
   b. Establish connections with experts you will be consulting with.
4. Decide whether you will track which individuals have been in releases.
   a. Sometimes, organizations track membership in different data releases to ensure that no one individual is present in too many releases. These databases can also be two-way in that they can track which audience members are accessing data releases.
   b. If you decide to use such a system, you will need to make sure it is being updated.
5. Identify the stakeholders and audience.
   a. The nature of the audience impacts the utility that your release will need to have.
   b. Is it even worth releasing, given the needs of the audience and the utility loss from privatizing?
   c. Is the privacy loss from the release too risky to justify?
   d. Who will see the release, and how will it be delivered to them?
6. Determine which regulations apply to the data release.
   a. Consult with legal and regulatory partners to ensure your release follows the proper protocols.
7. Identify the unit of privacy (See "Privacy Unit" on page 27 in Chapter 2).
   a. Make sure you know what aspect of the data you are protecting with DP.
   b. For tabular data: is each row an individual, a group, or an event? You may still want to protect groups or events even if the data is individual-level.

8. Define the privacy risk.

   a. Check if there is a clear guideline for your organization or industry. If not, look for similar releases for precedent.

   b. The established standards for privacy loss parameters will depend on the nature of the data you are releasing.

9. Plan the release.

   a. List all the public-facing outputs that are based on private data values: machine learning model, data description, data statistics, synthetic data, etc.

   b. Some of these outputs might require higher utility than others. Create a utility ranking for all the outputs.[1]

   c. Collect public information, such as the expected bounds on the data, key sets, certain marginals, or the number of individuals in a population.

   d. Define what you will not protect in the release. For example, you may decide to only protect user data from the past six months, even if data has been collected for 10 years.

10. Create the query.

   a. Choose your DP mechanism(s).

   b. Identify libraries and other tools.

   c. Check for privacy leakages, and make sure your query satisfies your chosen privacy loss parameters.

   d. Define the final privacy loss budget, if not already set.

   e. Build the DP pipeline with your chosen library. Consider trying it on public data as a test.

   f. Is the statistic giving you the utility you need? If not, you may want to return to an earlier step and revisit the privacy-utility trade-off in your approach.

11. Release the statistics.

   a. Run your DP pipeline on the private data set and release the statistics to your audience.

   b. If you are using a tracking database, update it with the members of the data set from this new release.

---

1 For example, you might be interested in publishing two different data statistics: the total number of people in a group, and the percentage of men and women in the group. In your example, you might be OK with a count of people that is not super precise, but the percentage of men and women might be of extreme importance, and you would like a very high utility for these percentages. You would rank your outputs as 1) percentage of men and women and 2) total number of people in a group.

In the checklist, step 10 was *create the query*; this is where the query is constructed, right before the statistics are released. There are multiple potential steps here, and it is important to go over them carefully. Note that data preparation is included as part of the query-creation step; this step isn't simply writing a query and running it. You should also consider your entire workload in this step—this is where prioritization of queries comes into play. You may find it beneficial to run the queries in a particular order. For example, if you know you want to run some basic statistics and train an ML model, you should run the basic statistics first, then spend the rest of your budget on the ML model.

Remember, the privacy semantics of the query need to tie to the unit of privacy that you selected in step 1. This means your queries need to be operations that respect the unit of privacy. For example, you can't define your unit of privacy to be individuals in the data set and then construct a query that returns row edits. Figure 13-2 shows the different operations that you have seen in the book so far.

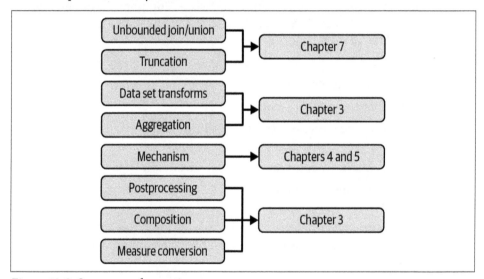

Figure 13-2. Summary of operations

Refer back to these previous chapters to review these concepts and make sure you are comfortable implementing them in OpenDP as needed.

An Example Project: Back to the Classroom

In Chapter 1, you saw a scenario where a professor unwittingly released a student's test score. Although he did not write the score on the board, he released the mean score before and after the student dropped the class. By now, it should be immediately apparent to you why this is a privacy violation, and you are ready to re-engage with this scenario and release this data privately.

As the professor, you have a notebook that reads a CSV of the student scores and calculates the mean:

```
import pandas as pd
df = pd.read_csv("student_exam_scores.csv")
df.mean()
```

How can you go about modifying this process to be differentially private? First, you need to identify the unit of privacy.[2] In this case, the unit of privacy is the students' test scores, where each student can contribute a maximum of one test score. Define a new variable that stores the maximum contribution:

```
import opendp.prelude as dp
input_metric, b_in = dp.unit_of(contributions=1)
```

In this scenario, we may consider an epsilon expenditure of $\epsilon = 1.0$ to be acceptable:

```
output_metric, b_out = dp.loss_of(epsilon=1.)
```

Now collect the public information that you know into the input domain. The input data consists of vectors of integers:

```
input_domain = dp.vector_domain(dp.atom_domain(T=float), size=class_size)
```

Using this information, you can create a measurement that uses Laplace noise to release the mean while protecting individual student exam scores.

Now that you have this transformation, you'll need to set your scale value for the Laplace noise and construct a measurement that will return a DP mean:

```
def make_mean_meas(scale):
    return (
        (input_domain, input_metric) >>
        dp.t.then_clamp((0., 100.)) >>
        dp.t.then_mean() >>
        dp.m.then_laplace(scale=scale)
    )
scale = dp.binary_search_param(make_mean_meas, b_in, b_out)
mean_meas = make_mean_meas(scale)
```

The binary search calibrates this measurement to satisfy $\epsilon = 1$. As you would expect, the *privacy map* emits an epsilon no greater than 1:

```
assert mean_meas.map(max_contributions) <= 1
```

Notice that, until this point, you still haven't touched the data—this has all been setting up the computation:

```
dp_mean = mean_meas(df["scores"])
```

---

2 You first saw this term in Chapter 2. Recall that the unit of privacy specifies what you are protecting.

You can understand the confidence interval using the following:

```
dp.laplacian_scale_to_accuracy(scale=scale, alpha=0.05)
```

This gives you a 95% confidence interval—that is, a $(1 - \alpha)100\,\%$ confidence interval for a value of $\alpha = 0.05$.

Proper Real-World Data Publications

Open data is data that can be "freely used, modified, and shared by anyone for any purpose" (*https://www.opendefinition.org*). Organizations that want to make their data open and publicly available will need to take privacy considerations into account. In this section, you will see two examples of a good data release. Recall in Chapter 11 that AOL released anonymized search logs in 2006, leading to the re-identification of users and a serious privacy violation. Improper data publishing practices erode trust in the data holders and can lead to significant reputational damage and legal consequences.

LinkedIn's Economic Graph and Microsoft's Broadband data release are two examples of high-quality data publications. These releases are effective because they provide transparency in terms of budget and mechanisms used and provide documentation describing their methods. Further, their unit of privacy is communicated, along with the privacy loss budget and timeline over which the privacy guarantees hold.

LinkedIn's Economic Graph

LinkedIn describes its Economic Graph (*https://economicgraph.linkedin.com*) as a "digital representation of the global economy." This project was a partnership with organizations including Eurostat and the Organization for Economic Co-operation and Development (OECD), and seeks to answer large-scale questions such as, "Who is hiring?" and "What jobs are available?" LinkedIn published this data with differential privacy to strike a balance between delivering important data to policymakers and protecting the privacy of their users. To answer the first question, researchers at LinkedIn queried the 1,000 employers (*https://oreil.ly/xC_aV*) with the most hires on LinkedIn over three months, across a variety of regions and industries,[3] and added Laplace noise to the count of new hires for each employer.

The researchers found that 95% of individuals won't be hired more than once by the same employer in three months and will appear in four reports: the country report, the region report, the country-industry report, and the region-industry report. Since each report has $\epsilon = 1.2$, the four top employer reports sum to $\epsilon = 4.8$. LinkedIn's

---

3 Ryan Rogers et al., "A Members First Approach to Enabling LinkedIn's Labor Market Insights at Scale," arXiv, October 27, 2020, *https://arxiv.org/abs/2010.13981*.

researchers utilized two variations of the exponential mechanism for querying the top-k employers: one variation when the data domain is known and an alternative variation when the data domain is unknown. Note that, when the data key set is unknown, the presence of a data element can leak privacy, regardless of the noise added to its count. Additionally, Economic Graph data releases utilize count queries with Laplace noise.

Microsoft's Broadband Data

The Broadband data set released by Microsoft in 2021 is an open data set that provides estimates on internet broadband usage for every zip code in the United States, as shown in Figure 13-3. To construct the data set, Microsoft's engineers and data scientists used aggregated and privatized data collected from Windows telemetry systems. DP COUNT queries were performed over the number of machines using and not using broadband internet in each zip code in the US, with the Laplace mechanism used to privatize the COUNT queries. The data was published to a GitHub repository (*https://oreil.ly/jONFI*), including detailed documentation on how the data set was constructed and the mechanisms and libraries used. The data set also provides error bounds related to the noise introduced by differential privacy.

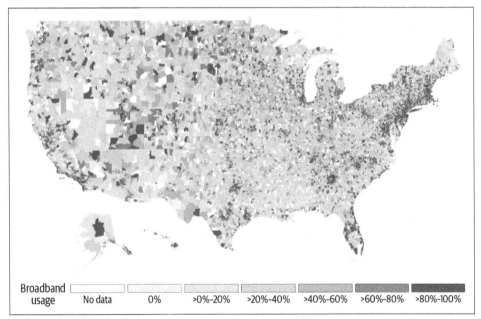

Figure 13-3. Broadband usage by zip code

DP Release Table: A Standard for Releasing Details About Your Release

Beyond including DP to protect user privacy, the LinkedIn and Microsoft releases were effective because they communicated clearly with the public. Important properties of the release were highlighted in online posts and white papers, such as the statistics calculated, algorithms used, ϵ values, and the total number of released reports. This release allows researchers and other privacy-concerned individuals to effectively analyze their workflows to understand how user data is being protected.

Within your organization, you may want to set a standard for how you will communicate key summary data about releases. For example, you may decide that releases should always have a table with privacy loss parameters and their values, along with the mechanism(s) used. In a situation where you need more details in your summary, you may decide to set a standard that each step of the DP pipeline is specified in the table so that your colleagues can see at a glance what DP processes were used in making the release. Table 13-1 puts the most important aspects of the LinkedIn DP data release into a single table.

Table 13-1. DP release table—LinkedIn

Name	Value
Project Scope	Reports on top jobs and skills for recent hires in 3-month period
Preprocessing methods	Tf-idf on skills keyset
ε	4.8
δ	$4 * 10^{-10}$
Unit of privacy	Hire
Mechanism	Laplace
Implementation	UnkLap
URL	*https://economicgraph.linkedin.com*

This is a central, standardized way to release DP metadata to the public so that releases can be efficiently compared and scrutinized. Similarly, refer to the Microsoft Broadband analysis (Table 13-2).

Table 13-2. DP release table—Microsoft Broadband

Name	Value
Project Scope	Reports on broadband usage in the USA by zip code
Preprocessing methods	None
ϵ	0.2
δ	0.0
Unit of privacy	Individual device
Mechanism	Laplace
Implementation	SmartNoise and OpenDP
URL	*https://github.com/microsoft/USBroadbandUsagePercentages*

That's All, Folks

We decided to write this book to present a practical yet in-depth introduction to DP. By now, you should be comfortable explaining key DP concepts and implementing DP data analyses in a variety of contexts. You should also be able to construct DP pipelines with OpenDP and ensure that they meet the privacy needs of your data. Given a DP mechanism, you should be able to reason about the privacy guarantees it makes and demonstrate simple proofs using privacy loss parameters like ϵ and δ.

Differential privacy can be a tool for putting sensitive data to work for researchers and society at large; however, sensitive data can only be shared privately when practitioners in the field can mindfully apply DP algorithms. This is where you come in: as a newly minted DP expert, you can now make the case within your organization for putting sensitive data to good use via DP releases. Such a release may take many forms, varying from statistical analyses to DP machine learning models. There is now a valuable opportunity to examine previously untouchable data for insights—now go forth and (DP) calculate!

If you've made it this far, please email us at *ethan@lakeside.tech*; we'd love to hear from you.

Further Reading

For further reading about DP, please see the following:

Theory

- Dwork, Cynthia and Aaron Roth. *The Algorithmic Foundations of Differential Privacy*. Boston: Now Publishers, 2014. *https://www.cis.upenn.edu/~aaroth/Papers/privacybook.pdf*.
- Dwork, Cynthia. "Differential Privacy." In *Automata, Languages and Programming*, edited by M. Bugliesi, B. Preneel, V. Sassone, and I. Wegener. Lecture Notes in Computer Science. Berlin: Springer, 2006, 1–12. *https://link.springer.com/chapter/10.1007/11787006_1*.

Applications

- Desfontaines, Damien. "Ted Is Writing Things." *https://desfontain.es/blog/*.
- Hay, Michael, Marco Gaboardi, and Salil Vadhan. "A Programming Framework for OpenDP." 2020. *https://salil.seas.harvard.edu/publications/programming-framework-opendp*.
- Near, Joseph P. and Chiké Abuah. *Programming Differential Privacy*. *https://programming-dp.com*.

Supplementary Definitions

Cardinality

The *cardinality* of a data set is the number of instances (rows) in a data set x, denoted $|x|_C$.

Metric

A *metric* $d(a, b)$ is a function $d: \mathbb{D} \times \mathbb{D} \to \mathbb{R}$ such that for any points a, b, and c in a domain $\mathbb{D}$, the following properties hold:

- $d(a, b) \geq 0$ and $d(a, b) = 0$, if and only if $a = b$ (non-negativity)
- $d(a, b) = d(b, a)$ (symmetry)
- $d(a, c) \leq d(a, b) + d(b, c)$ (triangle inequality)

Keep in mind that some of the metrics used in differential privacy don't satisfy all of these axioms. For instance, in the setting of unbounded contributions where data sets have user IDs (see "Data Sets with Unbounded Contributions" on page 177), two different data sets may still have an identifier distance of zero.

Multisets

Multisets are data sets that can have multiple instances of each record. Unlike vectors, multisets don't care about row ordering.

Symmetric difference

The symmetric difference between multisets x and x' is the multiset of elements that are either in x or x', but not in their intersection. The symmetric difference between sets x and x' is denoted $x \triangle x'$. That is, the symmetric difference consists of those elements that do not have matches in the other data set.

Rényi Differential Privacy

Here, we present a series of theorems demonstrating the relationship between RDP and (ϵ, δ) differential privacy.

Theorem: RDP Is Immune to Postprocessing

For a mechanism f that is (α, ϵ)-RDP, and a randomized mapping g, the composition $g(f(x))$ is also (α, ϵ)-RDP.

Proof

See Mironov[1] for a proof of this claim, building on van Ervan and Harremoës.[2]

Now, let's demonstrate the equivalence between RDP and (ϵ, δ)-DP. First, we will need some mathematical preliminaries.

Theorem: Young's Inequality

If $a, b \geq 0$ and $\frac{1}{p} + \frac{1}{q} = 1$ with $p, q > 1$, then $ab \leq \frac{a^p}{p} + \frac{b^q}{q}$

Proof via Calculus

Define $f(x) = \frac{x^p}{p} + \frac{1}{q} - x$ and take the derivative to determine the minimum of the function.

---

1 Mironov, "Renyi Differential Privacy," 263–75.

2 Tim van Erven and Peter Harremoës, "Renyi Divergence and Kullback-Leibler Divergence," *IEEE Transactions on Information Theory* 60, no. 7 (July 2014): 3797–820.

The derivative is $f'(x) = x^{p-1} - 1$, and setting this equal to 0:

$$f'(x) = x^{p-1} - 1 = 0$$

$$x^{p-1} = 1 \Rightarrow x = 1$$

We know this is a minimum by the second derivative test: $f''(x) = (p-1)x^{p-2} \geq 0$. So we know that the minimum of $f(x)$ occurs at $x = 1$ and that this minimum is $f(1) = 0$.

This means that:

$$f(x) \geq f(1) = 0 \Rightarrow \frac{x^p}{p} + \frac{1}{q} - x \geq 0$$

Without loss of generality, assume $a > b$. Then $a^p b^{-q} \geq 1$. This further implies that:

$$f\left(a^p b^{-q}\right) \geq f(1)$$

$$\frac{a^p b^{-q}}{p} + \frac{1}{q} - ab^{-\frac{q}{p}} \geq \frac{1}{p} + \frac{1}{q} - 1$$

and we know that $\frac{1}{p} + \frac{1}{q} = 1$, so:

$$\frac{a^p b^{-q}}{p} + \frac{1}{q} \geq ab^{-\frac{q}{p}}$$

Multiplying both sides by b^q:

$$\frac{a^p}{p} + \frac{b^q}{q} \geq ab^{-\frac{q}{p}}b^q$$

and simplifying the exponent:

$$-\frac{q}{p} + q = -\frac{qp + q}{p} = q\left(1 - \frac{1}{p}\right) = 1$$

Therefore:

$$ab \le \frac{a^p}{p} + \frac{b^q}{q}$$

Elementary Proof

For this proof, you will only need to know a few facts about logarithms and exponentials.

The exponential and logarithms are inverses of each other—that is, applying them both to a function does nothing:

$$f(x) = exp(ln(f(x)))$$

The logarithm of a product becomes the sum of two logarithms:

$$log(ab) = log(a) + log(b)$$

The logarithm of a power is the same as the product:

$$log(a)^p = p * log(a)$$

The exponential is *strictly convex*. This means that, for real $\alpha, \beta > 0$ where $\alpha + \beta = 1$ and $x \ne y$:

$$exp(\alpha x + \beta y) < \alpha * exp(x) + \beta * exp(y)$$

Using these facts, start by noting that:

$$ab = exp(log(ab))$$

$$ab = exp(log(a) + log(b))$$

$$ab = exp\left(\frac{p}{p}log(a) + \frac{q}{q}log(b)\right)$$

By the logarithm of a power rule:

$$ab = exp\left(\frac{1}{p}log(a^p) + \frac{1}{q}log(b^q)\right)$$

Because the exponential is strictly convex and $\frac{1}{p} + \frac{1}{q} = 1$:

$$ab = exp\left(\frac{1}{p}log(a^p) + \frac{1}{q}log(b^q)\right) \leq \frac{1}{p}exp(log(a^p)) + \frac{1}{q}exp(ln(b^q))$$

and since exp and log are inverses of each other:

$$\frac{1}{p}exp(log(a^p)) + \frac{1}{q}exp(ln(b^q)) = \frac{a^p}{p} + \frac{b^q}{q}$$

Therefore:

$$ab \leq \frac{a^p}{p} + \frac{b^q}{q}$$

Theorem: Holder's Inequality

Let $p, q \in [1, \infty]$ and $\frac{1}{p} + \frac{1}{q} = 1$. Then for functions f and g:

$$\| fg \|_1 \leq \| f \|_p \| g \|_q$$

Proof

To prove Holder's inequality, we will build upon the previous proof of Young's inequality.

Let $A = \| f \|_p$ and $B = \| g \|_q$.

Then we can define $a = \frac{|f(x)|}{A}$ and $b = \frac{|g(x)|}{B}$.

Now let's apply Young's inequality to this a and b:

$$ab = \frac{|f(x)g(x)|}{AB} \leq \frac{|f(x)|^p}{pA^p} + \frac{|g(x)|^q}{qA^q}$$

and using the definition of a and b:

$$ab = \leq \frac{|f(x)|^p}{pA^p} + \frac{|g(x)|^q}{qA^q} = \frac{a^p}{p} + \frac{b^q}{q}$$

Summing over x:

$$\frac{\Sigma_x |f(x)g(x)|}{AB} \le \frac{\Sigma_x |f(x)|^p}{pA^p} + \frac{\Sigma_x |g(x)|^q}{qA^q}$$

and since the magnitudes of f and g are just A and B:

$$\frac{\Sigma_x |f(x)g(x)|}{AB} \le \frac{1}{p} + \frac{1}{q}$$

Since we know that $\frac{1}{p} + \frac{1}{q} = 1$:

$$\frac{\Sigma_x |f(x)g(x)|}{AB} \le \frac{1}{p} + \frac{1}{q} = 1$$

Multiplying both sides by AB:

$$\sum_x |f(x)g(x)| = \| fg \|_1 \le AB$$

Recall that we defined $A = \| f \|_p$ and $B = \| g \|_q$ at the beginning. This means that:

$$\| fg \|_1 \le \| f \|_p \| g \|_q$$

Theorem: Probability Preservation

For distributions P and Q, an event A, and $\alpha > 1$:

$$P(A) \le exp[D_\alpha(P||Q) * Q(A)]^{\frac{(\alpha - 1)}{\alpha}}$$

Proof

We will use Holder's inequality and by cleverly setting $p = \alpha$, $q = \frac{\alpha}{\alpha - 1}$, $f(x) = \frac{P(x)}{Q(x)^{\frac{1}{q}}}$,

and $g(x) = Q(x)^{\frac{1}{q}}$, we have a scenario where $\frac{1}{p} + \frac{1}{q} = 1$. This means we can apply Holder's inequality:

$$\| fg \|_1 = \| P(x) \| \leq \left\| \frac{P(x)^{\alpha}}{Q(x)^{\frac{\alpha}{\alpha-1}}} \right\|_{\frac{\alpha}{\alpha}} \| \| Q(x)^{1-\frac{1}{\alpha}} \|_{\alpha}$$

$$\leq \| P(x)^{\alpha} Q(x)^{1-\alpha} \|_{\alpha} \| Q(x)^{1-\frac{1}{\alpha}} \|_{\alpha}$$

$$\leq exp[D_{\alpha}(P||Q)]^{\frac{\alpha-1}{\alpha}} Q(A)^{\frac{\alpha-1}{\alpha}}$$

Theorem: RDP to (ϵ, δ)-DP

A mechanism that is (α, ϵ)-RDP is also necessarily $\left(\epsilon + \frac{log\left(\frac{1}{\delta}\right)}{\alpha-1}, \delta\right)$-DP.

Proof

This proof is highly indebted to Mironov's paper, titled "Rényi Differential Privacy" (*https://oreil.ly/tX_uh*).

Given adjacent data sets D and D', we want to demonstrate that:

$$Pr[f(D) \in S] \leq exp(\epsilon')Pr[f(D') \in S] + \delta$$

By probability preservation, we know that:

$$\text{Pr}\,[f(D) \in S] \leq (e^{\epsilon}Pr[f(D') \in S])^{1-\frac{1}{\alpha}}$$

Consider the situation where:

$$(e^{\epsilon}Pr[f(D') \in S])^{1-\frac{1}{\alpha}} > \delta^{\frac{\alpha}{\alpha-1}}$$

This means that:

$$(e^\epsilon Pr[f(D) \in S]) \le (e^\epsilon Pr[f(D') \in S])^{1 - \frac{1}{\alpha}}$$

$$\le (e^\epsilon Pr[f(D') \in S]) \delta^{\frac{-1}{\alpha - 1}}$$

$$= exp\left(\epsilon + \frac{log\frac{1}{\delta}}{\alpha - 1}\right) Pr[f(D') \in S]$$

Now consider the other case:

$$(e^\epsilon Pr[f(D') \in S])^{1 - \frac{1}{\alpha}} \le \delta^{\frac{\alpha}{\alpha - 1}}$$

This means that:

$$Pr[f(D) \in S] \le (e^\epsilon Pr[f(D') \in S])^{1 - \frac{1}{\alpha}}$$

$$\le \delta$$

The Exponential Mechanism Satisfies Bounded Range

An exponential mechanism $EM_S(\cdot)$ with quality score S satisfies bounded range with 2ϵ. If S is monotonic over the data, then EM_S satisfies bounded range with ϵ.

Proof

When $M(\cdot)$ is the exponential mechanism $EM_S(\cdot)$, then given adjacent inputs x and x' and outcomes y and y', it suffices to show that:

$$\frac{\Pr\left[M(x) = y\right]}{\Pr\left[M(x') = y\right]} \frac{\Pr\left[M(x') = y'\right]}{\Pr\left[M(x) = y'\right]} \le e^{2\epsilon}$$

By the definition of the exponential mechanism, this becomes:

$$\frac{\exp\left(\frac{\epsilon S(x, y)}{\Delta S}\right) \exp\left(\frac{\epsilon S(x', y')}{\Delta S}\right)}{\exp\left(\frac{\epsilon S(x', y)}{\Delta S}\right) \exp\left(\frac{\epsilon S(x, y')}{\Delta S}\right)}$$

Since ΔS is the sensitivity of the scoring function, we know that $\left|\frac{S(x, y) - S(x', y)}{\Delta S}\right| \le 1$ and $\left|\frac{S(x', y') - S(x, y')}{\Delta S}\right| \le 1$:

$$\exp\left(\frac{\epsilon(S(x, y) - S(x', y))}{\Delta S}\right) \exp\left(\frac{\epsilon(S(x', y') - S(x, y'))}{\Delta S}\right) \le e^\epsilon e^\epsilon = e^{2\epsilon}$$

To demonstrate that EM_S satisfies bounded range with ϵ when S is monotonic, consider what this means for adjacent inputs x and x'. Monotonicity means that $S(a) \geq S(b')$ when $a > b$, so there are two possible outcomes:

- If $x \geq x'$, then $S(x, y) - S(x', y) \geq 0$ and $S(x', y') - S(x, y') \leq 0$, meaning that:

$$\exp\left(\frac{\epsilon(S(x, y) - S(x', y))}{\Delta S}\right) \exp\left(\frac{\epsilon(S(x', y') - S(x, y'))}{\Delta S}\right) \leq e^{\epsilon} \cdot 1 = e^{\epsilon}$$

- If $x \leq x'$, then $S(x, y) - S(x', y) \leq 0$ and $S(x', y') - S(x, y') \geq 0$, meaning that:

$$\exp\left(\frac{\epsilon(S(x, y) - S(x', y))}{\Delta S}\right) \exp\left(\frac{\epsilon(S(x', y') - S(x, y'))}{\Delta S}\right) \leq 1 \cdot e^{\epsilon} = e^{\epsilon}$$

This concludes the proof.

Structured Query Language (SQL)

For our purposes, a *database* is a collection of tables containing data that you can query data from. A *table* is a collection of data with a known structure, and a *query* is a statement about what you want from the table.

For example, consider a database of students in a school, where each table is a class (Tables D-1 and D-2).

Table D-1. ComputerScience101

student_id	first_name	last_name	major	grade
58394	Doy	Easterbrook	computer science	80
29485	Merridie	Blockwell	history	85
92554	Denys	Phorsby	physics	95
02359	Coreen	Otley	english	90
02945	Merci	Wiszniewski	history	95

Table D-2. History101

student_id	first_name	last_name	major	grade
09528	Teodoro	Anscombe	english	85
10394	Kala	Tidcombe	english	85
85422	Theodosia	Kelson	computer science	90
25925	Saunderson	Dunlap	english	90
29485	Merridie	Blockwell	history	95
92554	Denys	Phorsby	physics	95
02359	Coreen	Otley	english	85
02945	Merci	Wiszniewski	history	95

To see the `student_id` for every student in History 101, you would use the following query:

```
SELECT student_id FROM History101;
```

and would receive this output:

```
+------------+
| student_id |
+------------+
| 09528      |
| 10394      |
| 85422      |
| 25925      |
| 29485      |
| 92554      |
| 02359      |
| 02945      |
+------------+
```

This type of SELECT statement works on any combination of the columns:

```
SELECT student_id, major FROM History101;
```

```
+------------+------------------+
| student_id | major            |
+------------+------------------+
| 09528      | english          |
| 10394      | english          |
| 85422      | computer science |
| 25925      | english          |
| 29485      | history          |
| 92554      | physics          |
| 02359      | english          |
| 02945      | history          |
+------------+------------------+
```

You can also read the entire table using a wildcard (*) in place of the column names:

```
SELECT * FROM History101;
```

```
+------------+------------+-------------+------------------+-------+
| student_id | first_name | last_name   | major            | grade |
+------------+------------+-------------+------------------+-------+
| 09528      | Teodoro    | Anscombe    | english          | 85    |
| 10394      | Kala       | Tidcombe    | english          | 85    |
| 85422      | Theodosia  | Kelson      | computer science | 90    |
| 25925      | Saunderson | Dunlap      | english          | 90    |
| 29485      | Merridie   | Blockwell   | history          | 95    |
| 92554      | Denys      | Phorsby     | physics          | 95    |
| 02359      | Coreen     | Otley       | english          | 85    |
| 02945      | Merci      | Wiszniewski | history          | 95    |
+------------+------------+-------------+------------------+-------+
```

The SQL standard also supports aggregations such as sums, averages, and counts. To count the number of students in a class:

```
SELECT Count(*) FROM History101;

8
```

To calculate the average grade in the class:

```
SELECT AVG(grade) FROM History101;

90.0
```

You can also filter the data before returning it. Suppose you only want to see the students in the class who are majoring in computer science:

```
SELECT * FROM History101 WHERE major=computer_science;

+------------+------------+------------+------------------+-------+
| student_id | first_name | last_name  | major            | grade |
+------------+------------+------------+------------------+-------+
| 85422      | Theodosia  | Kelson     | computer science | 90    |
+------------+------------+------------+------------------+-------+
```

To see the students who currently have an A in the class:

```
SELECT * FROM History101 WHERE grade >= 90;

+------------+------------+------------+------------------+-------+
| student_id | first_name | last_name  | major            | grade |
+------------+------------+------------+------------------+-------+
| 85422      | Theodosia  | Kelson     | computer science | 90    |
| 25925      | Saunderson | Dunlap     | english          | 90    |
| 29485      | Merridie   | Blockwell  | history          | 95    |
| 92554      | Denys      | Phorsby    | physics          | 95    |
| 02945      | Merci      | Wiszniewski| history          | 95    |
+------------+------------+------------+------------------+-------+
```

What if you want to see the history majors with an A in the class? You can combine WHERE clauses using the AND statement:

```
SELECT * FROM History101 WHERE major=history AND grade >= 90;

+------------+------------+------------+------------------+-------+
| student_id | first_name | last_name  | major            | grade |
+------------+------------+------------+------------------+-------+
| 29485      | Merridie   | Blockwell  | history          | 95    |
| 02945      | Merci      | Wiszniewski| history          | 95    |
+------------+------------+------------+------------------+-------+
```

Composition Proofs

This appendix contains proofs for several theorems from Chapter 2: basic sequential composition, general sequential composition, parallel composition, and immunity to postprocessing. While you won't need to memorize these to prepare a DP release, working through each step can give you a deeper understanding of the behaviors of a DP mechanism. Further, knowing how to use composition and postprocessing will help you address more DP scenarios and build more complex pipelines.

Theorem: Basic Sequential Composition

Given an ϵ_0-DP mechanism $M_0(D)$ and an ϵ_1-DP mechanism $M_1(D)$, then applying each mechanism in sequence to a data set D provides $(\epsilon_0 + \epsilon_1)$-differential privacy.

Proof

For notational simplicity, let's start with the following scenario: you have an ϵ_0-DP mechanism called M_0, an ϵ_1-DP mechanism called M_1, and a data set D. If you apply M_0 to D, and then apply M_1 to D, the result is $(\epsilon_0 + \epsilon_1)$-DP, that is, the privacy loss sums. In fact, the order doesn't matter here, so long as they are independent.

For some outcome Y, you can use independence and know that:

$$Pr[M_0(D) = Y, M_1(D) = Y] = Pr[M_0(D) = Y]Pr[M_1(D) = Y]$$

and for an adjacent data set D', this also holds:

$$Pr[M_0(D') = Y, M_1(D') = Y] = Pr[M_0(D') = Y]Pr[M_1(D') = Y]$$

Dividing these two statements yields:

$$\frac{Pr[M_0(D) = Y]Pr[M_1(D) = Y]]}{Pr[M_0(D') = Y]Pr[M_1(D') = Y]]}$$

Now, you can group M_0 and M_1 together:

$$\left[\frac{Pr[M_0(D) = Y]}{Pr[M_0(D') = Y]}\right]\left[\frac{Pr[M_1(D) = Y]}{Pr[M_1(D') = Y]}\right]$$

By the definition of ϵ-DP, the first term is less than or equal to e^{ϵ_0} and the second term is less than or equal to e^{ϵ_1}:

Now, you can group M_0 and M_1 together:

$$\left[\frac{Pr[M_0(D) = Y]}{Pr[M_0(D') = Y]}\right]\left[\frac{Pr[M_1(D) = Y]}{Pr[M_1(D') = Y]}\right] \le e^{\epsilon_0}e^{\epsilon_1}$$

Since $e^{\epsilon_0}e^{\epsilon_1} = e^{\epsilon_0 + \epsilon_1}$:

$$\left[\frac{Pr[M_0(D) = Y]}{Pr[M_0(D') = Y]}\right]\left[\frac{Pr[M_1(D) = Y]}{Pr[M_1(D') = Y]}\right] \le e^{\epsilon_0 + \epsilon_1}$$

Therefore, the mechanisms M_0 and M_1 together are $(\epsilon_0 + \epsilon_1)$-DP.

Now, let's look at the general formulation of basic sequential composition as seen in Chapter 2. This statement is an extension of the previous proof, for i mechanisms instead of 2.

Theorem: General Sequential Composition

For a batch of k differentially private queries $M_i(D)$ applied to a data set D, the batch of queries provides $\sum_i^k \epsilon_i$-differential privacy.

Proof

For some outcome Y, you can use independence and know that:

$$Pr[M_0(D) = Y, \ldots, M_k(D) = Y] = Pr[M_0(D) = Y]\cdots Pr[M_{k-1}(D) = Y]$$

and this product can be expressed more succinctly as:

$$\prod_{i=0}^{k-1} Pr[M_i(D) = Y]$$

Similarly, for an adjacent data set D':

$$Pr[M_0(D') = Y, \ldots, M_k(D') = Y] = \prod_{i=0}^{k-1} Pr[M_i(D') = Y]$$

Now dividing these two statements yields:

$$\frac{\Pi_{i=0}^{k-1} Pr[M_i(D) = Y]}{\Pi_{i=0}^{k-1} Pr[M_i(D') = Y]} = \prod_{i=0}^{k-1} \frac{Pr[M_i(D) = Y]}{Pr[M_i(D') = Y]}$$

By the definition of ϵ-DP, the ith term in this product is less than or equal to ϵ_i:

$$\prod_{i=0}^{k-1} \frac{Pr[M_i(D) = Y]}{Pr[M_i(D') = Y]} \le \prod_{i=0}^{k-1} e^{\epsilon_i} = e^{\epsilon_0 + \epsilon_1 + \cdots + \epsilon_{k-1}}$$

Therefore, this mechanism satisfies ϵ-DP, where $\epsilon = \epsilon_0 + \epsilon_1 + \cdots + \epsilon_{k-1} = \Sigma_{i=0}^{k-1} \epsilon_i$.

Theorem: Parallel Composition

For a sequence of k ϵ_i-differentially private queries $M_i(D)$ and a sequence of disjoint subsets D_i of database D, the sequence of queries $M_i(D_i)$ provides $\max_i \epsilon_i$-differential privacy.

Proof

Similarly to sequential composition, let's start with a case where there are two mechanisms M_0 and M_1, which is ϵ_0-DP, and M_1, which is ϵ_1-DP. In parallel composition, each mechanism is run over a disjoint (non-overlapping) subset of the data set D. For two mechanisms, this means you need two subsets—let's call them D_0 and D_1. Since these subsets are disjoint, each item in D is either in D_0 or D_1, but not in both.

Suppose that M_0 is applied to D_0 and M_1 is applied to D_1. Then data points in D_0 are guaranteed to be protected by ϵ_0-DP, while data points in D_1 are guaranteed to be protected by ϵ_1-DP. To provide a measure of the privacy loss for the parallel mechanism (M_0, M_1), you have to use the worst-case scenario: you can only guarantee that privacy is preserved to the largest level of privacy loss experienced by a single subset, which is the largest value $\{\epsilon_0, \epsilon_1\}$: $max\{\epsilon_0, \epsilon_1\}$. More generally, the privacy loss of a parallel composition mechanism M_i (each with privacy loss parameter ϵ_i) over disjoint subsets D_i of D is $\max\limits_i \epsilon_i$.

Theorem: Immunity to Postprocessing

Let M be an ϵ-differentially private mechanism and $g: R \to R'$ be an arbitrary mapping. Then the composition $g \circ M$ is ϵ-differentially private.

Proof

Since a random mapping can always be described as a linear combination of deterministic functions $\sum_i a_i f_i(x)$ and a linear combination of DP mechanisms is DP, it suffices to show that this is true for a deterministic function g.

First, define S as a subset of R', and T as a subset of R such that T is the set of points for which $g(x)$ is in S: $T = \{r \in R : g(r) \in S\}$. S and T contain the mechanism outcomes we will be examining in the remainder of the proof. When $M(x) \in T$, then g(M(x)) maps the value M(x) to an element of S.

Since g is deterministic, it does not affect the probabilities:

$$Pr[g(M(x)) \in S] = Pr[M(x) \in T]$$

By the definition of ϵ-DP:

$$Pr[M(x) \in T] \le e^\epsilon Pr[M(y) \in T]$$

And again we know that these probabilities are equal:

$$e^\epsilon Pr[M(y) \in T] = e^\epsilon Pr[g(M(y)) \in S]$$

This means that:

$$\frac{Pr[g(M(x)) \in S]}{Pr[g(M(y)) \in S]} \le e^\epsilon$$

therefore, the postprocessor g applied to M preserves ϵ-DP.

Machine Learning

This appendix highlights the basic terminology of machine learning, outlines several varieties of machine learning, and summarizes the use of gradient descent to learn parameters.

The process of fitting a machine learning model is called *training*. Given a function with some unknown parameters, the training process tries different parameter values until it finds the values that allow it to most closely match the data. To understand how accurate the model is, you perform *testing*; this is the part of the process where you use your parameters to make predictions based on the input data and compare the predictions to the true values. If the tests show that your model is accurate, you've trained the computer to *learn* a model about the data. The trained model can be used to make decisions or predictions.

Supervised Versus Unsupervised Learning

Machine learning is often broken into two broad categories: *supervised* and *unsupervised*. Supervised learning describes a scenario where the data comes with labels to learn from. These labels aid the model in learning patterns between the different categories. For example, Table F-1 shows a data set of fruit measurements.

Table F-1. Fruits in a grocery store

Height (cm)	Diameter (cm)	Type
6.2	6.7	Apple
7.0	6.9	Orange
9.0	6.2	Pear
6.3	6.5	Apple
7.1	6.8	Orange

Height (cm)	Diameter (cm)	Type
6.4	6.8	Apple
9.1	6.1	Pear
9.2	6.2	Pear
7.2	7.4	Orange

Now imagine you are given a task—you know the height and circumference of a fruit and want to predict its type. In this case, the column *Type* is the *label* of the data set—it is what your model wants to predict. This is an example of *supervised learning*; the word *supervised* is used here because you are "supervising" the model's learning process by giving it labels to learn from. Supervised learning is common in scenarios where you have large amounts of preexisting data that was labeled by humans.

If, on the other hand, you are given the data set without this column, then your learning objective is different (Table F-2).

Table F-2. Fruits in a grocery store

Height (cm)	Diameter (cm)
6.2	6.7
7.0	6.9
9.0	6.2
6.3	6.5
7.1	6.8
6.4	6.8
9.1	6.1
9.2	6.2
7.2	7.4

You know that each row represents a fruit, but you do not know which type it is. In fact, this data doesn't even tell you how many types of fruit there are in the data set. With a data set like this, you can perform an *unsupervised learning* process, which will try to infer how many categories there are in the data and which category each member belongs to. Thus, it may notice that there are three fruits in the data set where the ratio of height to diameter is large—the fruit is taller than it is wide. These rows will be clustered together, and the model will tell you, "These objects seem similar." The model can therefore identify pears based on height and diameter without even knowing what a pear is; it simply looks at patterns in the data and makes its best estimate.

Unsupervised learning is more common in cases where you have data that hasn't been human reviewed. Sometimes, you will want to understand the global structure of the data as a first pass before doing further analysis on it. In a case like this, unsupervised learning can be a helpful first step to estimate how many clusters exist in the data. In other cases, the unsupervised learning is the main event—a classic example is handwritten digit detection that clusters images of digits into like categories, without any preexisting labels or human guidance.

Gradient Descent

Training a machine learning model is fundamentally about minimization. At each step of the training process, the model tries a set of predictions and calculates error from the true values. It then modifies its parameters and tries again. How does it modify the parameters? By taking a step in the direction of fastest change.

Imagine standing at the top of a mountain. If you want to get to the bottom as quickly as possible, do you zigzag left and right as you go, or do you follow the pull of gravity and walk straight down? Conversely, if you are at the edge of a canyon and want to find the lowest point, you will also walk straight down the side of the canyon, rather than run laps around its edge as you descend.

What is the connection between canyons and machine learning? In this case, if you construct an error function that gives you the difference between your model output and true values, you want to find the parameters that minimize the error. This is a crucial concept moving forward: machine learning is about optimizing parameters that minimize the error between the model prediction and the true values in the data. Ideally, this function should be *convex*—that is, have only one minimum value. In practice, this isn't always the case, and there may be multiple local minima in the error function.

For example, consider the function $f(x, y) = (x - 2)^4 + (y + 3)^2$. If you are given the point (1,1) and asked to find the quickest path from the point to the minimum of $f(x, y)$, how will you proceed? First, calculate the gradient $\nabla f(x, y) = \left(4(x - 2)^3, 2(y + 3)\right)$. This vector will point in the direction of the steepest descent. At a given point (x_i, y_i), take a step by calculating $(x_{i+1}, y_{i+1}) = (x_i, y_i) - \gamma \nabla f(x, y)$. Here, γ determines the size of the step taken in each iteration and is called the *learning rate*.

An implementation of this algorithm follows. In this case, the code will only stop iterating once the difference in f changes by an amount specified by the variable tol. In other cases, you may want to set a fixed number of iterations in a for loop:

```
import numpy as np


def f(x,y):
    return (x - 2)**4 + (y + 3)**2


def gradient(x,y):
    return np.array([4 * (x - 2) ** 3, 2 * (y + 3)])


if __name__ == '__main__':
    x_old = 10
    y_old = 10
    gamma = 0.01
    tol = 1e-16

    x_new, y_new = np.array([x_old, y_old]) - gamma * gradient(x_old, y_old)

    while np.abs(f(x_new, y_new) - f(x_old, y_old)) > tol:
        x_new, y_new = x_old, y_old
        x_old, y_old = np.array([x_old, y_old]) - gamma * gradient(x_old, y_old)
        print(x_new, y_new, f(x_new, y_new))
```

If you run this code, you will see the *x* and *y* values descend from *(10, 10)* down to values increasingly close to *(2, –3)*. Change the gamma value; what do you see?

These numbers are in close agreement with our expectation! Since the function is differentiable, we can know that $4(x - 2)^3 + 3(y + 3)^2 = 0$ is a local minimum and can simply check that this is true when $x = 2$ and $y = -3$. This is a luxury you will rarely (if ever) have: to check the minimum of a function using its derivative.

Using Gradient Descent to Learn Parameters

In the previous example, you found the point (x, y) that minimized a function *f*. In this case, the data points (x, y) were your data—the inputs to your function. A more useful scenario is finding *parameters* for a function that minimize error relative to a data set. This means that instead of finding a point (x, y) that minimizes a function, you will find the parameters α and β that minimize a function *f* relative to a data set $(x_0, y_0), (x_1, y_1), \ldots, (x_N, y_N)$.

Consider simple linear regression, where you want to learn the best parameters for $f(x) = \beta_0 + \beta_1 x_1 + \beta_2 x_2$. Here, you aren't minimizing this function itself; you are instead minimizing the function that calculates the error between the regression's estimation and the observed data. For example, let's use the mean squared error as a starting point:

$$E = \frac{1}{n} \sum_{i=0}^{n} \left(y_i - \left(\beta_0 + \beta_1 x_1^i + \beta_2 x_2^i \right) \right)^2$$

where y_i is the true observed value.

Since you want to find the best parameters to match the data, you will take the gradient relative to the parameters themselves:

$$\frac{\partial E}{\partial \beta_0} = \frac{-2}{n} \sum_{i=0}^{n} \left(y_i - \beta_0 - \beta_1 x_1^i - \beta_2 x_2^i \right)$$

$$\frac{\partial E}{\partial \beta_1} = \frac{-2}{n} \sum_{i=0}^{n} x_1^i \left(y_i - \beta_0 - \beta_1 x_1^i - \beta_2 x_2^i \right)$$

$$\frac{\partial E}{\partial \beta_2} = \frac{-2}{n} \sum_{i=0}^{n} x_2^i \left(y_i - \beta_0 - \beta_1 x_1^i - \beta_2 x_2^i \right)$$

Then at each step, you update the parameters $\beta_0, \beta_1, \beta_2$ using the now-familiar gradient descent:

$$(\beta_0, \beta_1, \beta_2) \rightarrow (\beta_0, \beta_1, \beta_2) - \gamma \left(\frac{\partial E}{\partial \beta_0}, \frac{\partial E}{\partial \beta_1}, \frac{\partial E}{\partial \beta_2} \right)$$

```
import numpy as np

# Prepare a data set
ideal_params = [4., 2., -3.]
data set_size = 100   # assuming known data set size

data_x = np.random.normal(size=[data set_size, 2])
data_y = np.hstack([np.ones(data set_size), data_x]) @ ideal_params

# Discover params via gradient descent
num_steps = 10

params = np.zeros(3)
for _ in range(num_steps):
    instance_level_grads = gradient(data_x, data_y) # n x 2 array
    df_dx = dp_mean(instance_level_grads[:, 0])
    df_dy = dp_mean(instance_level_grads[:, 1])

    params -= gamma * np.array([df_dx, df_dy])
```

Stochastic Gradient Descent

Although gradient descent is a powerful tool for finding the minimum of a function, it has its limitations. The examples shown so far require iterating over the entire data set for each of the parameters. This is only practical for small data sets over a low number of dimensions. Otherwise, the process can become computationally burdensome.

Imagine you are trying to minimize the error over hundreds of parameters and a data set with millions of entries; this would quickly become untenable. For example, a problem with 100 parameters and a data set of 100,000 rows would mean 100 * 100,000 = 10,000,000 calculations to compute the gradient. Further, this step will often be carried out hundreds or thousands of times in order to converge to an approximation of the minimum. Even 100 steps would mean doing 100 * 10,000,000 = 1 billion calculations! We clearly need something more efficient.

Thankfully, there is a technique called *stochastic gradient descent*, where the gradient is approximated via a random shuffling of the data. Rather than iterate over the entire data set, this algorithm first randomly permutes the data set, then takes a random sampling of the permuted data. Gradient descent is then performed on this random sample, leading to an approximation of the true gradient. Consider the efficiency challenge mentioned in the previous paragraph: if you have a problem with 100 parameters and 100,000 data points, the total number of calculations needed becomes unreasonable. However, if you take a random sample of 1,000 data points and approximate the gradient, your total number of calculations drops from 1 billion to (100 parameters) * 1,000 (data points) * 100 (iterations) = 10 million, a substantial improvement in speed over regular gradient descent.

When using multiple small subsets of the data (often called *batches*), the process is called *mini-batch gradient descent*. In mini-batch gradient descent, each iteration involves splitting the data set into multiple small subsets and calculating the gradient for each batch. This technique lends itself easily to parallelization; imagine you have 10 mini-batches to calculate gradients over. You can have each calculate in parallel, then average the results together.

Where to Find Solutions

Solutions to all exercises are presented in the book's repository (*https://oreil.ly/HODP_GitHub*), along with data sets and other materials relevant to the book.

For questions and comments related to the exercises, please don't hesitate to reach out to the authors at *ethan@lakeside.tech*.

Index

Symbols

τ-thresholding, 193

A

above threshold mechanism, 105-108
absolute distance metric, 35, 55
acceptance regions, 136
accuracy, of private mechanisms, 39
adaptive composition, 151-153
advanced composition, 120-123
aggregators, 75-81
analytical Fourier accountant, 136
annotation, 277
approximate differential privacy
    advanced composition, 120-123
    versus probabilistic differential privacy, 115
    propose-test-release (PTR) mechanism, 118, 193
    truncated noise mechanisms, 116
    δ (delta) parameter, 114
attacks (see privacy attacks)
averaging attacks, 4

B

B-Tree mechanism, 145-149
background knowledge attacks, 8
batching, stochastic, 225-229
Bayesian network, 244
Bernoulli distribution, 30
between-cluster separation (BCSS), 166
bias-variance trade-off, 183-188, 208
BigQuery platform, 20
bounded differential privacy, 57
bounded range (BR), 130, 313

bounds estimation, 143-145
Broadband data set, 297
browser logs example, 175-177
budget accountability, 290
budget-friendly exploratory analysis, 239

C

c-stable transformations, 58-61
Calinski-Harabasz index, 166
cardinality, 303
categorical naive Bayes, 211
Census Bureau data releases, 175, 265
central model, 34
centroids, 166
CH utility score, 167
chaining
    B-Tree mechanism, 145-149
    bounds estimation, 143-145
    building differentially private algorithms, 142
    definition of term, 142
    illustration of using OpenDP, 142
    transformations, 68
    use of term, 80
characteristic functions, 135
clipping transformations, 67
cluster sampling, 275
code examples, obtaining and using, xviii
codebooks, 277
combinators
    chaining, 142-149
    composition mechanisms, 151-155
    definition and concept of, 141
    partitioned data, 156-161

G

GANs (generative adversarial networks), 246-249
Gaussian mechanism, 123-126, 225
Gaussian noise, 5
general data access, 239
generative adversarial networks (GANs), 246-249
generators, 246
geographic spine, 145
geometric mechanism (discrete Laplace mechanism), 93
global sensitivity, 15, 35
gradient descent, 221-224, 325-327
gradient of the loss function, 221
graphical models, 243-246
grouped data, 80
Gumbel distribution, 102

H

Hamming distance metric, 57
histograms, 193
Hölder's inequality, 308
homogeneity attacks, 8
hospital visits example, 183-188
hyperparameters
    definition of term, 223
    private fitting, 200
    selecting, 208
    tuning, 227-229
hypothesis testing interpretation, 136-138

I

identifier distance metric, 177
image synthetic data, 238
immunity to postprocessing, 44-46, 305, 322
income prediction example, 233-236
inference, 200
inference problem, 4, 256
information norms, 279
input space, 76
interactive models, 256
interactivity, 104
interleaving queries, 151

K

k-anonymity, 7, 267-269
k-means, 166

known-size mean transformations, 72
known-size sum transformation, 70-72

L

Laplace distribution, 17
Laplace mechanism, 37-43, 91-94, 123
Laplace noise, 5
Laplace Noisy Max (LNM), 104, 106
latent dimensionality, 246
least squares solution, 262-265
linear regression, 200
linkage attacks, 258-260
LinkedIn data release, 171, 296
linking, 7
Lloyd's algorithm, 166
LNM (Laplace Noisy Max), 104, 106
local model, 34
local sensitivity, 15
local stability, 118
lossy conversions, 150

M

machine learning (ML)
    attacks on, 269
    definition of term, 219
    differentially private gradient descent (DP-GD), 221-224
    differentially private stochastic gradient descent (DP-SGD), 225-229
    gradient descent, 325-327
    importance of differential privacy in, 219
    private aggregations of teacher ensembles (PATE), 230-232
    stochastic gradient descent, 328
    supervised versus unsupervised learning, 323-325
    terminology used in, 220
    training models with PyTorch, 232-236
MAPE (mean absolute percentage error), 185
marginal-based synthetic data generators, 240-243
max-divergence, 87
maximum absolute distance, 35
mean absolute percentage error (MAPE), 185
mean sensitivity, 15
mean transformations, 72
mechanisms, definition of term, 85
membership attacks, 220, 257
metadata parameters, 275

About the Authors

Ethan Cowan worked on software and research topics as part of the OpenDP team from 2020 to 2022. In particular, he focused on privatizing machine learning models and developing platforms for analyzing sensitive data with built-in differential privacy. Ethan now studies the history and ethics of emerging technology.

Michael Shoemate is the architect for the OpenDP Library, a widely used open source library for differential privacy. His work involves collaborating with researchers to adapt differentially private methods into trustworthy and accessible software tools, and communicating how these tools can be used.

Mayana Pereira works on applying machine learning and privacy-preserving techniques to a diverse range of practical problems at Microsoft's AI for Good Team. Mayana is also an active collaborator of OpenDP, an open source project for the differential privacy community to develop general-purpose, vetted, usable, and scalable tools for differential privacy.

Colophon

The animal on the cover of *Hands-On Differential Privacy* is a slate pencil sea urchin (*Heterocentrotus mamillatus*). Other common names for the creature include brown pencil urchin, slate pencil urchin, and red pencil urchin.

The slate pencil sea urchin can be found throughout the coral bottom and waters of the Indo-Pacific region and is especially abundant in Hawaii. It hides in caves that reach up to 32 feet deep. Juvenile slate pencil sea urchins can be found hiding under rocks.

In general, sea urchins are globe-shaped and covered in a spiky skin. The slate pencil sea urchin's longer spines are 12 centimeters in length and can be 1 centimeter thick, which is considered stout enough for writing. The creature can vary in its color, with its longer dorsal and lateral spines being light brown to dark brown in shade, and its shorter spines appearing drastically different in either dark purple-black or white.

The animal eats mostly encrusting coralline algae but has also consumed other types of algae, such as Pterocladia and Ulva. Although the slate pencil sea urchin has a predominantly sedentary lifestyle, as it primarily eats the algae in closest proximity to it, the species is somewhat active compared to other urchins. It has been known to travel up to 600 centimeters away from its starting point, moving an average of 96 centimeters a day.

Although some species of sea urchin are considered near threatened in regards to their conservation status, the sea pencil urchin is not considered threatened or endangered at this time. Many of the animals on O'Reilly covers are endangered; all of them are important to the world.

The cover illustration is by Karen Montgomery, based on an antique line engraving from a loose plate, source unknown. The series design is by Edie Freedman, Ellie Volckhausen, and Karen Montgomery. The cover fonts are Gilroy Semibold and Guardian Sans. The text font is Adobe Minion Pro; the heading font is Adobe Myriad Condensed; and the code font is Dalton Maag's Ubuntu Mono.

O'REILLY®

Learn from experts.
Become one yourself.

60,000+ titles | Live events with experts | Role-based courses
Interactive learning | Certification preparation

Try the O'Reilly learning platform
free for 10 days.

www.ingramcontent.com/pod-product-compliance
Lightning Source LLC
Jackson TN
JSHW052004131224
75386JS00036B/1189